LEND-LEASE AIRCRAFT IN WORLD WAR II

LEND-LEASE AIRCRAFT IN WORLD WAR II

ARTHUR PEARCY

Airlife
England

Copyright © 1996 Arthur Pearcy

First Published in the UK in 1996
by Airlife Publishing Ltd

British Library Cataloguing in Publication Data
A catalogue record for this book
is available from the British Library

ISBN 1 85310 443 4

Typeset by Phoenix Typesetting, Ilkley, West
Yorkshire

Printed in England by
Butler & Tanner Ltd, Frome and London

Airlife Publishing Ltd

101 Longden Road, Shrewsbury, SY3 9EB, England

Contents

Foreword

HERE, in this remarkable story of 'Lend-Lease', Arthur Pearcy adds further to his valuable earlier books on Anglo–American co-operation in aviation. He tells of the monumental agreement forged between President Franklin D. Roosevelt of the United States and Winston Churchill, Prime Minister of Britain – an agreement which contributed so greatly to the winning of the Second World War.

The Lend-Lease Bill, passed by the United States Congress on 11 March 1941, cleared the way for the supply to the Royal Air Force and its allied services of a steady flow of American aircraft, equipment and other munitions without which we in Britain might well have been overwhelmed by German military might during the gap of 18 months or more between the decisive victory of the Battle of Britain and the effective entry into the War by United States after Pearl Harbor in December 1941.

The concept of Lend-Lease had first emerged in the Spring of 1941 from the fact that, up to November 1940, Britain had paid in full for everything we had received of the large orders for war materials placed in the United States. Thereafter, British financial resources were beginning to run dry.

In that precarious situation following the defeat of France at a time when the United States was wholly unprepared for War or for its own defence against the stark German ambitions, both the President and the Prime Minister came to share – through an interchange of secret telegrams – the conviction that unless Hitler's agressive intentions could be halted, there would be no future for Anglo–American civilisations as we knew them. Britain remained the last bastion of freedom while the United States re-armed.

When the War began in September 1939 Britain had possessed some $4,000 million – in dollars or in gold. Sixteen months later, by 1 January 1941, we had earned an additional $2,000 million through exports and the sale of investments in the US and elsewhere. But, even so, having paid out more than $4,500 million in cash, we were down to no more than $1,500 million, while our requirements for military munitions were increasing faster than ever.

Fighting alone, we were ordering everything we could lay our hands on in useful war materials on the principle that to worry about what might happen when the dollars ran out made little sense while we were fighting for our lives under constant air attack and the threat of imminent invasion.

Hence, on 8 December 1940, Winston Churchill wrote a long and candid letter to President Roosevelt, with whom he had already formed a cordial – though long-distance – rapport. He placed the dollar situation before the President without reservation, and that our vital trans-Atlantic shipping lanes, upon which we relied both for the feeding of the British people and for the delivery of war materials, had by now incurred grievous losses beyond any prospect of replenishment from home resources.

That letter brought an immediate response through the British ambassador in Washington DC, Lord Lothian.

At a meeting of the US Defense Advisory Commission on Shipping Resources, Secretary Henry Morganthau of the Treasury Department – and a convinced supporter of the Allied cause – recalled a Statute of 1892 whereby the Secretary for War had been empowered to lease government property 'at his discretion whenever he was convinced that it would be for the public good – but limited to a period of five years'. A number of precedents for action under this Statute had been established.

That struck a chord with President Roosevelt. He saw in it 'a means of enabling Britain to defend itself', and thus assist the United States in its own defence, through the lease to Britain of weapons and raw materials.

In a radio 'fireside chat' on 30 December 1941, the President said:

'There is danger ahead, danger against which we must prepare. We know that we cannot escape danger by crawling into bed and pulling the covers over our heads. Now, if Britain should go down, all of us in all the Americas will be living at the point of a gun, a gun loaded with explosive bullets, economic as well as military. We must produce arms and ships with every energy and resource we can command. We must become the arsenal of democracy.'

Along these lines action was already in hand for the transfer to Britain of 50 US destroyers of First World War vintage in return for the 99-year lease to the United States of air and naval bases in Newfoundland, Bermuda, the Bahamas, the Caribbean and in British Guiana.

Harking back to 1892, an important principle of leases had thus been re-established.

The President now extended it to the preparation of a new and helpful Lend-Lease agreement between America and Britain.

Early in January 1941, the wise and personable Harry Hopkins arrived in Britain as President Roosevelt's emissary specifically to discuss the future with the Prime Minister. He and Churchill immediately hit it off together; the emissary was briefed to inform the President what Britain would need from the USA and to report on the country's morale.

While Hopkins was in England the Lend-Lease Bill, No. 1776 – 'an Act to promote the defense of the United States' – was drafted; its passage through Congress greatly helped by Hopkins's statement back to the President of what he found in Britain. He wrote to the President; 'People here are amazing – from Churchill down. If courage alone can win, the result will be inevitable. But they need our help desperately and I am sure you will permit nothing to stand in the way. Churchill *is* the government in every sense of the word. He controls the grand strategy and often the detail. Labour trusts him. The army, navy and air force are behind him to a man. I cannot emphasise too strongly that he is the one and only person over here with whom you need to have a full meeting of the minds. This island needs our help now, Mr President, with everything we can give them.'

Later, at a dinner in Glasgow with the PM, Hopkins said: 'I suppose you wish to know what I am going to say to President Roosevelt on my return. Well, I am going to quote you one verse from the Book of Books on which my own Scottish mother was brought up: "Whither thou goest, I will go. And where thou lodgest I will lodge. Thy people shall be my people and thy God my God." '

Then he added very quietly, 'through to the end'.

Along such a line, when he returned to Washington, Hopkins advocated powerfully the passage of the Lend-Lease Bill.

While all this was going on the gifted and influential British ambassador to the United States, the Marquis of Lothian – immensely helpful as an intermediary between the Prime Minister and the President – died suddenly, on 12 December 1940, in Washington, at the age of 58 – a blow to both nations. He was succeeded by the equally distinguished Lord Halifax – former Foreign Secretary – who arrived in Washington in time for the signing, by the President, of the Lend-Lease Act on 11 March 1941 – passed by 317 votes to 71 – thereby fulfilling the Prime Minister's exhortation:

'Give us the tools and we will finish the job.'

Thus was set in motion what Churchill described as: 'The most unsordid act in the history of any nation' which transformed immediately the whole position. There was no provision for any repayment. There was not even account kept in dollars or in sterling. What we had was lent or leased to us because our continued resistance to the Hitler tyranny was deemed to be of vital interest to the great Republic. According to President Roosevelt, 'the defence of the United States, and not dollars, was henceforth to determine where American weapons were to go'.

As a result, (following-up the 200 Harvard trainers and the 200 Hudson reconnaissance bombers already ordered and paid for by the British Air Commission), there began a great, and increasing, flow of more than 75 different types of aircraft for the Royal Air Force, its allied air services and for the Empire Air Training Schools being developed around the World. During the next five years the United States aircraft industry, (backed by the approval by Congress of the allocation, on 27 March 1941, of a first tranche of $7,000 million of Lend-Lease finance) supplied to the United Kingdom a total of more than 38,800 aircraft, eventually to the tune of more than $50,000 million of Lend-Lease finances.

Nor was Lend-Lease applied solely to aircraft. Under its terms it covered every form of land, sea and air equipment of service to the prosecution of the War – and food as well.

Numerically, the 'top dozen' of military aircraft supplied under Lend-Lease were:

1. 5,019 North American NA.16 Harvard trainers

2. 3,512 Curtiss Kittyhawk single-seat fighters (for the Far East theatre)
3. 2,539 Lockheed 414 Hudson reconnaissance bombers
4. 2,450 Consolidated Vultee LB-30 Liberator bombers
5. 2,227 Fairchild PT-2B Cornell primary trainers (for Canada)
6. 2,002 Chance-Vought F4U Corsair naval fighters
7. 1,810 North American NA.73 Mustang 2 single-seat fighters
8. 1,790 Douglas C-47 Dakota transports
9. 1,250 Douglas A-20 Boston medium bombers
10. 1,190 Cessna AT-8 Crane light-twin trainers (for the RCAF)
11. 1,175 Martin 187 Baltimore light bombers
12. 1,172 Grumman F6F Hellcat naval fighters.

Officials at a conference held in the offices of the Office & Production Management, the US equivalent of Britain's Ministry of Supply (MoS) in Washington DC on 19 August 1941. Left to right: John Lord O'Brien, General Council OPM: Edward K Stettinius Jr, Director of Priorities OPM: Lord Beaverbrook, Britain's Minister of Supply: William S Knudson, Director General OPM, and W. Averill Harriman, Lend-Lease Administrator in London. (IWM OEM 250).

Those 26,136 aircraft made up nearly 70 per cent of the massive total of Lend-Lease aircraft. They were reinforced, after the War, by an additional batch of 430 North American F.86E Sabre F.4 single-seat jet fighters, built by Canadair Limited in Montreal to arm 12 squadrons of the Royal Air Force; ten in Germany and two with RAF Fighter Command.

There can be no doubt about the immense value to the allied war effort of these aircraft. Not only that, but also the existence of large numbers of reliable transport 'work-horses' – the Douglas C-47 Dakotas – of which more than 10,650 were built between 1935 and 1947. They became the foundation of post-War civil air transport in Europe, as elsewhere, after the War.

Lend-Lease thus carried forward from war into peace the tradition of Anglo–American co-operation in aviation which had begun in February of 1909, when the Wright brothers granted a first licence for manufacture of a batch of six Short-Wright 'Flyer' biplanes at Leysdown on the Isle of Sheppey in Kent. That initiative was carried forward in the opposite direction when the United States entered the First World War in April 1917.

In the 15 months between August 1917 and the end of the fighting on 11 November 1918, a total of 3,220 de Havilland D.H.4s were built in the United States, although only a few hundred had, by then, been delivered to the American Expeditionary Force in France. In all, 4,846 D.H.4s (most of them with American Liberty engines) were built in the US,

3,106 by Dayton-Wright, 1,600 by Fisher Body and 140 by Standard.

Thereafter, between 1920 and 1925, a further 354 D.H.4s were built by the Boeing Company, powered with Liberty engines and equipped with welded steel-tube fuselages in place of the original wood construction. They were delivered to the US Army Air Corps and to the US Marine Corps, and later flown extensively on US air mail services.

When the United States entered the Second World War in December 1941 an urgent need arose for a proven and powerful liquid-cooled aero-engine to supersede the original Liberty engines and to add to supplies of the liquid-cooled Allison. Already, in September 1940, the Packard Engine Division of the Packard Motor Car Company of Detroit, Michigan, had undertaken to build the Rolls-Royce Merlin for both the American and British governments.

From 1942 onwards, the R.R. Merlin 28 was in production in Detroit for the Curtiss P-40F Warhawk, the D.H. Mosquito and the Avro Lancaster built in Canada. In 1944 the Packard-built R.R. Merlin 61 was installed in the North American P-51D Mustang and in the RAF's Mustang IIIs, built by North America to a British specification – and one of the foremost single-seat fighters of the War.

Nor did this effective 'Lend-Lease in reverse' end

there. The development of the Whittle jet engine in England, and the first British jet to fly – the single-engine, single-seat, Gloster E.28/39 – was shown to General Hap Arnold, Commanding General of the US Army Air Forces, by Winston Churchill at Cranwell in May of 1941.

Arnold, much impressed, on his return to the USA telephoned Larry Bell of the Bell Aircraft Company and D.R. Schoults of the General Electric Engine Company, and, shortly afterwards, a team from Power Jets of Lutterworth went to General Electric in Massachussets in the US with a Whittle W1.X engine and a set of drawings – all this before Pearl Harbor in December 1941.

President Franklin D Roosevelt seen signing the Bill to extend further the life of the Lend-Lease Act on 11 March 1943. Second from the right, witnessing the signature, is Edward R Stettinius Jr. who in 1941 became Administrator of Lend-Lease. (IWM NYP 25934).

Thanks to these British jet engines flown to the United States in 1941 – to General Electric at their Lynn Works near Boston, and to Lockheed Aircraft at Burbank, California – the first two American jet aircraft were able to fly in March 1942 and January 1944.

First to fly was the rather uninspired Bell XP-59A 'Airacomet' single-seat twin-engine fighter-trainer. It was powered with a GE-J31 jet engine derived from a Whittle W.1-X sent from England to the G.E. Works in a packing case, together with drawings for the later W.2-B.

The job was tackled with enthusiasm by the G.E.

team, with whom Whittle got on exceptionally well. The prototype Bell XP-59A began flight tests on 1 October 1942 at Muroc (later named the Edwards A.F.B.). Eventually 30 P-59Bs were built for the US 412th Fighter Group for test work and operational evaluations.

At Lockheed Aircraft the first prototype XP-80 'Shooting Star' fighter was flown for the first time on 8 January 1944, also at Muroc, powered with a de Havilland-Halford H-1 jet engine of 3,000 lb static thrust.

The 'Shooting Star' went into large-scale production for the US Air Forces with General Electric J.33 engines. It took part in the Korean War and in 1947 set up a World's air speed record of 623.8 m.p.h.

The story of Anglo–American post-War co-operation, stemming from the Lend-Lease epic agreement, has continued ever since. It remains well in train to extend onwards through the completion of the first 100 years of powered flight and of 'Wings Across the Sea'.

Evolved from Sydney Camm's and Ralph Hooper's P.1127 vertical take-off-and-landing

In 1944 Edward R Stettinius Jr. was appointed Under-Secretary of State after holding the position as Administrator of Lend-Lease since 1941. Prior to that he served as a member of the US Defense Advisory Committee and Chairman of the US War Resources Board. Photo depicts Prime Minister Winston S Churchill shaking hands and saying 'goodbye' to Edward Stettinius at 10 Downing Street after his new appointment as US Under-Secretary of State. (IWM H 37960).

This RAF Transport Command Liberator Marco Polo *in July 1944 made a round trip from Montreal to London and back to Washington DC in three days. Seen at RAF Northolt on Thursday evening 20 July 1944 are the passengers flying to the USA. Left to right: Mr Peter G Masefield, Mr G M Thomson, Mr Geoffrey Lloyd, Parliamentary Secretary to the Ministry of Fuel & Power; Sir William Brown, Secretary of the Oil Mission: Lord Beaverbrook: Mr Ralph Assheton, Financial Secretary to the Treasury, and Mr V Butler. The Liberator made a record crossing to the USA in 19 hours 44 minutes. (IWM CH 13545).*

prototype of 1961 has now come the sophisticated British Aerospace/McDonnell Douglas AV-8B Harrier II, manufactured in both Britain and the United States. And so, more than 30 years after the first hovering flight of the P.1127, this jointly produced VTOL aircraft is in service with the Royal Air Force and the US Marine Corps – and more to come.

As it happens, I was able to glean much of the foregoing at first hand from the time when, in 1945, I was appointed by Sir Winston Churchill to be Britain's first Civil Air Attaché at the British Embassy in Washington DC under Lord Halifax.

That followed a stint in 1943 and 1944 of flying on operations in B-17s of the 96th Bomb Group of the US 8th Air Force. General Hap Arnold then gave me the opportunity to fly to the United States and, with a Lockheed Lodestar and a US Air Force crew, to fly from Coast to Coast to speak to the personnel of training bases and aircraft production centres on the importance of the Allied round-the-clock air offensive against Germany. In that way, I was privileged to see the fruits of Lend-Lease at first hand – as recounted here – and to emphasise some of the results.

The fact is that Lend-Lease cleared the way forward to a two-way collaborative enterprise which not only helped to win the War, but the results of which will endure well into the 21st Century. Has history seen the like?

Peter Masefield
Reigate, Surrey
January 1996

Preface

History is always studied after the fact. It just cannot be otherwise. Sometimes during long periods of reflection this study elicits regret or sorrow, and more often, nostalgia. It is now over fifty years since the commencement of Lend-Lease, and in this volume I have relived some of the World War Two years, during which time the many US-built aircraft types delivered under Lend-Lease first appeared, initially on paper as silhouettes in the Air Ministry official recognition handbook – AP 1480. Being based in the East Riding of Yorkshire, surrounded by airfields, a wide variety of types was logged, and despite wartime restrictions on keeping a diary, one was kept. Lend-Lease aircraft for the Fleet Air Arm were active in and out of Brough, the home of Blackburns which modified nearly 4,000 aircraft including Martlets, Avengers, Corsairs and Hellcats.

It was the pre-war Purchasing Commissions from Britain and other European countries that were responsible for what was to be a large, transatlantic flow of US-built warplanes purchased in North America, all needed to help counteract the threat posed by the German forces. Unfortunately orders placed by France and Belgium were only partially delivered, and in some cases not at all, due to the war clouds which burst over Europe in 1939. Fortunately the British were quick to take over these orders so it was not too long before strange aircraft types were being shipped to the UK.

The original French contract for Consolidated Liberators was not signed until 4 June 1940, only two weeks before France capitulated. When the UK took over the French B-24 contract the number of aircraft was reduced from 175 to 159. These 159 aircraft, plus the six LB-30s already on order under Contract A-5068, were allocated RAF serials AL503 to 667. The last twenty-six numbers of this allocation were cancelled and new serials allocated when the earlier and different Liberator models were later substituted under US–UK contract exchange. This explains why the LB-30As and Liberator Is had numerically higher RAF serials than the Liberator IIs.

In the autumn of 1940, over a year before Pearl Harbor, the US government took a look at the automobile industry with a view to augmenting aircraft production capacity. The intention was not to employ this industry as plane-makers, but as parts-makers. With one major exception this decision went uncontested throughout World War Two; the exception was the Ford Motor Company, which operated a government-financed plant at Willow Run, Michigan. As the war progressed the Liberator was being produced by Consolidated at San Diego and Fort Worth, by Douglas at Tulsa, Oklahoma, by Ford and by North American Aviation at Dallas. Costs came down as production mounted. Each B-24A cost $341,960 to build, whilst a typical B-24J cost $210,943.

There were many incidents affecting Lend-Lease aircraft at the factory. On 2 June 1941, the first Liberator II (AL503) took off from Lindbergh Field, San Diego on its final acceptance flight before delivery. As the prototype it had been fitted with two Boulton & Paul power turrets (other aircraft received their armament after delivery in the UK). During take-off a loose bolt jammed the elevator control in the up position and the aircraft stalled into San Diego Bay, killing the company's chief test pilot,

William B. Wheatley, and all others on board. In order to fulfil Contract F-677, another Liberator II was built and assigned RAF serial FP685. It is coincidence that RAF serial FP686 was allocated as a replacement for Vultee V-72 Vengeance AN679, which crashed before delivery.

Aircraft Names

A quick look at the aircraft names allocated to Lend-Lease aircraft for the RAF and Royal Navy reveals that there was a continuing tradition of assigning geographical names – Boston, Hudson, Ventura, Harvard, Cornell, Baltimore, Maryland, Cleveland, Chesapeake etc. Curtiss introduced the Hawk series, so it was practical to name successive fighters Mohawk, Tomahawk, Kittyhawk. Grumman preferred bird names for its amphibious flying boats – Goose, Gosling, Widgeon etc. – and cat names for its fighters – Wildcat, Hellcat, Tigercat. Although there are two states with the name Dakota, North and South, some sources claim the name for the ubiquitous transport is an acronym for 'Douglas Aircraft Company Transport Aircraft'.

From the beginning the name Liberator was commonly used in association with the early procurement of the type by the British, so the general impression was formed that the name was British in origin. In fact, this appeared to be confirmed in 1942 when Consolidated placed a full-page advertisement in several popular US aviation magazines which stated, in part, 'We always thought of her by her US Army designation – the Consolidated B-24 . . . Then we discovered she had already won a name. The British were calling her the Liberator . . . So, from now on, Liberator is official.'

The advertising agency was obviously not in direct touch with Major Reuben H. Fleet, president of Consolidated. On 25 October 1940, Air Commodore B.G.A. Parker RAF of the British Purchasing Commission had written to Major Fleet to ask what name Consolidated had given to the bomber the company would soon start delivering to them. In his reply, dated 28 October 1940, Fleet stated the name was 'Consolidated Liberator', adding, 'We chose Liberator because the airplane can carry destruction to the heart of the Hun, and thus help you and us to liberate those nations temporarily finding themselves under Hitler's yoke.' It was later revealed that the name Liberator

was suggested by Fleet's children's governess, Miss Edith Brocklebank. She was British.

Initially the Bell P-39 was named Caribou, later changed to Airacobra. This is one of the many names jointly adopted by the Allies on both sides of the Atlantic. As far as is known neither the Waco CG-13A glider or the Pitcairn PA-34A autogyro ever received names. The Douglas Boston is a type connected with more than one name, indicating modification. The Boston II name was given to the ex-French DB-7s powered by 1,100 hp R-1830-S3C4-G engines. Upon arrival in the UK the aircraft became Havoc Is. These were completed in two basic versions: the Havoc I (Intruder) version, also known as Moonfighter, Ranger and Havoc IV; and the Havoc I night-fighter version. Then there was the Havoc I (Pandora) modified to carry in the bomb bay a Long Aerial Mine, and the Havoc I (Turbinlite) fitted with a 2,700 million candlepower Helmore/GEC searchlight in the nose.

Initially the Grumman G-36 was known as the Martlet. No fewer than 1,123 of the fighter type were obtained for the Royal Navy, entering service with the Fleet Air Arm by courtesy of the French Navy (Aéronavale) which had ordered a batch of eighty-one to equip the squadrons intended for service on the new 18,000-ton aircraft carriers, *Joffre* and *Painleve*, both of which failed to materialise, the former being still on the stocks in June 1940 and the latter not even started.

In June 1940, with the collapse of France, the French order was transferred to the UK and the first Martlet was delivered on 27 July, before the type had gone into service with the US Navy, and assembled at Prestwick. It operated from Skeabrae in the Orkney Islands providing fighter defence for the fleet anchorage at Scapa Flow. Falling within the criteria for the Battle of Britain, the Martlet became the only US-built aircraft officially to participate in the Battle of Britain and the first in RAF service to destroy an enemy aircraft.

In addition to 100 ordered for the UK, over 100 were taken over from French and Greek contracts, whilst the rest, just under 1,000, were delivered under Lend-Lease. On 13 January 1944, to conform to US Navy nomenclature, the name was changed to Wildcat. Many Lend-Lease Wildcats were dumped at sea after World War Two as both the UK and the US already had too many aircraft in the surplus market.

The name Tarpon was initially given to the Grumman TBF-1B of which 402 were received by the Royal Navy for use by the Fleet Air Arm. Later the US name Avenger was adopted for the type in service with the FAA.

I can vividly recall the many official amendments which arrived for inclusion in the AP 1480 aircraft recognition manual. These increased as more Lend-Lease information on types was released. One must remember that both the Lockheed Hudson and the North American Mustang owed their origin to a British requirement and were ordered by the British Purchasing Commission. With many equivalent models in production for both the UK and the US, the designations posed a problem which was further complicated by the different equipment installed. All aircraft requisitioned on a British direct purchase order were flown with RAF or RN serial numbers, and so received no US Army Air Corps serial.

The table in Appendix C was taken from a World War Two aircraft spotter's book and emphasises the designation and name problem. This problem disappeared with the introduction of production Lend-Lease aircraft which were paid for by American funding, even when no equivalent model was being developed for the US.

Lend-Lease aircraft destined for the RAF, as distinguished from those for the Royal Navy (Fleet Air Arm), were ordered through US Army Air Corps procurement channels and so had allocated standard Air Corps designations and serial numbers. Lend-Lease types equivalent to their US models were still fitted quite often with British-specified equipment. Late Douglas and Boeing-built DB-7 Bostons became designated A-20Cs to distinguish them from the considerably different A-20As built for the USAAC. When any of the A-20Cs were diverted for US service they retained the British camouflage and often the RAF serial and fin flash. They had US stars painted over the roundels, sometimes on both wings in preference to the standard US practice of only one star on the upper port and one on the lower starboard wings, the US serial being added on the tail whilst still retaining the RAF serial.

Only one source can be found with a reference to the Lockheed B-37 Lexington, named Ventura by the RAF, of which an initial order for 675 was placed by the BPC, first flight being on 31 July 1941. When included in the Lend-Lease programme it became designated B-34 with the USAAC for procurement purposes. Early examples requisitioned from Lend-Lease allocations were known as the B-37, whilst others were designated B-34A. Under the original British contract, 188, later increased to 300 (AE658 to 957), Model 37-21-01 Venturas were ordered; some, including AE659 and AE662, were flight-tested in US markings, with AE662 being retained by Lockheed as a test-bed for the new powerplant installation of the Constellation nacelle. This aircraft, powered by two 2,200 hp Wright R-3350s fitted in Constellation-type nacelles, was nicknamed 'Ventellation', a part combination of the Ventura and Constellation names. Deliveries to the UK commenced in September 1941; RAF aircraft were ferried across the North Atlantic, with three crashing during the delivery flight.

Air Publications

A small booklet for the vest pocket entitled 'Spot them in the Air' was published by the *Daily Mirror* late in 1939 costing three pence. Of the twenty-seven Allied and enemy silhouettes featured there are just two Lend-Lease types – Harvard and Hudson. My copy of the 1940 'Confidential' copy of 'Silhouettes of British Aircraft' is more revealing as it includes the Buffalo, Lightning, Mohawk, Vultee Vanguard 48, Curtiss SBC-4, Northrop A-17A, Vought 156, Boston, Liberator, Martin 167, Hudson, Harvard, Cessna, Douglas DC-3, Lockheed 12, Lockheed 14, Lockheed Electra, Stinson 105 and Stinson Reliant.

The Curtiss SBC-4 was the Cleveland, Northrop A-17A the Nomad, Vought 156 the Chesapeake, Martin 167 the Maryland, Stinson 105 the Sentinel. The Cessna silhouette was listed in the civil section of the document and was the Cessna Airmaster first produced in 1934 as the C-34. A number of later models, C-145 and C-165, were pressed into USAAF service as utility transports during World War Two, designated UC-77 and UC-94. Eleven UC-77s were impressed and only three C-165s as the UC-94.

As a very young and enthusiastic ATC cadet with 1233 Squadron (Driffield), I first encountered Lend-Lease aircraft in 1942 on visits to the gunnery school located at RAF Catfoss which was equipped with Mustang and Thunderbolt fighters, visitors being the Boston and Mitchell. Later the Northrop P-61 Black Widow was demonstrated at the station. One wonders how near the RAF were to having the Black

Widow included in the Lend-Lease programme, as the type was fully evaluated by a test pilot friend at Boscombe Down.

Located between RAF Driffield, my home station, and RAF Leconfield was RAF Hutton Cranswick, some four miles south of my home, opened in 1942. During World War Two the Lend-Lease Mustang was flown with various squadrons including 170 Squadron in September 1942, 168 Squadron in September 1943, and 26 Squadron in April 1944. In September 1943 both 168 and 170 Squadrons arrived in order to evaluate a steel mesh runway laid out at Huggate Wold, and after flight tests with the Mustang both units moved in on 10 and 11 October. This was in preparation for the first landing on such strips in Normandy in June 1944.

Hutton Cranswick became No. 16 Armament Practice Camp (APC), this resulting in a large, noisy, single-engine Lend-Lease type arriving – the Vultee Vengeance target-tug. In August 1945, 288 Squadron equipped with the type was resident, but earlier in December 1943, Vengeance aircraft from 291 Squadron had been resident for a while. I recall looking over HB528 and discovering it was ex-USAAF 41-101361.

Finally, a few days after the fiftieth anniversary of D-Day, I enquired of a good friend, Les Clark, who served in the Royal Navy, where he was on 6 June 1944. He was in Glasgow docks aboard the Lend-Lease escort carrier HMS *Fencer*, ex-CVE-14, loading up with British Seafires and Lend-Lease Grumman Martlets. He later went with this wooden-decked aircraft carrier to Australia.

It must be remembered that nearly forty escort carriers were operated by the Royal Navy under Lend-Lease with the loss of only two: HMS *Avenger*, ex-BAVG-2, on 15 November 1942 and HMS *Dasher*, ex-BAVG-5, on 27 March 1943. They played their part operating with the Atlantic convoys carrying Lend-Lease material including aircraft. Their presence was vital.

INTRODUCTION

Lend-Lease commenced early in 1941, when the US Congress passed HR 1776 – the famous Act stipulating that any kind of defence material might be put at the disposal of other governments anywhere in the world, without cash payment, for purposes essential to the defence of the United States. The first transfers of defence material to Britain were arranged three hours after the Act became law. Two years later expenditure under it had reached eleven thousand million dollars, and a further six thousand million dollars had been earmarked for supplying aid to the United Nations.

Lend-Lease was a weapon of war. It was forged at a time when the freedom-loving peoples of the world were in mortal peril. It was a concrete recognition of the truth that those freedom-loving peoples can defend their freedom only by working and fighting together. That is how the Allies turned the tide of Axis aggression. Lend-Lease was a new and important development in the foreign policy of the United States. The huge Lend-Lease administration was only a small part of the machinery which the United States had built up for sending war supplies to those nations fighting the Axis forces. Lend-Lease was a vital mechanism of war supply.

During March 1938, Adolf Hitler seized Austria. In London, the government quickly approved a plan for the British aircraft industry to be expanded. At the same time, a British air mission was dispatched to North America. Among the members of that unique mission was an unknown Air Commodore named Arthur T. Harris, later to be the Commander-in-Chief of RAF Bomber Command, and Sir Henry Self, who later served as chief of the British Air Commission in the USA.

The mission found the American aircraft industry in April 1938 operating only in skeleton fashion. Many of the companies were barely able to keep going at all on the thin stream of orders then coming in. The US Army was still limited by statute to an air force of 2,300 aircraft, and the US Navy to one of 1,000. In the twelve months ending 30 June 1938, the armed services together had appropriations to purchase only 900 aircraft.

After visiting most of the large aircraft companies, the British mission placed only two orders, both having important consequences. The first was for 400 of the new advanced trainers that North American Aviation Corporation had developed for the US Army Air Corps. This was just the beginning of a long series of orders for many thousands of these Harvard trainers which were used in the training of tens of thousands of pilots all over the world under the huge Commonwealth training programme.

The other order was for long-range reconnaissance bombers. When the mission visited the Lockheed Company's plant in Burbank, California in the spring of 1938, they found nothing that would satisfy British military requirements and prepared to move on. But Lockheed, like most other aircraft companies in the USA, needed orders badly. Robert Gross, the president, asked for forty-eight hours to allow his engineers to work up plans for a military adaptation of one of their commercial types, the Lockheed 14 Super Electra airliner. Naturally the mission was sceptical, but forty-eight hours later they were presented with a full-scale mock-up of a long-range bomber. They were impressed and were satisfied that it had great possibilities and placed an order for 200 aircraft. This was the birth of the famous Lockheed Hudson bomber, which filled an important gap in RAF Coastal Command and made a great contribution to the harrying of the U-boat during the early stages of World War Two. Total deliveries to the RAF of the Hudson were just over 2,000, the type being followed by the Lockheed Ventura.

The orders placed with North American and Lockheed led also to some of the largest engine orders placed in many years with the two principal aircraft engine manufacturers – the Wright Aeronautical Corporation and Pratt & Whitney.

Before World War Two the United States was governed by the pre-war Neutrality Act, which obliged President Roosevelt on 3 September 1939 to place an embargo on all shipments of arms to any of the belligerent nations. Ten days later he had called Congress to a special session to consider the removal

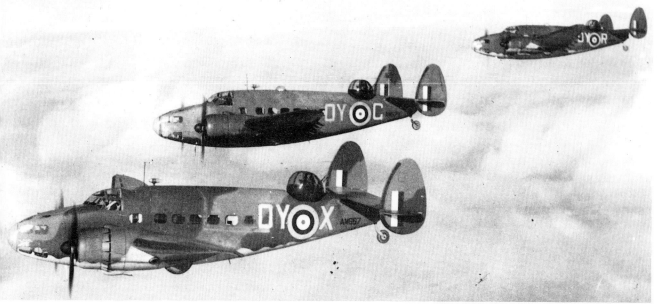

Over twenty squadrons of the RAF were equipped with the Hudson during World War 2. 48 Squadron aircraft shown here, were supplied in June 1941 being based in the Shetlands. The type was hard at work from the first day of World War 2, their main task being to keep a watch for German surface raiders attempting to escape into the Atlantic between Scotland and Norway. (MAP).

of this ban, which, under the appearance of impartiality, virtually deprived Great Britain and France of all the advantages of the seas in the transport of munitions and supplies. It was not until the end of November 1939, after many weeks of discussion and agitation, that the Neutrality Act was repealed and the new principle of 'Cash and Carry' substituted. This still preserved the strict neutrality on the part of the United States, for Americans were as free to sell weapons to Germany as to the Allies. Three days after the passage of the new law the British Purchasing Commission, headed by Arthur Purvis, a man of outstanding ability, began its work.

In the United States, the long debate on HR1176 – the Lend-Lease Bill – was in its final stage of a national debate that had been going on with increasing vigour since the fall of France. The Senate version of the Bill went back to the House for concurrence in minor changes, and on Tuesday, 11 March 1941 the House accepted them by a vote of 317 to seventy-one. As soon as the vote was completed, the House Minority Leader Representative Martin and Republican Senator Vandenberg, both of whom had been active in opposition, issued unity statements pledging full bi-partisan support of the Lend-Lease programme, now it was the law of the land. Within three hours of signing the Lend-Lease Act on the afternoon of 11 March 1941, President Roosevelt issued two directives putting the Lend-Lease programme in motion.

The ferrying of aircraft from the United States by the RAF commenced late in 1940. To operate the service ATFERO was formed (Atlantic Ferry Organisation), ferry crews being recruited from Imperial Airways, Canadian and even US airlines. On 20 July 1941, ATFERO became RAF Ferry Command, the change not affecting operations or staff. A mixture of civilian and service personnel continued to work together.

Orders for aircraft continued to be placed with both British and American companies for operational and training types needed in the years ahead, for which Winston Churchill had offered no prospect but blood, toil, tears and sweat. Some aircraft were diverted from French and Belgian orders.

To handle the large volume of US aircraft being ferried across the North and South Atlantic during World War Two, special arrangements were made, especially in the United Kingdom. British aircraft companies were appointed as 'sister firms' to American aircraft manufacturers, with responsibilities for specific types of Lend-Lease aircraft destined for both the RAF and the Royal Navy.

Anomalies

There were many anomalies in relation to Lend-Lease contracts with repossession on both sides of aircraft types as and when required in different theatres of operations. There were the odd aircraft not listed in the Lend-Lease contracts, but nevertheless involved. During 1941 the British government purchased for one million dollars each three huge Boeing Model 314A Clippers from the US government for BOAC to operate from Poole, Dorset, via Bathurst and Lisbon to Africa and the United States. In six-and-a-half years up to January 1948, these three flying boats averaged 18,000 flying hours, flew over 4,258,876 miles including 596 Atlantic crossings, and carried 40,042 passengers including Mr Winston Churchill. They were definitely servants of Lend-Lease.

Another anomaly which does appear in the official Lend-Lease listing is quoted as being a Curtiss C-46 Commando, but actually it was the prototype CW-20T transport completed in 1940 and fitted with twin fins, registered as NX19436 c/n 101. The US Army became very interested in the CW-20, purchasing the prototype for $361,556 in June 1941 and assigning the designation C-55 and serial 41-21041. In a very unusual move, the US Army Air Corps soon returned the transport to Curtiss and allowed it to be sold to BOAC in September 1941, which registered it G-AGDI and named it *St Louis*. After BOAC service it was scrapped in the United Kingdom on 29 October 1943. Under the Lend-Lease programme it was allocated the requisition No. 2991 and Contract AC-15802.

Prior to the inauguration of Lend-Lease in March 1941, Curtiss P-40 sales were made to both France and Britain under separate designation and serial number systems. The US Army Air Corps purchased the type under the US designation P-40 with appropriate US serial numbers, whilst the United Kingdom, which placed its own orders and took over the initial French orders, bought similar Curtiss 81s and 87s under the RAF names Tomahawk and Kittyhawk with appropriate RAF serials.

After Lend-Lease became effective, all procurement was through the Air Corps – US Army Air Force after 20 June 1941 – using US designations and serials. Even though a particular aircraft was intended for Britain, was equipped to meet RAF requirements and to carry RAF markings and serial number, it also had a US designation and serial number.

There were examples of the US recalling loaned Lend-Lease equipment, one being when the US Army Air Force took over some of the P-40s delivered to the RAF for use in North Africa during January 1943. These repossessed P-40F-20s from RAF Kittyhawk II orders had the US national star insignia painted over the RAF roundel and the US serial number added to the tail. Other RAF models repossessed included a number of P-40K and P-40L fighters.

The Curtiss P-40 series is an excellent example to use in an attempt to clarify the anomalies covering Lend-Lease aircraft. The RAF had numerous fighter squadrons using the type at various periods during World War Two, whilst the RAAF and RNZAF had eight and seven squadrons respectively. The RCAF used many at home in defence and training roles, whilst four RCAF squadrons flew Tomahawks overseas and three used Kittyhawks in Alaska and the Aleutians. While the French never received any of the early Tomahawks that they ordered in 1939, Free French forces were well supplied with Lend-Lease

Rare photo taken at Takoradi, Gold Coast, West Africa, showing three RAF Tomahawk fighters awaiting delivery after assembly. The type was delivered from the USA to both the UK and West Africa in crates by sea. Deliveries commenced late in 1940 prior to Lend-Lease. The Tomahawk was a development of the earlier Mohawk, differing mainly in having an Allison liquid-cooled 1,040hp V-1710-33 engine. (MAP)

Bearing British style camouflage and RAF tail flash, this Kittyhawk IIA 41-14216 or P-40F-20 coded 'X6-0' is from a batch of fighters initially destined for the RAF but repossessed for use in the invasion of North Africa in January 1943. Over 3,000 Kittyhawks were delivered to the Commonwealth Air Forces under Lend-Lease, the first being delivered to the RAF late in 1941. (Via Peter M Bowers).

P-40s and operated three squadrons in North Africa after November 1942.

Other Curtiss P-40s were supplied through Lend-Lease or diverted from RAF direct-purchase and Lend-Lease orders for use by China, the USSR, South Africa, the Netherlands East Indies, neutral Turkey, Brazil and Egypt. One RAF P-40M Kittyhawk III transferred to the Soviet Union was captured by the Finnish Air Force and then used against the Russians.

Curtiss P-40E-1s were Kittyhawk IAs procured for the RAF with Lend-Lease funds, the odd one being retained for US Army Air Corps use having US markings applied over the British camouflage. The -1 suffix was added to formalise the differences between the 1,500 Kittyhawk IAs supplied to the RAF fitted with British equipment early in the Lend-Lease programme, and the USAAC P-40E.

Of the 586 Kittyhawk IVs built for the RAF, the first 130 were delivered to the USSR, whilst a further forty-one were sent to Brazil. These were equivalent to the P-40N. Twelve Kittyhawk IA fighters which went to the RCAF lost their RAF identity and were taken on RCAF charge on 10 April 1942, and were allocated serials 720 to 731; ex-ET845, 847, 849, 850, 852, 854, 856, 858, 860, 862, 863 and 866 with Curtiss c/n 1306, 1308, 1310, 1311, 1313, 1315, 1317, 1319, 1321, 1323, 1324 and 1327. A total of 1,500 aircraft, ET100 to EV699 is recorded, being listed as Kittyhawk I/IAs, equivalent to the P-40D/E. Their US serials were 41-24776 to 41-25195 and 41-35874 to 41-36953. There were many diversions, some by ship to Australia and New Zealand direct, and by rail over the border to Canada. Later others were diverted to the South African Air Force. At least thirty-four were lost at sea en route to the United Kingdom.

RCAF records reveal that in January 1943 fifteen Kittyhawk III fighters were acquired on Lend-Lease contract, having their US serials only prior to being allocated 831 to 844 with the RCAF. These were followed by thirty-five Kittyhawk IVs during 1943–4, again ex-US and allocated RCAF serials 845 to 880. Earlier in the war, seventy-two Kittyhawk I fighters with RCAF serials 1028 to 1099, received in 1941–2, were all ex-RAF with serials in the AK and AL range. Twenty-one were transferred to Turkey out of this batch of 560 aircraft carrying RAF serials AK571 to AL230. This batch in the RAF serial sequence was preceded by an earlier batch of 471 Tomahawk IIB fighters, AK100 to 570. Of these AK210 to 224 and AK226 to 241 were lost at sea en route. Of these 125 were shipped to Russia and nine transferred to the RCAF and one to the Turkish Air Force. Thirty-six were diverted to China for use by the American Volunteer Group – AVG, known as the 'Flying Tigers'. Britain released a total of 100 Tomahawks to the AVG which adopted the famous shark's teeth nose emblem originating with the RAF which used the marking on its Tomahawks in North Africa during 1940.

These references are used only as an example of the anomalies within the huge Lend-Lease contract programme involving not only aircraft destined for the United Kingdom, but those destined for the Commonwealth. It would require a large volume or possibly two to record all the RCAF Lend-Lease aircraft.

Scene on board the USS Ranger, *a small escort carrier, seen at sea on 9 March 1943 as Curtiss Kittyhawk P-40F-20 fighters of the USAAF are prepared for action in a joint USAAF-US Navy mission during the Allied invasion of North Africa. The fighters were originally destined for Britain under Lend-Lease as Kittyhawk II and they retain the British camouflage.*

Export Hawks

Other than the US Army Air Corps, France was the first customer for the Curtiss Model 81, and during April 1940 the first export aircraft was completed in French markings, but could not be delivered. The United Kingdom took over the French contracts and accepted the Curtiss aircraft under the name Tomahawk. The later Model 87, also ordered by France, was used by Britain as the Kittyhawk. When Curtiss introduced the P-40F powered by the Rolls-Royce Merlin engine, the new name Warhawk was applied to distinguish it from the Allison-engined P-40D and P-40E. This name was not adopted by the RAF for the re-engined model, and the name Kittyhawk was retained for both versions of the Model 87.

Although the Curtiss P-40 was used by many nations during World War Two, the United Kingdom was the only purchaser of the type other than the USAAC. Many RAF models were released for use by other Allied air forces and taken from the original direct-purchase orders of 1939–40. Those ordered after March 1941 were Lend-Lease models delivered as described earlier with US designation and serial numbers in addition to RAF serial numbers and markings or camouflage. With such complexity surrounding just one aircraft type, the Curtiss P-40 series, it is obvious that discrepancies and contradictions exist within the manufacturer's records when an attempt is made to match Tomahawk and Kittyhawk designations to the appropriate RAF serial allocations and the equivalent USAAC P-40 models.

The following information has been extracted from British official records. In some cases it supplements information on the type to be found in the appendices. A similar situation can be found in the material covering the Douglas DB-7 and A-20 Havoc/Boston. The first aircraft made its maiden flight on 17 August 1939, and DB-7s were first accepted by the French Purchasing Commission at Santa Monica on 31 October with deliveries being made by ship to Casablanca. Before the fall of France in June 1940 less than half of the DB-7 order had been accepted, a number never reaching the Armée de l'Air as they were still in transit aboard ship. Sixteen from the first French production batch were diverted to Belgium, and France thus actually took delivery of only seventy DB-7s. The United Kingdom took over the French DB-7s, twenty being designated Boston I with the RAF, whilst later DB-7s were designated Boston II but upon arrival in the UK became Havoc I aircraft.

Tomahawk/Kittyhawk Models

Tomahawk (Model 81) A total of 1,180 delivered under British direct-purchase contracts. In addition, the RAF took over ten P-40C fighters from the USAAC, these being 41-13389, 41-13390, 41-13396, 41-13397, 41-13398, 41-13399, 41-13400, 41-13401, 41-13406 and 41-13407. The RAF operated them as Tomahawks of an unspecified mark and without RAF serial numbers.

Tomahawk I (Model H81-A) A total of 140 equivalents to the USAAC P-40, except for four wing guns, were ordered on two contracts with deliveries commencing in April 1940. It was decided that these were unsuitable for combat use and they were relegated to training roles. Three were used by the RCAF retaining RAF serials AH774, AH793 and AH840, becoming instructional airframes. RAF serials were AH741–840 c/n 14446–14545 (100); AH841–880 c/n 14091–14130 (40).

Tomahawk II Designation not used officially for specific aircraft, but was a generalisation for improved Tomahawks delivered during October and November 1940.

Tomahawk IIA (Model H81-A2) Protective armour and externally-covered self-sealing fuel tanks on 110 aircraft equivalent to the P-40B. Twenty-three transferred to the USSR and AH938 to Canada as an instructional airframe. RAF serials AH881–990 c/n 14131–14220 (90); c/n 14582–14601 (20).

Tomahawk IIB (Model H-81-A2, -A3) A total of 930 in four lots. These were generally equivalent to the P-40C and were used extensively by the RAF and SAAF in North Africa as from 16 June 1941. Of these, 100 fighters unofficially designated H81-A3 were released to China and used by the AVG. A further twenty-three went to the USSR, and unspecified numbers went to Turkey and Egypt. RAF serials AH991–999 c/n 14658–14666 (9) to Russia; AK100–570 c/n 14582–14951, 15423–15522 (471) of which thirty-six went to China; AM370–519 c/n 15823–15972 (150) of which sixty-four went to China; AN218–517 c/n 17817–18116 (300).

Kittyhawk The French contract for Curtiss Model 87s was taken over by Britain prior to construction commencing. The airframe and engine changes justified the new name – Kittyhawk. A total of 560 was procured on direct-purchase contracts and a further 2,432 were supplied by the Lend-Lease programme, bringing the total to 2,992.

Kittyhawk I (Model A87-A2) Fitted with four .50 inch calibre wing guns, the 560 fighters were comparable to the P-40D. The United Kingdom took over the initial French order and deliveries commenced in August 1941, with seventy-two diverted to Canada, as mentioned earlier, and seventeen to Turkey. RAF serials AK571–870 c/n 14952–15251 (300), five to Turkey; AK871–950 c/n 15342–15421 (80), three to Turkey; AK951–999 c/n 18695–18743 (49), four to Turkey; AL100–230 c/n 18744–18874 (131), five to Turkey. Seventy-two to the RCAF allocated serials 1028 to 1099 all ex-RAF serials. Example: 1028, ex-AK752, taken on charge 9 October 1941, struck off charge 16 August 1946 and served with 132 Squadron.

Kittyhawk IA (Model H87-A3, -A4) The 1,500 fighters were direct equivalents of the P-40E and were delivered under the US Army Air Corps designation P-40-1 to distinguish the British equipment etc. from those for US service. Many were diverted to Canada, Australia and New Zealand. The RAAF serials were A29-1–163 (163); RNZAF serials NZ3001–NZ3044 (44); NZ3091–NZ3098 (8); NZ3100–NZ3108 (9) and NZ3271. Twelve went to the RCAF as detailed earlier.

Kittyhawk II (Model H87-B3) World War Two British sources identify the 330 RAF P-40Fs and P-40Ls as Kittyhawk IIs; later records list the first 230 as

Kittyhawk IIAs. Eighty-one were transferred to the USAAC overseas and seven, FL263/270/276/280/283/305/307, were given to the Free French Air Force. The RNZAF had one P-40L with serial NZ3074. RAF serials P-40F FL219–368 (150); FL369–448 (80); P-40L FS400–499 (100).

Kittyhawk III Of the 616 Kittyhawk IIIs, the first 192 were P-40K-1s, the next 160 were P-40Ls, and the final 264 were P-40Ms. The last 170 were diverted to the USSR. Nine P-40K-1s were delivered to the RCAF on 26 November 1942 retaining their US serials – 42-45921, 42-45944, 42-45945, 42-45951, 42-45952, 42-45954, 42-45977, 42-46003 and 42-46004. The RAF serials of the 170 P-40Ms which went to Russia were FS100–269. Type was widely used by the RAAF and RNZAF. Fifteen went to the RCAF as 831–845.

Kittyhawk IV (Model H87V, W) The final 586 Kittyhawks were USAAC P-40Ns delivered from March 1943 to January 1944 of which 130 were diverted to the USSR. The RAF serials were FS270–399 (130) to Russia; FT849–954 (106); FX498–847 (350). The type was used by the RAAF, the RNZAF and the RCAF.

Export Model Designations
The following are export model designations used for the Curtiss Model 81 and 87 with reference to British Purchasing Commission and Lend-Lease orders.

Model H81-A1 Two French orders for 100 and 85 equivalents of the P-40 except for French instruments and equipment plus the unique reverse movement French throttles. The first few were completed in French markings but none delivered to France, with Britain taking them all as Tomahawk Is.

Model 81-A2 Improvement Model 81-A fighters equivalent to the P-40B. Britain ordered 865 on direct-purchase orders as the Tomahawk I and IA and released 100 identified as H81-A3s to China for the AVG.

Model 81-A3 Unofficial designation for the 100 fighters from the British 81-A2 contract diverted to the AVG. This was a Curtiss 'paper' designation.

Model 81-AC Forty conversions of the P-40C type airframe to British requirements and was an unspecified Tomahawk mark.

Model 87-A1 Unspecified order from France but not delivered and designation cancelled.

Model 87-A2 Twenty equivalents of the P-40D for Britain as Kittyhawk Is.

Model 87-A3 Covered 540 equivalents of the P40E to Britain as Kittyhawk IIs.

Model 87-A4 Curtiss P-40Es with British equipment provided under Lend-Lease as P-40E-1s designated Kittyhawk IAs.

Model 87-A5 Unspecified number made as part of 87-A4 order.

Model 87-B3 This covered 1,311 USAAF P-40Fs with 230 intended for Britain as Kittyhawk IIAs. The -B3 designation was retained for 700 P-40Ls.

Model 87-V, 87-W Total of 5,220 USAAF P-40Ns and 456 British Kittyhawk IVs.

Losses at Sea

It is a well known fact that the British Merchant Navy played a crucial role in World War Two. In March 1942 a total of 273 British and Allied merchant ships was lost, some carrying vitally needed Lend-Lease aircraft types as deck cargo. By November 1942 the Germans had 200 U-boats on patrol with a further 170 in training, and Admiral Dönitz was in sight of his target of 300 U-boats operating in the Atlantic. Fortunately the tide turned before that target was reached.

Records reveal that as late as August 1942 RAF Coastal Command was allocated just five Consolidated B-24 Liberator aircraft to protect the Atlantic convoys. Aircraft fitted with airborne radar assisted in making it nearly impossible for U-boats to surface in their attacks on Allied merchantmen.

One must recall the disaster which befell PQ-17 convoy when the U-boat packs sank twenty-four out of the convoy's thirty-five merchant ships in freezing Arctic waters. The subsequent loss of Lend-Lease material included 4,246 lorries and gun carriers, 594 tanks and 297 aircraft. It was a major disaster.

1. Pattern for Victory

On 17 December 1940, President F. D. Roosevelt was talking to reporters crowded in his oval office in the White House for the weekly press conference. He told the story of the man helping his neighbour with a fire that had broken out. It was told for a purpose. At this time the most terrible conflagration the world had ever seen was raging. It had started in 1931 with a small fire in Manchuria, a region in north-east China that seemed far away and of no great concern to the rest of the world. In 1937, the fire of Japanese aggression broke out again with new fury, eventually to grow so big that it threatened to overwhelm all of China and to spread over eastern Asia and far out into the Pacific. Here in Europe, ever since 1933, there had been another smouldering fire that consumed one nation after another in sudden bursts – Ethiopia, Spain, Austria, Albania and Czechoslovakia.

In September 1939, fire suddenly broke out into a furious blaze of Nazi aggression, and in the ten months that followed, Poland, Denmark, Norway, Holland, Luxembourg, Belgium and finally France were consumed. By December 1940, the British were fighting a desperate, lone battle to keep the fire from spreading across the English Channel and eventually out into the Atlantic towards both North and South America. The nations battling the Axis powers, Britain, China and others, could not get sufficient arms from the United States. Something much bigger was needed than loans to China, sales of old World War One guns to Britain after Dunkirk and the trading of fifty aged destroyers for naval bases. It is true the United States was co-operating more and more closely with these nations in their purchasing programmes, but the definitive solution proposed to the US nation at that press conference on 17 December was the essence of what came to be called 'Lend-Lease'.

During the three months that followed, the American people debated Lend–Lease as no issue in US foreign policy had ever been debated before. It reached from the halls of Congress to every fireside in America. When the vote in Congress was taken, Lend-Lease was approved by a large majority. The Act was signed on 11 March 1941. Under its original terms it would have expired on 30 June 1943, but on 9 March 1943 the House of Representatives voted 407 to six to extend the Act. Two days later, on the second anniversary of the signing of the original Act, the Senate extended it without a single dissenting vote.

Cash & Carry

In Britain the news of the passing of the Lend-Lease Act was received with the utmost enthusiasm. Rising in the House of Commons on the afternoon of 12 March 1941, Winston Churchill said that he was sure the House would wish him to express on their behalf, and on behalf of the nation, '. . . our deep and respectful appreciation of this monument of generous and far-seeing statesmanship. The government and people of the United States have in fact written a new Magna Carta, which not only has regard to the rights and laws upon which a healthy and advancing civilisation can alone be erected, but also proclaims by precept and example the duty of free men and free nations, wherever they may be, to share the responsibility and the burden of enforcing them.'

General George C. Marshall, the US Chief of Staff, was responsible for a defence programme which dated from 16 May 1940, six days after the Nazis had begun their offensive on France and the Low Countries. On that day, the President sent a special message to Congress. 'These are ominous days,' he began. Then he asked the Congress for the first of two special appropriations which he requested that month for Army and Navy expansion, totalling more than 2,500 million dollars. With one eye on the Maginot Line and the other on the fate of five nations which had found within the past five weeks that neutrality and good intentions would not save them for aggression, the President said, 'No old defence is so strong that it requires no further strengthening, and no attack is so unlikely or impossible that it may be ignored.'

Then he sprang on them a figure that electrified

the Congress and the nation: 'I should like to see this nation geared up to the ability to turn out at least 50,000 planes a year.' Production the year before, 1939, numbered 2,100 military aircraft of which most were trainers.

About the same time as the first British Air Mission with Air Commodore Harris came to the United States, the French placed their first order for 100 Curtiss-Wright P-36 fighters, the predecessor of the world-famous P-40 of World War Two. The US government played no role in these foreign purchases, although it was customary for official foreign missions to pay courtesy calls on General H. H. 'Hap' Arnold, the Chief of the US Army Air Corps, and other officials in Washington. In September and October of 1938, however, two visitors arrived in the US from opposite sides of the world whose missions resulted in the first steps of active US assistance to the nations opposing aggression.

From China, Generalissimo Chiang Kai-shek sent K. P. Chen, adviser to the Finance Ministry, to seek a loan for the purchase of supplies essential for the continued struggle against Japan. From France came Jean P. Monnet, a banker and businessman well known in the US, to gauge for the French government the possibilities of a large-scale aircraft and aero-engine purchasing programme.

As early as the Spring of 1939, France had begun considering the Lockheed P-38 Lightning for the Armée de l'Air. In April 1940 the Anglo-French Purchasing Committee placed a contract for 667 aircraft thus boosting production, as the USAAC had only ordered 80 P-38s. Model 322-61-03 or 322-F for France and 322-61-04 or 322-B for Britain were to be powered by Allison V-1710-C15s, rated at 1,090 hp at 14,000 ft. After the fall of France in June 1940, the entire contract for Model 322s was taken over by the United Kingdom, amended to provide for delivery of 143 Lightnings for the RAF. Depicted is the Lockheed P-38 assembly line located at Burbank, California early in 1940. (Lockheed).

French Order

When Jean Monnet arrived in the US in the autumn of 1938 to make a survey of plane production capacity, the President requested Secretary Henry L. Morgenthau to represent the US government. Morgenthau was the chief fiscal officer of the Federal Government, and it was his duty to keep up-to-date with the financial state of foreign governments buying in the United States; he had to make certain they had the money to pay for the goods they ordered. Monnet talked with both War and Navy Department officials and made a rapid survey of the aircraft industry in the US. He was soon convinced that the placing of large orders could rapidly expand aircraft production, and he returned to France with his report. By the end of 1938 he returned with a new air mission that immediately went into action.

On 26 January 1939, the French Air Mission placed its first contract, for 115 of the Glenn L. Martin Company's medium bombers, these being forerunners of the RAF Baltimore. Within two months the French ordered 700 more aircraft plus hundreds of additional aero-engines. By the end of 1939 the French order had reached almost 2,000 aircraft, these including Curtiss-Wright P-36 Hawks and P-40 fighters, Douglas twin-engined bombers, Martin medium bombers and North American Harvard trainers.

The greatest contribution of the French orders was in the aero-engine field. This was a bottleneck in the production of aircraft, and the orders for engines, which included a large number for use in French-designed and -built aircraft, gave the United States an important head start. By the end of 1939, France had ordered over 6,000 Wright and Pratt & Whitney engines which not only helped keep the manufacturers busy, but made it necessary to expand plant facilities: Pratt & Whitney had to double the size of their engine plant during the summer of 1939 in order to handle the French orders.

On 3 September 1939, when the United Kingdom and France declared war on Germany, the President had no choice but to enforce an arms embargo. It was not, however, in keeping with the sympathies of the US Senate and Congress which, on 4 November 1939, passed an Act permitting both the United Kingdom and France to purchase arms for cash and then carry them away in their own ships – this

became known as the 'Cash and Carry' Act.

Three days later, a new British Purchasing Commission was established in the United States under Arthur B. Purvis, a remarkably able and vigorous man who had emigrated to Canada from Britain after the First World War. Unfortunately he was killed in an air accident in Britain during August 1941. A similar French mission was established under Jean F. Bloch-Laine. Soon afterwards the supply programmes of the two Allies were co-ordinated by the establishment of the Anglo-French Co-ordinating Commission under Jean Monnet in London, and the Anglo-French Purchasing Board under Arthur Purvis in the United States.

On 6 December 1939, the President appointed a Liaison Committee to assist and watch over the entire foreign purchasing programme. The policy had now changed. Instead of selecting a few US types for acquisition, the Purchasing Board set out with the intention not only of obtaining aircraft and other essential equipment, but also of gearing the American industry machine up to large-scale production. Money was spent, not only on the equipment required but also on the establishment of manufacturing facilities. Entire factories were built in some US locations with British money. It was decided to place orders for many types of aircraft with all companies that had available capacity.

Three times as many orders were placed for aircraft by the French and British in the first half of 1940 as in the whole of 1939 – over 8,000 aircraft and 13,000 aero-engines. This brought the total of orders placed in the US by the two Allies for military aircraft in the eighteen months from 1 January 1939 to 30 June 1940 to 10,800. In the same period the US Army Air Corps and the US Navy were able to order 4,500 aircraft out of their appropriations.

However, by May 1940, despite the US war production having a good start, thousands of aircraft ordered by Great Britain and France were not yet delivered. In fact only 104, the last of those ordered in 1938, had actually been shipped across the Atlantic to Great Britain since the first of the year, whilst France had actually received only 557 aircraft.

So far as France and Britain were concerned, they and the United States had been too late with too little. The Maginot Line had been outflanked and the Nazis were already on the French coastline overlooking the English Channel.

2. Early Days of Darkness

The first detachment of the Dunkirk survivors came ashore at Dover on 29 May 1940. An urgent message was sent to President Roosevelt by Prime Minister Winston Churchill. Could anything be done to send more arms at once for the defence of England and what was left of France – if France held out? The need was immediate, but it could not be answered by arms which were not yet manufactured.

On 4 June 1940, Winston Churchill went before the House of Commons and delivered his magnificent challenge:

> 'We shall defend our island, whatever the cost may be; we shall fight on the beaches, we shall fight on the landing grounds, we shall fight in the fields and in the streets, we shall fight in the hills; we shall never surrender, and even if, which I do not for a moment believe, this island or a large part of it were subjugated and starving, then our Empire beyond the seas, armed and guarded by the British fleet, would carry on the struggle, until, in God's good time, the New World, with all its power and might, steps forth to the rescue and the liberation of the Old.'

During this critical period the US attempted to assist France by allocating some aircraft in service with the US Army Air Corps and the US Navy. They were not the number Premier Paul Reynaud of France desperately imagined might be sent when he made his last appeal for aid to President Roosevelt on 13 June 1940. At this time the US had no quantity of aircraft to send. However, the US Navy agreed to release fifty of its Curtiss-Wright SBC-4 Helldiver dive-bombers in response to a government desire to aid France. Early in 1940 France had ordered ninety export versions of the SBC-4. The aircraft were returned to the factory from the US Navy for refurbishment and application of French markings. At the same time the US Army Air Corps released ninety-three of its Northrop A-17A light attack bombers which had been in service for only eighteen months. In June 1940 they were returned to the factory for re-sale to France.

Most of the aircraft were ferried to Halifax, Nova Scotia where the French aircraft carrier *Bearn* was docked. But the aircraft never reached Europe. Sailing on 17 June 1940, this coincided with Marshal Pétain asking for an armistice. Whilst at sea Admiral Darlan ordered the ship to change course and run for Martinique in the French West Indies. Here the aircraft carrier and its aircraft remained rusting in ineffectual neutrality until three years later, when the French National Committee took over control of the island from Vichy.

In addition to the threat of invasion the disasters in France confronted Great Britain with another emergency. On 15 June 1940, the day after German troops marched down the Champs Élysées in Paris, Arthur Purvis received in New York a secret cable from London. The surrender of France, it said, might come at any moment. The British Purchasing Commission in the US must be ready to deal with the emergency which this could create in the supply programme.

Purvis immediately conferred with Sir Henry Self and Thomas Childs, the Commission's General Counsel, on the critical situation they faced. Over the past five months, the British and French purchasing programmes in the USA had been more and more closely merged together. If France should capitulate and drag into inaction with her all her supply assets in the United States, Britain would face Germany alone with the joint air programme wrecked and all the other joint contracts subject to endless legal disputes. Purvis knew that if the French contracts were cancelled, the American industry might be reluctant to go ahead with British orders. Apparently for several weeks, as the military situation grew worse, the French mission had been experiencing increasing trouble trying to persuade manufacturers in the United States to accept contracts. They had naturally begun to look like a bad risk. It would be fatal if this attitude also spread to British contracts.

To Arthur Purvis and Sir Henry Self, there was but one answer. If France fell, the French contracts must not be allowed to fall with her. They immediately sent a cable to London requesting recommendations and for discretionary powers to take any steps necessary to protect the British position. At that time outstanding French commitments in the US totalled over five hundred million dollars. Many of the contracts covered supplies for Britain which were necessary if they were to carry on. Others were for special equipment for France and would be worthless.

It would take weeks to examine the thousands of contracts covering aircraft, machine tools, raw materials, transports, aero-engines, explosives and guns. It would mean picking out what the British needed and then negotiating with the manufacturers on individual contracts. Time was a vital element and Purvis believed the British must be prepared to take on all the contracts.

At midnight on 15 June 1940, Arthur Purvis received an answer from London. He and Sir Henry Self had authority to do whatever was necessary. There were no other instructions – the full responsibility was with them.

Contract Take-over

By early Sunday morning 16 June, it was clear from radio bulletins that a Cabinet crisis was coming to a head in Bordeaux between supporters of Prime Minister Reynaud, who wanted to continue the fight, and the Pétain–Laval faction, which had decided the war was over. It was decided negotiations must start immediately with the French Air Commission. At the Commission headquarters in the Rockefeller Center, New York, Colonel Jacquin, head of the Air Commission, was dejectedly listening to the news on the radio. Thomas Childs informed him that the British wished to take over all the French contracts. There was no hesitation and he confirmed that all French air contracts would go to the British. Jacquin held no authority over the ground contracts, but he immediately contacted the French Purchasing Commission officials to arrange a meeting with the British. Later in the day Prime Minister Reynaud resigned and Pétain had decided to capitulate. The British team under Arthur Purvis worked hard drafting and re-drafting the necessary documents ready for signature. They were accepting six hundred million dollars in obligation for the British Government. The French signed knowing that the government that had appointed them had gone.

One condition was attached. The documents were to be kept secret until it was confirmed that France had finally fallen. Purvis agreed, and by the afternoon of 17 June the transfer was complete. All French assets in the US were frozen by the US Treasury Department.

Arthur Purvis admitted he was not sure that the American manufacturers would accept the documents which had been signed by the French. The Pétain government, under Nazi pressure, might repudiate the agreement in an effort to immobilise the French supplies. Purvis approached a few American companies to get their reaction. There was some hesitation at first. Then Donald Wills Douglas, president of the Douglas Aircraft Company located in Santa Monica, California, blazed the way for American industry by accepting it. The rest of the American business fell in line. The arms that had been destined for the French would now pass into the hands of the British.

Allied Bases

For over a century it had been the policy of the United States to prevent any non-American power from obtaining new territory in the western hemisphere. With the advent of the Good Neighbour policy the US made it clear that they wished to co-operate with other American republics as sovereign equals in the common defence of the hemisphere. This co-operation was advanced markedly in December 1938 by the Declaration of Principle at the conference in Lima, Peru, where all the American republics agreed to consult together whenever foreign intervention threatened part of the Americas.

After Dunkirk, the United States went a step further. On 16 June 1940, Congress authorised the Secretary of War and the Secretary of the Navy to manufacture in government-owned arsenals or shipyards, or to purchase on the open market, munitions of war for direct sale to the government of any American republic. This law, known as the Pittman Act, was a forerunner of Lend-Lease. It did for the American republics most of what the Lend-Lease Act did later for all nations whose defence was vital to the US, except relieve them of the necessity of paying cash for goods.

The United States had a strong navy, and were preparing to build up a large army and army air corps, so the possibility of getting task forces to

South America in the event of an attack was limited. If Hitler should obtain control of French Guiana, Martinique and Guadeloupe, he would immediately have bases which could be used to cut any lines of communication to the south, and even to attack the vital Panama Canal.

This danger was discussed at a meeting of foreign ministers of the American republics on 21 July 1940 in Havana, Cuba. The Panama Canal, Puerto Rico and the Virgin Islands were the most southerly bases of the United States. These were further from the hump of Brazil, where many thought Hitler was most likely to strike, than Brazil was from Dakar, the most likely point from which an attack would be launched. Moreover, the bases were hardly adequate to protect the Atlantic approaches to the vital Panama Canal without the support of the British Navy. If the US could get a base in British Guiana, they would be nearly a thousand miles closer to Natal. With additional bases on the outer islands of the Caribbean stretching from the Bahamas in the north to Trinidad in the south, they would be in a far better position to defend the Panama Canal. Most of these islands were British-owned.

Both Iceland and Greenland offered inviting bases for German operations against the North American continent. During the summer of 1940 Nazi bombers were already appearing over Iceland, and, as discovered later, a Nazi weather station had been set up in Greenland. Neither island had any defences worthy of mention. Canada, like the United States, had no North Atlantic outposts.

President Roosevelt and Prime Minister Mackenzie King met at Ogdensburg, New York on 17 August 1940 to discuss the danger of attack from the North Atlantic. They established the Permanent Joint Board of Defense to consider the defences of the northern part of the western hemisphere. Strong sea and air bases in the outlying islands of Newfoundland and Bermuda were essential to the defence of Canada and the United States. Both Bermuda and Newfoundland were British possessions.

Opinion in the United States ranged from those who were for all-out aid to Britain in the interests of American security, and those who were committed to a continental defence alone. Some groups, however, hoping to halt the transfer of US destroyers to the Royal Navy, urged that the bases in question

be given in exchange for cancellation of old World War One debts. The US Government took up the matter of Atlantic bases with Britain, and Winston Churchill's government agreed to make them available. The President stated that in the interests of US defence the over-age destroyers should be transferred to the Royal Navy. As this would tie into one transaction the destroyers and the bases, the proposal was supported vigorously by the Secretary of the US Navy, Frank Knox, and others. The United States would lease the base sites for ninety-nine years.

A temporary delay in concluding the negotiations occurred in the middle of August 1940, but a compromise was marked out in Washington and accepted in London whereby Great Britain would 'freely give' the rights to bases in Newfoundland and Bermuda, which would be of special value to the defence of Canada as well, and would trade for the aforementioned destroyers the West Indies and South American base sites located on the Bahamas, Jamaica, St Lucia, Trinidad, Antigua and British Guiana. Many of these proved to be useful on both sides for Lend-Lease deliveries.

The documents were drafted and were ready for signature on Labour Day, signed by Lord Lothian and US Secretary Cordell Hull. At this time, Winston Churchill reaffirmed the pledge given in his Dunkirk speech that the British fleet would never be scuttled or surrendered, but would fight on from overseas bases if the waters surrounding the British Isles became 'untenable'. Churchill could not, however, resist coupling the assurance with a jab at the pessimists in the United States who were then giving Britain a small chance of survival: 'These hypothetical contingencies,' he observed, 'seem more likely to concern the German fleet or what is left of it, than the British fleet.'

US Industry Growth

During the second half of 1940 and the beginning of 1941, the United States was heavily involved in the build-up of her war industry. So as to develop further the policy announced in his rearmament speech of 16 May 1940, the President, on 10 July 1940, asked Congress to appropriate funds to equip a mechanised army of 2,000,000 men and to purchase 15,000 more aircraft for the US Army Air Corps plus 4,000 for the US Navy, in addition to the 7,000 authorised for both armed services in June.

For the very first time in the history of the United States steps were taken to create a powerful army to defend North America in the face of an armed attack. The decision came none too soon. On 27 September 1940, Germany, Italy and Japan signed an alliance in which each agreed to protect the 'new order' in Europe and Asia – a 'new order' made possible only by totalitarian aggression – and to come to each other's aid in case of attack by another power. This treaty of the three Axis aggressors, disguised so thinly as a defensive alliance, was a threat of war against the United States if it continued to take steps to defend itself.

In January 1940, a Dutch Purchasing Commission travelled to the United States, but bought only a few aircraft plus a small amount of other military equipment. After the loss of their homeland in May 1940, the Dutch still retained a great overseas empire in the Netherlands East Indies, for whose defence they required all the munitions they could obtain. Five days after the Netherlands government escaped to London, a Purchasing Commission arrived in the US from the East Indies seeking aid and ordered more than $50,000,000 worth of war stores before the end of the year. Many other small nations followed suit. During the summer and autumn of 1940, Purchasing Commissions from most of the American republics and other neutral nations appeared in the United States. All sought to buy aircraft, tanks, guns and other arms, as well as tools and materials for the manufacturer of arms. Orders for China and Great Britain, the two great nations left fighting the Axis powers on opposite sides of the globe, poured into the United States at a fast-increasing rate. Loans for China were negotiated in the US by T. V. Soong on a special mission for his brother-in-law, Generalissimo Chiang Kai-shek.

Here in the United Kingdom, the country faced an entirely new strategic situation. Important sources of essential supplies from the continent of Europe were cut off with the fall of Norway, Denmark, Holland, Belgium and France. At the same time the need for arms to defend the British Isles against direct attack by Germany, and the Suez Canal in Egypt against direct attack by Italy, had multiplied. On the other side of the globe in the face of Japanese infiltration into French Indo-China, the governments of Australia and New Zealand were also thinking of arms for the defence of Singapore and the south-west Pacific.

Meanwhile, in the United States arms orders poured in and were increasing month by month. Congress appropriated huge sums for the defence programme. Aircraft orders for the US Army Air Corps and the US Navy in the two-and-a-half years from 1 January 1938 to 30 June 1940 totalled only 5,400. In the next six months alone, they amounted to 21,401.

During 1941 the Curtiss Airplane Division expanded its manufacturing area by approximately 400 per cent and it totalled 4,268,410 square feet. The total work force numbered 45,000. This expansion included the construction of a second factory located at Buffalo, New York, known as Plant Two and totalling some 1,200,000 square feet of working area, and a newly created plant at Columbus, Ohio with a floor area of 1,156,000 square feet. The original facility at St Louis, Missouri was producing in excess of eight aircraft per day, and production of the whole airplane division eventually reached sixty aircraft per day.

3. Aircraft Production and HR 1776

Two important organisations around which careful planning was centred were the National Defense Advisory Commission and the President's Liaison Committee. The Advisory Commission was charged with the responsibility of planning for the necessary expansion of production, consulting constantly with the Army, the Navy, the Air Corps, the foreign Purchasing Missions and the President's Liaison Committee acting on their behalf. The latter organisation had been created as early as December 1939.

During July 1940, Arthur Purvis, Secretary Henry L. Morgenthau and his assistant Philip Young began to discuss informally the relationship between the US aircraft production programme and the rising needs of the United Kingdom. At this time the US was turning out military aircraft at the rate of in excess of 550 per month, of which nearly half were training aircraft. Between them the British and French had ordered more than 10,000 aircraft up to 1 July 1940, but only about 250 a month were being produced during the second half of 1940 for shipment overseas. Tentative plans called for a production target of roughly 3,000 aircraft a month by the end of 1941 – 1,000 earmarked for British orders and 2,000 for the US armed services. Arthur Purvis had remarked casually several times to Secretary Morgenthau, however, that by the end of 1941 the British would require 4,000 aircraft a month from the United States instead of the 1,000 scheduled.

The requirement for aircraft came to a head during the early morning of 24 July when the future needs of Britain were initially discussed between Morgenthau, Young and Purvis in order that the latter could make a request at a meeting with US Secretary Henry L. Stimson, Knox, William Knudson and General H. H. 'Hap' Arnold. Henry L. Morgenthau was also present. Purvis increased the 1,000 aircraft a month by the end of 1941 to 1,500, but was soon reminded of the 4,000 figure. Plans were being formulated for the next eighteen months' production so there was an immediate need to know. Arthur Purvis had first to confer with Morris Wilson who was Lord Beaverbrook's representative

in the United States. It was agreed the figure be 4,000 aircraft which meant doubling the entire production programme. All workers in the US would have to pitch in and help. William Knudson stated that the new figure would never be reached by the end of 1941, but by another year it could be achieved. He was not far wrong. By the end of 1942, aircraft production was 5,400 a month, and by August 1943 the figure had risen to 7,500 a month. United States industry had accepted the challenge and come through with flying colours.

Here in the United Kingdom, Lord Beaverbrook broadcast to tell the good news to the British public. The promise of even greater aid helped and gave the country courage to face the Battle of Britain which began two weeks later on 8 August 1940. However, although the United Kingdom received many aircraft, the number was nothing like the agreed figure of 4,000 per month. Long before the United States reached the production figure of 6,000 a month, both Russia and the US had been attacked.

With the aircraft production programme doubled overnight, plans had to be laid to expand the production of components. Aero-engines still continued to be one of the worse bottlenecks. During the summer of 1940, the US Army Air Corps was using air-cooled radial engines, but had turned to liquid-cooled engines for use in fighter aircraft. A new engine developed and built by Allison was going into production; it held promise, but 'bugs' were still appearing and took time to eliminate. Realising the predicament the Air Corps became interested in the battle-proved Rolls-Royce Merlin engine used with great success in both the Supermarine Spitfire and Hawker Hurricane fighters plus Vickers Armstrong Wellington and Handley Page Halifax bombers.

Secretary Morgenthau telephoned Lord Beaverbrook, who had just been appointed Minister of Aircraft Production, and requested a licence to produce Merlin engines in the United States. This was approved immediately. On 3 September 1940, a contract was signed with the Packard Motor Company to produce 9,000 Merlin engines of which 3,000 were for the US Army Air Corps and 6,000 for the United Kingdom where they were needed to step up bomber production. However, a factory had to be built and tooled up. The cost of this was split between the two Allies, one-third borne by the US and two-thirds by the British. Prior to the plant being completed, the UK government had paid over $24,900,000 for the construction and had submitted the design of the engine. The Packard-Merlin was produced for the US Army Air Corps without a royalty charge and this engine powered the later North American P-51 Mustang and some of the Curtiss P-40 Tomahawk fighters.

More committees were created with representatives from the Allied armed services, including a Joint Aircraft Committee whose task was to standardise aircraft and their armament. The first aircraft attended to was the Curtiss P-40 which was in full-scale production for both the United States and Great Britain. The two models were basically the same, but had innumerable differences in detail, with each government constantly changing specifications independently of the other. This was giving the manufacturer more than a headache and was resulting in a low rate of production. In September 1940 the committee met at the Buffalo, New York plant of the Curtiss-Wright Corporation resulting in a two-day meeting and an agreement to standardise the model and freeze the design for a period of three months. The result was an immediate increase in production. Similar meetings were held at other aircraft factories, again resulting in an increase in production.

Also in September steps were taken towards standardisation of other arms besides aircraft when Sir Walter Layton was sent to the United States as a special envoy for the newly formed British Ministry of Supply (MoS). Plant expansion was to commence at once, with effect from 29 November 1940. The decision to purchase American-type equipment, embodied in the Stimson–Layton Agreement, was much more than a simple acceptance of US standard items. The British also offered to work with the United States in the development of new weapons or the re-design of older ones for both nations. This was a form of co-operation or mutual aid in ideas which became accepted throughout World War Two and was an indispensable part of the joint war effort.

Prior to the Lend-Lease Act being passed, other methods were tried. The United States arranged to buy from the United Kingdom certain war plants built by British funds which were now needed for the US defence programme. However, these were stopgap measures. By the end of 1940, the British dollar position was so serious that something larger than could be accomplished under existing law was needed if the flow of arms to Britain and the other democracies was to continue. It was up to Congress and the American people to make the decision on further aid.

HR 1776

By the end of 1940, a large majority of the American people had made up their minds that it was in their national interest to continue the flow of aid, including arms, to nations fighting the Axis powers. It was quite remarkable that there had been no real issue over this in the presidential campaign during the autumn. In his Cleveland, Ohio speech on 2 November, the President said that 'our policy is to give all possible material aid to the nations which still resist aggression, across the Atlantic and Pacific Oceans'. Wendell Wilkie, in his final campaign speech at Madison Square Garden, New York on 3 November, declared that 'all of us – Republicans, Democrats and Independents – believe in giving aid to the heroic British people. We must make available to them the products of our industry.' The majority of the American people now expected this policy, supported unequivocally by both candidates, to be translated into action.

Unfortunately there were still many who were far from convinced that the United States' national interest demanded such a policy. There were also a very few who could grasp the magnitude of the steps that would have to be taken if aid from the United States were to be effective.

Three days after the US election, the President publicly announced a 'rule of thumb' for the division of American arms output. As the weapons came off the many production lines, they were to be divided roughly fifty-fifty between the United States armed services and the British and Canadian forces. That same day, the Priorities Board approved a British request to order 12,000 more aircraft in addition to the 11,000 already ordered. The promise of material aid to keep Britain in the fight was day by day being translated into a definite plan. But the huge machinery of organisation for carrying out the plan had still to be devised.

Edward R Stettinius Jr., who, in 1941, became Administrator of Lend-Lease, and who during his three years in that office, was responsible for distributing £4,652,000,000 worth of material to the Allied war fronts of the world, is seen pointing to a map showing the flow of Lend-Lease material from the USA to the Allies. His predecessor as Lend-Lease Administrator was Harry Hopkins. (IWM HU 65898).

Dollars were the most immediate problem. In September 1939, the British had started with roughly 4,500 million in dollars and gold, and in United States investment that could be turned into dollars. Much of this belonged to private citizens, but after the outbreak of World War Two the British government commenced the taking over of private dollar balances and United States investments, compensating the owners in sterling. The dollars all went into a single war chest. Replenishment of this came from our export trade with the United States. It must have seemed strange to many Americans that

Britain, a nation struggling for survival, should be making such strenuous efforts to export such luxury goods as whisky, fine woollens and pottery. These goods were sold in the US for dollars, which in turn were used to purchase American-made weapons.

Unfortunately the fall of France put an end to this policy. The take-over of the French contracts had doubled the rate of British spending overnight, and in addition thousands of new orders had to be placed immediately. By the end of 1940, the war chest of dollars was down to almost 2,000 million, and of this nearly 1,500 million was already pledged to pay for war materials ordered in the US but not yet delivered. The majority of British production was centred for war use, meaning that the country could not export sufficient goods to obtain all the dollars badly needed. By January 1941 Britain had used up the reserve of dollars and the gold supply, and were forced to stop purchasing war goods in the United States.

By the middle of December, new British contracting in the United States had practically come to a halt. Secretary Morgenthau and Philip Young, a highly ranked British Treasury official, had been meeting every week to discuss the dollar position and the volume of British orders. A strict weekly budget of dollars was imposed for the British missions based in the US. No matter the priority for weapons and supplies, it could not be ordered if the weekly budget had already been spent.

To meet the dollar problem, the US could have made loans, but loans between Allies in a major war of survival seldom worked out satisfactorily. Meanwhile munitions capacity was growing tighter every day, machine tools were becoming scarce, and raw material shortages began to loom ahead. By 1 December 1940 only 2,100 of the 23,000 aircraft ordered by the British had been delivered. To deliver all these aircraft, and at the same time to build up the air strength for the safety of the United States, would strain plant facilities to the limit. Only a single, unified US government procurement policy for all defence purposes could accomplish the tremendous task that lay ahead. This meant that the US government should place all the orders for arms.

Solution

A search had been on in US government circles all summer and autumn for the best solution to these problems. Finally it was the President himself who suggested that it should not be necessary for the British to use their own funds and have ships and aircraft built in the United States, or for the US to loan the necessary money for this purpose. In his opinion there was no reason why the United States could not lease a finished product to the Allies for the duration of the emergency. It was a fruitful starting point.

Early in December 1940, Franklin D. Roosevelt left Washington DC for a short cruise on the USS *Tuscaloosa*. One purpose of the trip was to visit some

of the naval bases in the Caribbean that had just been leased by the British. But the President also wanted an opportunity to think over all the problems which were now becoming more critical every day under the pressure of events abroad.

The United Kingdom had at this time in Washington a singularly gifted and influential ambassador. He was the Marquess of Lothian, Philip Kerr, a friend of Winston Churchill who had been closely involved with negotiations for transfer of naval bases in the Caribbean to the United States. In December 1940, shortly after his return to Washington from a visit to London, he was taken seriously ill and on 12 December died. His successor was Lord Halifax who discharged the work of ambassador to the United States with conspicuous and ever-growing influence and success. President Roosevelt, Cordell Hull, and other eminent personalities in Washington were extremely pleased with the selection.

It was fully evident that the Nazis were definitely intent on dominating the globe. Hitler counted on Britain surrendering in the spring of 1941; then Germany and Japan would take on the United States together. That apparently was the strategy brought to the notice of US government officials by Secretary Cordell Hull. With Britain out of the war, Axis naval forces might suddenly appear in the North American hemisphere, one on either side of South America, or even at the vital Panama Canal. The US government was doing its best to tell the American people of the grave threat to their national safety. As the march of aggression continued abroad, the US was coming to appreciate more fully the imminence of the threat if Britain should collapse. But a plan for furnishing her with the arms she needed had still to be agreed upon. When the President returned from his trip to the Caribbean on 16 December 1940, he was ready to make a proposal to the American people. First, he outlined it at a press conference the next day.

To the reporters gathered before him, Franklin D. Roosevelt laid down what he took to be the clear policy of the United States:

'There is absolutely no doubt in the mind of a very overwhelming number of Americans that the best immediate defence of the United States is the success of Great Britain defending itself, and that, therefore, quite aside from our historic and current interest in the survival of democracy in the world as a whole, it is equally important from a selfish point of view and for American defence that we should do everything possible to help the British Empire to defend itself.'

The President reminded the press conference that no major war in all history had ever been won or lost because of money. In 1914 the bankers had assured us that the war would probably not go on for more than three months because of lack of money, he said, and if it did, the bankers would stop it within six months: 'There was the best economic opinion in the world that the continuance of war was absolutely dependent on money in the bank. Well, you know what happened . . . Now, what I'm trying to do is to eliminate the dollar sign.' That was the heart of the proposal.

Then the President explained his solution fully but in simple terms. Factories in the United States were turning out munitions, some of which were being bought by the British, the rest going to the US armed services. From now on, the United States government should place all the contracts for munitions to be manufactured in the United States. If we needed them when they came off the line, the President said, we could use them ourselves; if we decided that they 'would be more useful to the defence of the United States if they were used in Great Britain than if they were kept in storage here,' we could 'either lease or sell the materials, subject to mortgage, to the people on the other side.' 'The defence of the United States', and not dollars, was henceforth to determine where US-made weapons were to go. The President went on to relate the famous story of the fire in a neighbour's house and the loan of a garden hose. Lend-Lease as a weapon for the defence of our vital interests was first proposed to the American people in everyday terms.

A few days after the press conference, on 30 December, a fireside chat on the radio network on the subject of national defence was announced. This resulted in letters and messages pouring into the White House from citizens all over the country. The President had spoken bluntly. If Britain should go down, he said, 'all of us, in all the Americas, would be living at the point of a gun, a gun loaded with explosive bullets, economic as well as military. We must produce arms and ships with every energy and resource we can command.' Then the President summed up the national policy in a world of aggression: 'We must be the great arsenal of democracy.'

On 6 January 1941, a week after the fireside chat, the President delivered his annual message to Congress on 'The State of the Union'. 'I find it unhappily necessary to report,' he said, 'that the future and the safety of our country are overwhelmingly involved in events far beyond our borders.' Then he asked Congress for the authority and the funds necessary to manufacture additional weapons and war supplies to be turned over to those countries actually at grips with the Axis powers.

The Lend-Lease Bill

On their return to the White House from the Capitol, Secretary Morgenthau and E. H. Foley, the General Counsel of the Treasury, called on the President to discuss a proposed Bill to carry out the policy of full aid to the democracies. The Bill had first been drafted four days earlier by Oscar C. Cox, a lawyer from Maine who had come down to the US Treasury Department in 1938 from the New York City Corporation Counsel's office. Since the earliest days Cox had worked on the problem of foreign purchases, and he was among the first to propose the trade-in as a method of transferring US rifles to Britain. Later in the summer of 1940 he had dug up the old statute, dating back to 1892, that had begun the thinking on aid to the democracies in terms of a lease. His draft of the Lend-Lease Bill was modelled in part on the Pittman Act, passed in the summer of 1940 in order to assist the other American republics to obtain arms in the United States.

After Oscar Cox had prepared the first draft, the Lend-Lease Bill was discussed and revised by Secretary Morgenthau and the Treasury staff, Secretary Stimson, Assistant Secretary McCloy and other US War Department officials, the Navy Secretary Knox, Secretary Cordell Hull and his legal adviser Green Hackworth, Attorney-General Jackson, by Ben Cohen and by many others in a series of day and night discussions and drafting sessions. Congressional leaders – Senators Barkley, George, Connally and Harrison, Speaker Rayburn, Representatives McCormack, Bloom and Luther Johnson – were also consulted. By the time the new Bill was brought to the President, it was the joint product of many different people. Out of every discussion came a new idea, a new word, or a change of phrase. The staff of the Congressional Legislative Council worked long hours massaging the language into its best possible form. US Treasury lawyers worked very long hours co-ordinating and reconciling all the many suggestions that had been made.

The President read the Bill slowly and carefully after he finally received it from Henry Morgenthau. After he had finished, he said that it provided for the aid which the US had determined to give in the most direct and clear-cut fashion possible. The President requested it be brought back to him as soon as possible initialled by Secretaries Cordell Hull, Henry L. Stimson and Knox, and by William Knudson and Secretary Morgenthau himself.

There was another rapid series of conferences the following day as Foley and Cox started round Washington for the final clearance on the Bill. A few more changes were made by the State and War Department, but by five o'clock in the afternoon Secretary Morgenthau and Foley were back at the White House with a Bill that everyone agreed on. It bore all the initials the President had requested. 'This is really a fast piece of work for Washington,' the President said with a grin as the draft was handed to him, 'and I'm not one to be outdone.' He read the Bill through carefully, asked a few more questions, and initialled the vital document himself.

Two days later, late in the afternoon, there was a final conference at the White House with members of the Cabinet and Congressional leaders. After he had read the Bill aloud, the President made several things clear. First, that there should be no limit in the Act itself on the amount of aid that could be given to foreign countries. The appropriations which would be asked for from time to time as money was needed

would limit expenditure. The Act itself should contain no maximum limit. This was an emergency; it could not be predicted how much aid would have to be given any more accurately than the course of the war itself could be defined.

One of the Senators present said he was worried about the provision in the Bill for lend-leasing US Army and Navy material already on hand. It was an important point, and the question was to be asked over and over again during the coming months. Roosevelt, however, stood firm:

> 'Take an example. It might be of tremendous importance to the defence of China or Greece if we could take airplanes off our carriers and fly them to those nations. We could replace them for our own use in a short space of time. By making them available now to countries fighting with their backs to the wall, we would help them and help ourselves too. Once you start excluding things from this Bill you are bound to end up forbidding something which we will find a few months from now absolutely must be done for our own defence.'

Finally, the President emphasised speed. The British had been forced to stop practically all contracting, and orders for delivery in late 1941 and in 1942 would have to be placed very soon. The war would not wait while the US debated.

On 10 January 1941, at noon on the day after the final debate, Senator Barkley introduced the Lend-Lease Bill in the Senate, and Representative McCormack introduced it in the House. The Clerk of the House of Representatives stamped it with the number HR 1776.

4. The Empire Air Training Scheme

Although South Africa did not join the Empire Air Training Scheme established in Canada, the South African Air Force (SAAF) placed training facilities, some of which had been planned as far back as 1937, at the disposal of the RAF. On 1 June 1940 a Joint Air Training Scheme came into existence in South Africa, and flying schools were immediately activated at Baeagwanath, Randfontein, Kimberley, East London, Oudtshoorn, Cape Town and Port Elizabeth. At its peak, the training scheme comprised thirty-six air training schools, the majority at new airfields, with extensive hangar and barrack facilities. By 31 December 1945, 33,347 personnel had been trained as pilots, observers, navigators, bomb aimers and air gunners. Of this total 20,800 were from the RAF, 12,221 were SAAF and 326 were Allied personnel. A very high standard of flying training was achieved with results comparable to the Empire Air Training Scheme in Canada, Australia and Southern Rhodesia. Principal aircraft used included British-built types as well as North American Harvards and Northrop Nomads, which came under Lend-Lease.

Like many other Allied countries, South Africa became dependent on American-built aircraft of a variety of types, some of which had been originally destined for the UK under Lend-Lease. Avro Ansons used on anti-submarine patrols and convoy escort duty were later replaced by Lockheed Ventura long-range bombers, these eventually equipping five SAAF squadrons. In March 1941 sixty-five Martin Marylands had been shipped to South Africa, and these joined Bristol Beaufort torpedo-bombers in equipping maritime reconnaissance units. They were assisted by Lend-Lease Consolidated PBY-5 Catalinas of the RAF and the Royal Netherlands Air Force (RNAF). Early in World War Two, two fighter squadrons were formed and equipped with Curtiss Mohawks and stationed at coastal bases for the air defence of South African ports.

P-40 Kittyhawks

In December 1941 when the Japanese Empire entered World War Two, the SAAF operational strength was concentrated in East and North Africa, mainly under RAF command. In the Union itself there was a mixture of British biplanes based in the Transvaal and Avro Ansons based with three reconnaissance flights along the coastline. The previously mentioned Mohawks, some seventeen in number, were at No.5 Air Depot, having been flown from Kenya, awaiting modification to Cyclone engines.

Considerable concern was felt in both Pretoria and London over the rapid occupational successes of Japanese forces, and in particular over the fall of Singapore. The defence of South African ports was vital, with Durban and its large dry dock of particular significance as it was the only one available in the Indian Ocean following the loss of Singapore. The ports were of great importance to the continued flow of material to the Middle East via the convoys routed via the Union. Many carried Lend-Lease supplies including much needed aircraft.

In Pretoria the Chief of General Staff proposed to Britain that it would require six new fighter and six torpedo-bomber reconnaissance units, plus two reserve fighter units, entailing a requirement of some 144 fighters and 108 TBR aircraft. Urgent signals followed on the subject and the United Kingdom insisted it was unable to supply any aircraft, as all production from British factories was needed by RAF units. It was suggested by South Africa that US-built Curtiss P-40s and Lockheed B-37 Venturas would be suitable for their requirement.

In preparation for the arrival of the US aircraft, three North American Harvard Mk Is were taken on charge to assist with training and attached to a SAAF Curtiss Mohawk squadron. On 16 June 1942 ten pilots from No.10 Squadron, with flight training completed on Harvards and flying Mohawks, were dispatched to Cape Town to collect the unit's first Kittyhawks assembled at No. 9 Air Depot at Brooklyn. Initially six out of sixteen aircraft were ferried to Groutville on 28 June, two other Kittyhawks being delayed en route due to technical problems and a landing accident. By the beginning of August the unit had sixteen aircraft on strength

Official photo dated May 1943 depicting Lend-Lease Ventura Gr.V FN957 from a batch of 12 FN956–967 which were ex US Navy PV-1 aircraft. Of the initial British Purchasing Commission deliveries, 16 crashed en route prior to delivery, 42 were held in Canada for the RCAF and 82 were diverted to the SAAF, whilst others were returned to the USAAF. (Via Philip Jarrett).

and took over all fighter defence duties in the area. The RAF Lend-Lease numbers allocated had been replaced by SAAF serials 5001 to 5022, the number of aircraft being increased to twenty-two.

In August 1942, six more Kittyhawks were delivered direct from the US. Although a total of forty-eight had been allotted to South Africa, it was to be some time before further deliveries could be effected as there was an urgent need to equip operational units in the Middle East. However, in March 1943 one of the convoys destined for the Middle East was attacked as it passed around the coast, and one of the ships, the *Sheafcrown*, was damaged and beached off East London. Amongst the stores that were salvaged were nine Kittyhawks; four – FR425/430/433/434 – were beyond repair, but the remainder were only slightly damaged (FR426/427/428/431/432) and were subsequently allocated SAAF serials 5023 to 5027. All went on the strength of No. 11 Operational Training Unit (OTU) in July 1943, this being the first SAAF operational fighter training unit in the Union.

There were further Lend-Lease Kittyhawk losses when no less than fifteen fighters – FT898–904, 907–909, 911–914 and 916 – were lost when U-510

sank the *Eldena* whilst en route in an Atlantic convoy. However, there were further shipments and by the end of 1943 some seventy-six Kittyhawks had been delivered, including those salvaged from the *Sheafcrown*. Attrition naturally was to account for quite a number of aircraft, and further allotments under Lend-Lease direct from the US were out of the question. In order to keep unit establishment at the required level, a final batch of nineteen Kittyhawks was withdrawn from No.163 MU located at Casablanca and ferried down to South Africa during March and April 1944.

The last of the SAAF Kittyhawks, some fifty-eight in total, were eventually struck off charge on 10 February 1948 and offered for scrap. An offer from the Israeli Defence Air Force (IDAF) was made to purchase the aircraft but could not be accepted as the Lend-Lease conditions under which these aircraft were supplied forbade such sales. The aircraft were sold by public tender to a scrap metal company.

Middle East

The most active theatre of operations for the SAAF was the Western Desert in North Africa. Martin

Marylands were moved from East Africa and by November 1941 the first light bomber Wing had been formed with squadrons equipped with Douglas Bostons. Earlier on 16 June the SAAF began accepting a number of Lend-Lease Curtiss Tomahawk Mk IIB fighters. The Martin Baltimore equipped one unit in the Wing.

On the first day of June 1943, the SAAF formed its first Douglas Dakota transport squadron which operated with the RAF in the Middle East. The ubiquitous Douglas transport entered SAAF service by way of the RAF. The SAAF had to struggle through the early war years with a motley collection of ex-South African Airways Junkers Ju 52/3ms, some creaky old RAF Vickers Valentias and a batch of Lockheed Lodestars which had initially been ordered for South African Airways, but were diverted for military transport use. A total of eighty-four Lend-Lease C-47 Dakotas were transferred to the SAAF during World War Two. The first of them was still wearing its factory-fresh USAAF serial 42-23630 painted on at the Long Beach factory in California on 6 May 1943, despite being allocated the RAF serial FD874. After its Atlantic ferry flight it was collected at Accra on the Gold Coast (now Ghana) by Captain Johannes Slabbert and his SAAF crew, on 21 June. Captain Slabbert flew it to South Africa by way of El Geneina, Juba and Kasama. The new Dakota and crew landed at Germiston in the Transvaal on 25 June after thirty-three hours thirty-eight minutes' actual flying time. The SAAF's pioneer Dakota was allocated a new serial – 6801. It was allocated to No.5 Wing, and went on to complete many years of yeoman service.

Initially No.28 Squadron SAAF in the Middle East had received Lend-Lease Dakotas from RAF stocks when the unit was formed on the first day of June 1943. The first entry in the Operational Record Book (ORB) reads, 'In humble surroundings at SAAF Base Depot, Almaza, Cairo, Middle East. 28 Squadron is born'. By the end of April 1944, 28 Squadron was equipped with no less than thirty ex-RAF Dakotas, and during that eventful year a total of 87,029 passengers and 33,692,361 lb of freight were carried, the total flying hours for the year amounting to 38,859. A second unit, No.44 Squadron, was formed on 27 April 1944 and both squadrons became heavily involved in the Balkans campaign. Both operated under No.216 Group RAF on service within the Mediterranean theatre of operations, flying as far as Karachi to the east and Takoradi on the Gold Coast to the west. This latter base was the terminal on the South Atlantic ferry route from the USA for Lend-Lease aircraft manufactured in North America.

As mentioned earlier, No.28 Squadron had received its Dakota transports from RAF stocks, the first three being FD906/7/8. Little time was wasted in putting the new transports to work, and getting them transferred to the SAAF inventory. From North Africa the SAAF moved north with the Allied forces for the invasion of Italy, who relied on air support provided by the SAAF transport squadrons equipped with Lockheed Lodestars and Dakotas.

Additional Lend-Lease aircraft received by the SAAF included Lockheed Venturas based at Gibraltar taking part in the Battle of the Atlantic, along with the Consolidated Catalinas. During 1944 the SAAF gained a heavy bomber component with the arrival in southern Italy of three squadrons equipped with Consolidated Liberators. Also received by the service were Martin Marauder tactical bombers, Lockheed Harpoon reconnaissance bombers, and a number of North American Mustang fighter-bombers.

Australia & Southern Rhodesia

During World War Two, Australia's greatest single achievement in administration and organisation was coping with the demands made on it by the huge Empire Air Training Scheme. Under an existing pre-war arrangement whereby twenty per cent of RAF pilots were recruited from British communities outside the United Kingdom, the RAAF had trained fifty pilots each year at Point Cook to serve with the RAF before reverting to reserve status back home. There was a new scheme in the offing which was far bolder in conception.

After the original plans for the Empire Air Training Scheme had been cabled to the Dominions by the British Government on 26 September 1939, and Australian representatives had attended the Allied conference in Ottawa, the RAAF undertook the tremendous responsibility of training 280 pilots each month to advanced standard, plus 184 air observers and 320 wireless operator/air gunners. Australia also accepted the responsibility of providing Initial Training Schools (ITS) and Elementary Flying Training Schools (EFTS) for eighty student pilots, seventy-two WOP/AGs and forty-two student observers per month, all of whom went on to advanced training in Canada.

Out of the total, mammoth annual Dominions output in the Empire Air Training Scheme of 20,000 pilots, 20,000 air gunners and 12,000 navigators for RAF service, the Australian contribution was to be about 10,000 aircrew every year, and it was planned that seven-ninths of the quota of airmen should be fully trained entirely within her own resources, the remainder being partially trained before going to Canada. By 5 October 1939 the scheme was approved in principle by Australia, and so rapid was subsequent progress that the first batch of thirty-four pilots graduated from the SFTS on 18 November. This was despite the fact that when World War Two began the RAAF had only twenty-seven flying instructors.

Apart from the personnel problem, there was the question of aircraft. It was estimated that initially some 1,728 training aircraft would be required to operate the scheme successfully in Australia. As a start ten Douglas DC-2 airliners were purchased from Eastern Air Lines by the British Purchasing Commission. These gave excellent service with the RAAF and were used to train aircrew at two of the wireless operator schools. These aircraft were delivered during late 1940 and early 1941, eventually being replaced by Lend-Lease Hudsons.

With Japan entering into the conflict there was a major build-up of US forces and aircraft in Australia from 1942 onwards. Douglas C-53 Skytrooper transports were initially loaned by the USAAF for service with the RAAF in May 1943, these being followed by 124 Douglas C-47 Dakotas supplied under Lend-Lease.

As the huge Empire Air Training Scheme expanded in Australia the RAAF created twelve elementary and eight advanced flying training schools, three air navigation, two air observer and three bombing and gunnery schools plus the necessary ancillary units. The total RAAF contribution to the EATS comprised 27,387 aircrew, of whom 10,882 were pilots, 2,282 navigators and 3,309 wireless operator/air gunners (WOP/AG) who were sent to Canada after receiving elementary training in Australia. In addition 674 pilots went to Rhodesia after initial training with the RAAF.

Meanwhile, here in the UK units of the RAAF became operational from 1940 onwards. Initially nearly 500 RAAF personnel served with the RAF,

and when 3 Squadron arrived it soon equipped with Lend-Lease Curtiss Tomahawks and Kittyhawk I, II and IIIs as well as North American Mustangs, with which it fought throughout the conflict in the Mediterranean theatre, through North Africa and the Levant, and so into Italy and Yugoslavia. It shot down more enemy aircraft than any other Allied squadron in the Mediterranean theatre of operations.

At the beginning of World War Two, the government of Southern Rhodesia offered to man and maintain a total of three squadrons with the RAF, and at the same time contributed materially to the huge Empire Air Training Scheme. The first EFTS to open under the EATS was the Southern Rhodesian Air Training Group in May 1940. Following rapid expansion, many thousands of pilots, navigators and air gunners from the UK, the African colonies, Australia, the Middle East and most of the Allied countries, qualified there during World War Two.

Little Norway

In a disastrous two months, May and June 1940, the Allied forces were forced to withdraw from continental Europe. The evacuation of Dunkirk began on 30 May and by 10 June the evacuation of Norway was likewise complete. The Norwegian government in exile were established in the UK and were prepared to carry on the battle against the Axis powers, now heavily augmented by a declaration of war by Italy against France and England.

The Norwegian government had hoped to start a flying training school in France, but, with the fall of that country and the shortage of available airfields in the British Isles, it was decided to accept an invitation received from the Canadian government to establish an air training camp in Toronto. Its purpose was to train flying and ground personnel to fight with the RAF and to provide a reserve to satisfy any future demands. Col Oscar Klingenberg of the Royal Norwegian Army Air Force, military attaché to the Norwegian Legation in Washington DC, was chosen to organise suitable training schools.

Accordingly, the municipal Island airport at Toronto, which afforded the advantage of having a floatplane harbour, was leased from the city to serve as a training base, with headquarters established in downtown Toronto. On 4 August 1940 the first contingent of 120 Norwegians reached Canada. They included Lt-Col Bjorne Oen as C-in-C of the Hoerens Flyverben and Vice-Admiral Hjalmar Riisen-Larsen as C-in-C of the Marinens Flyverben. This first contingent comprised partially trained and fully trained pilots from both the Army and Naval air forces. The base was to serve as a joint training school, the main objective being to train sufficient naval personnel to operate a reconnaissance squadron out of Iceland, and enough army personnel to send a fighter squadron to the UK as soon as possible.

Orders for aircraft from the US which had been unfulfilled at the time of Germany's attack on Norway were transferred to the Canadian base, and the first Fairchild PT-19 Cornell primary trainer, a gift from Swedes living in the US, arrived on 23 August 1940. Known as 'Little Norway' the first official flying training course was initiated on 21 September 1940. Advanced training was carried out at Patricia Bay, British Columbia for the Navy in readiness to form 330 Squadron with twenty-four Northrop N-3PB twin-float seaplanes, ordered prior to the invasion of Norway. On 1 August 1941 the Squadron became operational and arrived in Iceland, where it came under RAF Coastal Command. In the summer of 1942 the Squadron received six RAF Lend-Lease flying boats.

On 10 November 1940 the Toronto camp was officially opened and by the end of the year twelve Fairchild PT-19 trainers, six Curtiss H-75A-8 Hawk fighters, thirty-two Douglas/Northrop 8A-5 light attack bombers, four Stinson SR9-C Reliants and one Waco on floats had arrived. Norway had ordered twenty-four H75-A6 Hawks during 1939 and deliveries had begun in February 1940. The Germans captured most of those received in Norway and sold eight to Finland. Norway ordered an additional thirty-six H75-A8s just before the German occupation and six were delivered to the Norwegian forces in Canada in February 1941; the remaining thirty were requisitioned by the US Army Air Corps as P-36G fighters.

The Douglas/Northrop 8A-5 had been ordered by the French Purchasing Commission and ninety-three of the type were returned to Douglas on 20 June 1940 to be refurbished and re-engined. However, following the fall of France, the contract was taken over by the British Purchasing Commission using the name Nomad. A total of thirty-six 8A-5s were ordered by the Norwegian government early in 1940. However, by the time the aircraft had been completed Norway had been occupied and the 8A-5s were delivered to Island airport on Lake Ontario. As arrangements were later made for the training of Norwegian aircrew in RAF and RCAF schools, the 8A-5s became surplus to requirement and thirty-one were taken over by the USAAF, designated A-33-DEs.

In April 1941 the two RNAF forces merged into one command as the Royal Norwegian Air Forces. Vice-Admiral Riisen-Larsen was appointed C-in-C in England, while Lt-Col Ole Reistad became Officer Commanding RNAF Training Centres in Canada. Following a call-up of all Norwegian nationals for military service in the spring of 1942, a 430-acre recruit training camp was carved out of the forest, sixteen miles from Huntsville in the Muskoka District, north of Toronto. The camp was named 'Vesle Skaugum' and was opened by Crown Princess Martha on 18 January 1942.

By mid-1942 Island airport had begun to prove too small to accommodate all Norwegian flying training operations. The airport at Muskoka, ten miles from Gravenhurst, had been leased in January and a 300-acre farm adjacent to it was purchased by the Norwegians; buildings were erected and it proved a very suitable elementary flying training establishment. It was officially opened by Crown Prince Olav on 4 May 1942. Fairchild PT-19s were supplemented by fifty Fairchild PT-26 trainers known as 'Canadianised Cornells' and fitted with a canopy. The open-cockpit PT-19 was hardly the ideal trainer to operate during the cold Canadian winter months. The first five PT-26s purchased against Lend-Lease arrived in August 1942, followed by a further five in October, twenty more during August and September 1943, and the final twenty in July of 1944, making a total of eighty-six.

Owing to the difficulties in purchasing advanced trainers, the Norwegian students were sent to RAF stations operating under the huge British Commonwealth Air Training Plan, at Moose Jaw or Medicine Hat in the Canadian prairie area. Upon receiving their Norwegian wings, they returned to Island airport for operational training on fighters or light bombers. Early in 1943, due to flying restrictions in the Toronto area, it was decided to concentrate all elementary flying at the Muskoka airport schools. On 5 April 1943 the Toronto camp was handed over to the RCAF and Muskoka took on the name 'Little Norway'.

There was a complete change of aircraft types in the Norwegian inventory in Canada. The US War Department purchased the twelve remaining Curtiss Hawks in May 1943 to be designated P-36G, whilst thirteen Douglas 8A-5s which remained were also disposed of; five had already been written off in flying accidents, and some Hawks had possibly been reduced as a source of spares or written off in accidents. The Wacos and Stinsons had been disposed of earlier to an American dealer, so by 1944 the total aircraft fleet comprised eighty-six Cornells and two Interstate L-8 or S-1A commercial Cadet lightplanes received as gifts in April 1942. One RCAF North American Harvard trainer was on loan to the Norwegians from September 1943 to April 1944.

As the flow of recruits diminished it was found to be an advantage to centralise the organisation. Students for advanced training were directed to No.16 SFTS at Hagersville for single-engine flying, assisted by Norwegian instructors attached to the school. By 1 June 1945 some 3,323 personnel – 677 aircrew – of all ranks and trades had been trained. Forty personnel had lost their lives during training, twenty-three as a result of flying accidents. A total of eleven Fairchild trainers had been written off during the four-and-a-half years of training. The remaining seventy-five trainers plus the two Interstate Cadets were shipped overseas, forty-six to the new RNAF training centre at Winkleigh, Devon between January and April 1945, and twenty-nine direct to Norway between June and July 1945. 'Little Norway' at Muskoka was officially closed on 16 April 1945.

Back home in Norway a flying school had been established at Gardermoen equipped with Fairchild PT-19, PT-26 and PT-26B primary trainers and North American Harvard II basic trainers. During World War Two, Norwegian crews wearing BOAC uniforms had assisted in operating fourteen Lockheed Lodestar transports, carrying refugees and mail between neutral Sweden and the UK. These transports had been purchased from the US, were eventually transferred to the RAF, and post-war were transferred to the Royal Norwegian Air Force to form 335 Transport Squadron. Eight of the Lodestars were Model 18-08s purchased for use in the Middle East and had BOAC/RAF regis-

tration/serials as follows: G-AGCV (AX717); G-AGCR (AX718); G-AGCW (AX719); G-AGCU (AX720); G-AGCP (AX721); G-AGCT (AX722); G-AGCS (AX723); and G-ACGX (HK981). The two Model 18-07 Lodestars were G-AGBP (HK980) and G-AGBO (HK973). Others were G-AGEH (HK851), ex-41-29635, and G-AGIL (HK855).

What was originally known as the Empire Air Training Plan was described by Prime Minister Winston Churchill as 'one of the major factors, and possibly the decisive factor' of World War Two. At its peak the British and Commonwealth Air Training Plan in Canada had thirty Elementary Flying Training Schools of which six were RAF; twenty-nine Service Flying Training Schools of which ten were RAF; sixteen navigation and air observer schools, and twelve bombing and gunnery schools of which one was RAF; and four wireless schools. In its short life, the BCATP trained nearly 140,000 aircrew, comprising 7,000 New Zealanders, 9,600 Australians, 47,400 British and 73,000 Canadians. More than 5,000 were pilots with a similar number of navigators and/or bomb aimers, and some 35,000 WOP/AG and air gunners. The various aircraft used to train this vast number of Commonwealth aircrew were supplied under the massive Lend-Lease programme, and the majority remained in Canada, many retaining RAF serials, although some were later listed with RCAF serials. The following aircraft from a consecutive serial batch provide good examples of this: FH618–650 (33), de Havilland PT-24 Tiger Moth; FH651–999 (349), Fairchild PT-26 Cornell I; FJ100–649 (550), Cessna AT-17A Crane; FJ650–700 (51), Fairchild PT-26 Cornell; and FJ741–FK108 (268), Boeing Stearman PT-27 Kaydet I.

At the Canadian Forces Base at Trenton there is today a fine set of memorial gates to the BCATP, bearing the arms of the four partners, with the RCAF badge appropriately on top. At the 1949 dedication, Canada's Prime Minister, St Laurent, said the gates were 'an enduring monument to the vision of those who conceived the Air Training Plan, to the energy of those who organised it and to the trained airmen from its schools who fought and won victory in the air'. Engraved at one side is an epitaph taken from the poetry of A. E. Housman:

Their shoulders held the sky suspended.
They stood, and the earth's foundations stay.

5. Commonwealth Expansion – Canada

In Canada a huge re-equipment and expansion programme commenced during 1937 when the political situation in Europe began to deteriorate, and more money became available for defence purposes. In 1937 the Royal Canadian Air Force was allotted over $C4½ million, the largest sum it had hitherto received, with the total being increased to over $C11¼ million the following year, while almost $C30 million was voted for appropriation just after the Munich crisis in 1939.

The Canadian aircraft industry also expanded to cope with the additional orders, and undertook the construction under licence of more British and American types of aircraft. After building Vedette and Vancouver flying boats for the RCAF, Canadian Vickers received an initial order for seven Supermarine Stranraer anti-submarine flying boats, this order later being increased to eighteen. During 1936, three Northrop Delta transport and reconnaissance monoplanes were built and delivered. Four Delta Mk IIs were built for the RCAF in 1937, and thirteen more were ordered for delivery by the end of 1939. In the United States, Boeing were not only established in Seattle in Washington State on the Canadian border, but had a factory at Vancouver which was awarded a contract for eleven British-designed Blackburn Shark torpedo-bomber biplanes in 1937, and this order was later increased to twenty.

Aircraft manufacturers in Canada were kept busy. Eighteen Westland Wapitis supplied by the United Kingdom were reconditioned in 1938 by the Ottawa Car Manufacturing Company and modified. Further expansion came with an initial order for eighteen Bristol Blenheim twin-engined bombers to be constructed by the Canadian Fairchild company. In the same year Noorduyn acquired the manufacturing rights in Canada for the North American NA-16-3 training monoplane, which later became well known as the Harvard. This trainer had been selected by the RCAF for advanced instruction training. Noorduyn also began building the Norseman single-engined transport monoplane for the RCAF.

A British Air Mission visited Canada during 1938 to investigate the potential of her aircraft industry for the supply of suitable types for the Royal Air Force. A central company was formed to operate two main establishments to contract directly with the British government. Several prominent organisations banded together to form Canadian Associated Limited which, in the autumn of 1938, received orders for eighty Handley Page Hampden twin-engined bombers for the RAF. This order was eventually doubled. One of the companies involved in Hampden production was the Canadian Car & Foundry Co. Limited which had previously had the licence from the United States to build the Grumman GE-23 Goblin two-seat fighter biplane. Fifty-two had been constructed in 1938, but only fifteen entered service with the RCAF, the remainder finding their way to Spain.

On 1 September 1939, Canada placed her armed forces on active service, and nine days later she declared war on Nazi Germany.

Over the next five years the RCAF expanded from a small air arm equipped with obsolescent equipment into the fourth largest Allied air force. During the same period under the huge Commonwealth Air Training Plan it provided for the largest aircrew training facilities ever achieved. Fifty pilots from the RAF on short-service commissions were already being trained in the country when delegations from Canada herself, Britain, Australia and New Zealand assembled in Ottawa towards the end of 1939 to set up the historic British Commonwealth Air Training Plan. The agreement signed on 3 December 1939 converted Canada, in the words of President Franklin D. Roosevelt, into 'the aerodrome of democracy'. The original expiry date was 31 March 1943, but during 1942 it was extended and finally expired on 31 March 1945, when no fewer than 131,553 aircrew had been trained.

Flying Training

Canada was initially responsible for setting up a total of seventy-four technical and flying training schools, with a monthly output of 520 pilots trained

LEND-LEASE AIRCRAFT IN WORLD WAR II

Nomad was the RAF name for the Northrop A-17A light-bomber of which 61 were allocated to the UK by the USAAC in 1940. Six were lost at sea in transit and only AS958/967/971/974 and AW421 went to the RAF, the rest going to the SAAF. Depicted is AS974 which was assembled at Burtonwood in August 1940 and flown to No. 20 Maintenance Unit at Aston Down. The type was powered by a single 825 hp Pratt & Whitney Twin Wasp Junior R-1535-13 radial. (Via Philip Jarrett).

to elementary standards, 544 to service standards, 340 as observers and 580 wireless operator/air gunners. Primary responsibility for this great plan rested solely with the RCAF, and involved a huge building programme of airfields and the purchasing of vast quantities of equipment. Instructors were provided by the United States, as well as by the RAF and RCAF, and more than 4,000 aircraft were ordered for the massive Canadian training programme, a large proportion being produced by Canada herself, but others coming out of the Lend-Lease programme. By the end of 1940 the flow of qualified aircrew from the Canadian schools began to reach Britain, most being posted to RAF units. Many graduates initially had to be retained in Canada as instructors for the further expansion of the British Commonwealth Air Training Plan. It was soon possible to organise new RCAF squadrons in Britain.

In Canada the home-based squadrons began to re-equip with thirty-two Northrop A-17A Nomads, some 247 Lockheed Hudson patrol bombers of various marks and twenty Douglas DB-280 Digby reconnaissance bombers for anti-submarine and convoy escort duties. For defence against the likely possibility of enemy air attack on Canada, a few fighter interceptor squadrons were also formed, using Canadian-built Hawker Hurricane fighters, and some seventy-two Curtiss Model 87A P-40D Kittyhawk Mk Is. Twenty-five more P-40s were sent by surface transport from the United States to Canada in March 1942.

The number of operational bases was gradually

increased, their location extending to the desolate extremities of the Canadian borders and outposts. In March 1940 the total personnel strength of the RCAF was 2,400 officers and 28,000 men, whilst a steady flow of recruits matched the arrival of new aircraft types.

For maritime reconnaissance work ten Consolidated Model 28 Catalina Mk I flying boats and the first of 224 Consolidated Model 28 Canso A amphibians had been ordered in 1941 for construction under licence by Boeing Aircraft of Canada and Canadian Vickers, while contracts for training aircraft were increased. De Havilland (Canada) began assembling Fairey Battle monoplanes for the training plan and Fleet Aircraft built a further 200 of their Model 16B Finch Mk II trainers in 1941. One hundred and sixty Fleet Model 60 Fort advanced trainers were completed for the RCAF before production by this company was switched to the US-designed Fairchild M-62 Cornell. A total of 541 Mk I, 917 Mk II and 107 Mk III Cornells were produced, and the Mk II replaced the 301 Boeing Model A/D-75NI Stearmans previously supplied from the United States, all but one being allocated RAF Lend-Lease serials. North American Harvards and Norsemans continued to be manufactured and supplied by Noorduyn, and for advanced twin-engined training the RCAF began to receive in 1941 the first of 826 Cessna T-50 Crane Mk Is and Mk IAs from the United States. The last eighty-two were allocated RAF Lend-Lease serial numbers. A number of aircraft ordered for the RCAF from the United States were handed over to Britain at this time, including Bell P-39 Airacobra fighters and Consolidated PBY-5 Catalina flying boats.

Further Expansion

At an early stage in the development of the huge British Commonwealth Air Training Plan, it was organised into four training commands with headquarters located at Toronto, Winnipeg, Montreal and Regina. Under an extended agreement which

1941, sixteen RCAF squadrons were fully operational in the United Kingdom and one in the Middle East. A month or two earlier a Canadian squadron had been formed within RAF Coastal Command equipped with Lockheed Hudsons supplied under Lend-Lease. Towards the end of 1941 the first RCAF intruder unit, 418 Squadron at Debden, Essex, was formed with Lend-Lease Douglas Boston aircraft.

In Canada most of the operational duties fell to

Striking air-to-air view of Douglas DB-7A Boston II AH433 in flight over the factory at Santa Monica on 17 December 1940 prior to flying to New York to be handed over to the British Purchasing Commission and then shipped to the UK. It was from a batch of 100 AH430-529 which were originally a French contract, hence the large fin flash. (Via Philip Jarrett).

was signed in June 1942, the number of training schools was increased to sixty-seven, including twenty-one double schools, and ten new specialist schools were added for operational training and other functions. In addition the administration of a further twenty-seven schools which the RAF had established in Canada was now entrusted to the RCAF.

About eighty per cent of the aircrew turned out in Canadian schools were native Canadians, and after qualifying they joined squadrons which were forming in the United Kingdom as well as on home ground in North America. The first unit formed overseas was 403 Squadron on 1 March 1941, equipped with Lend-Lease Curtiss Tomahawk Mk Is, and this was followed in the course of the year by no fewer than seventeen more squadrons including the first RCAF bomber squadrons. By November

Eastern Air Command, engaged in long patrols over the north-western Atlantic, where, from the spring of 1941 onwards, the war against marauding U-boats became increasingly fierce. There was a steady expansion of strength in Canada. To meet this expansion, which was matched by the overseas build-up, about 10,000 aircraft were on order at the beginning of 1942, from all sources.

During 1942–3, the Boeing Aircraft Company of Canada delivered fifty-five Model 28-5A Canso amphibians to the RCAF commands in Canada, and these were subsequently joined by 137 Lockheed-Vega-built V-146 Ventura GR Mk Vs for coastal patrols. A further 149 Venturas were supplied to the RCAF with RAF Lend-Lease serials. Initially some eighty-six Consolidated Model 32 Liberator Mk III/IVs and GR Mk VIs went to the RCAF for use on very long-range anti-submarine operations over the Atlantic. Some Boeing (Canada)-built Catalinas, or Cansos as they were known, 193 in number, plus some converted for air-sea rescue duties, were constructed for the RCAF.

It is interesting to record that along with aircraft from the United States armed services, which came under Canadian control for operations in the north-western Atlantic, the Lend-Lease Consolidated B-24 Liberators of the RCAF and other maritime reconnaissance types of Eastern Command sank six submarines during World War Two. Although there was much less U-boat activity on the Pacific seaboard, one Japanese submarine was damaged and subsequently sunk by the RCAF. In the Spring of 1942 several RCAF bomber-reconnaissance and fighter squadrons of Western Air Command were sent north to Alaska and the Aleutians to assist the US forces in checking a Japanese attack from that quarter. For several months the RCAF aircraft completed patrols and strafing missions in that isolated theatre of operations, during which a Canadian Lend-Lease P-40 Kittyhawk pilot shot down a Mitsubishi Zero-Sen fighter, the only enemy aircraft to be destroyed by Canadian home-based units during World War Two. The RCAF remained in the Aleutians, flying alongside the USAAF, until the Japanese withdrew from Kiska during August 1943.

Ferry & Staging Route

In order to move aircraft and supplies from the United States north to Alaska and the Aleutians, a north-west ferry and staging route was pioneered within RCAF Western Command. The volume and high priority of the traffic, particularly of Lend-Lease aircraft en route to the USSR, finally led to the formation during June 1944 of the new North-West Air Command, with headquarters located at Edmonton, in order to administer the chain of airfields, navigation facilities, etc. In order to provide a transport support service the RCAF received eighteen Lockheed Model 18-56 Lodestars and 169 Douglas C-47 Dakota Mk I/III/IV transports under Lend-Lease from the United States, with most of the latter type having RAF serials.

When the expansion had reached its peak during October 1943 there were ninety-seven flying schools and 184 ancillary units operating in the British Commonwealth Air Training Plan which was twice the number originally planned, and more than 10,000 training aircraft of many types were in use. Each month more than 3,000 aircrew were turned out, and so large was the reserve of new aircrew that it became possible to commence reducing the training output early in 1944. In October 1944 the closing down of the schools was accelerated, and at the end of March 1945 the huge British Commonwealth Air Training Plan was officially terminated. During its operation in Canada it had produced fighting men in eight different aircrew categories, from pilots to flight engineers, totalling 72,835 for the RCAF, 42,110 for the RAF (including 3,333 for the Fleet Air Arm), 9,606 for the RAAF, and 7,002 for the RNZAF.

The RCAF contributed three transport squadrons equipped with Lend-Lease Douglas C-47 Dakotas overseas, two of which initially operated in Air Command South-East Asia (ACSEA), and one in Europe. In the Far East the two RCAF squadrons flew in support of the 14th Army in operations in Burma, and were the last RCAF units to operate against the enemy since their vital work continued until the Japanese surrender in August 1945. They then transferred to Europe to work with the third RCAF Dakota squadron with the Canadian occupation forces, and it was the end of June 1946 before they flew their Lend-Lease Dakotas back home to Canada.

During the latter stages of the war years home-based squadrons of the RCAF received new equipment from both Canadian and United States aircraft manufacturers, all under Lend-Lease. From the US came the first of 164 North American B-25C Mitchell Mk II light bombers and photographic aircraft, together with 341 Beech C-45F Expeditors and a number of Lockheed Lodestar transports, plus some thirty-two Waco CG-4A Hadrian gliders. Soon after the end of World War Two, aged Curtiss P-40 Kittyhawk fighters, still giving stalwart service, were supplemented by 130 North American F-51D Mustang fighters from the United States. These equipped both regular and auxiliary fighter squadrons and training units.

As a loyal member of the British Commonwealth, Canada naturally maintained close ties with the United Kingdom, and close liaison between all her defence partners was simplified by the formation of the North Atlantic Treaty Organisation (NATO), which came into effect on 24 August 1949.

6. ATFERO, Ferry and Transport Commands

As 1940 drew to a close, the United Kingdom desperately lacked the necessary equipment to enable it to carry an offensive war to the enemy. In North America, the factories were now in full stride, producing a variety of excellent aircraft, fully capable of measuring up to the heavy demands required of them in the European theatre of operations. Unfortunately a great deal of this valuable effort by the United States was to no avail. The marauding German U-boats in their packs were taking a savage toll of both men and material, the latter including aircraft which were often deck cargo.

With the fall of France the last land front in Europe was lost, but the war in the air continued with growing violence. By flying the bombers which Britain had ordered from the United States instead of sending them on slow ship convoys, the striking power in the air could be reinforced far more quickly, and increasingly valuable shipping space could be released for other essential supplies. On 10 November 1940 seven Lockheed Hudsons, crewed by personnel from Canadian Pacific Air Services (CPAS), made a non-stop flight across the Atlantic, pioneering what was to become the Royal Air Force Ferry Command which by VE Day in 1945 had delivered over 10,000 aircraft.

The possibility of a regular airmail crossing of the

After a rough crossing of the Atlantic the British merchantman Nailsea Court *is seen on arrival at the mouth of the River Mersey in April 1941, with four early Lockheed Hudson patrol bombers stowed on the deck. The Hudson was ordered before Lend-Lease, the first arriving by sea at Liverpool on 15 February 1939 and being assembled at Speke Airport. Normal loading port in the USA was Philadelphia. In March 1943 the* Nailsea Court *was sunk with only three survivors. (Via David J Smith).*

Atlantic had in 1939 been discussed by the postal authorities of the United States, Canada and Great Britain. It was not considered feasible to carry mail by air during the winter months and the project was abandoned. Discussions were revived early in 1940 when the Lockheed Hudson had been chosen as the weapon the RAF Coastal Command vitally needed. Britain was purchasing them and shipping them by sea from the USA under a 'cash and carry' system. Something like three months was elapsing between test flights at the factory in California and arrival at

In the early days of Lend-Lease in July 1940, there was pressure to increase the monthly rate of aircraft to Britain from 1,000 to 4,000. Mr Morris W Wilson, President of the Royal Bank of Canada, was appointed Lord Beaverbrook's representative in the USA. He is seen here with Air Chief Marshal Sir Frederick Bowhill with a Lend-Lease Liberator in the background. (IWM CAN 2804).

operational destination in the United Kingdom, usually Aldergrove in Northern Ireland. Between April 1939 and January 1940 some 200 Lockheed Hudsons had been shipped across the Atlantic, although one or two were delivered direct to Canada. By ferrying the new bombers across the Atlantic, shipping space was saved and the three months was reduced to less than ten days.

It was suggested that the best agency to operate a ferry service was the Canadian Pacific Railway Company. The British Purchasing Commission in New York issued the necessary contracts for the first delivery by air, BOAC assisting with technical experience and the Air Ministry paying all expenses. Flying personnel who could be spared formed the new Canadian Pacific Air Service with its headquarters in Montreal.

By mid-September 1940 the first of the Hudsons for delivery by air was ready and deliveries of fifty within two months were promised. The aircraft were flown to Pembina in North Dakota on the international border about sixty miles south of Winnipeg, and there, since the United States was not yet at war and Custom proprieties had to be observed, they were towed across the frontier into Canada by tractor and often by horse. The crews employed to ferry these aircraft came from many countries and many walks of life.

The first Atlantic ferry crews were returned from the United Kingdom by boat, a journey which took anything from ten days to a fortnight. This caused hold-ups and on several occasions so many ferry crews were tied up at sea that there were none to fly the aircraft waiting. The first Consolidated Liberators to be produced for the RAF were flown across the Atlantic during March 1941. Six were diverted to transport duties for use on the recently instituted Transatlantic Return Ferry Service between Prestwick in Scotland, Newfoundland and Montreal. The first westbound Liberator left Prestwick on 4 May 1941. These unarmed transports were designated LB-30 and were initially operated by BOAC.

Quick expansion of the ferry service, together with political and military considerations in North America and Britain, made it essential that control should be directly rested in a ministry of the British government, and in May 1941 the Canadian Pacific Railway were notified of the termination of the agreement.

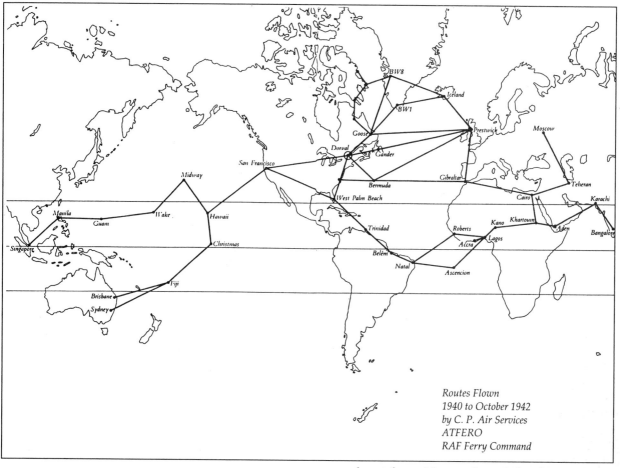

*Routes Flown
1940 to October 1942
by C. P. Air Services
ATFERO
RAF Ferry Command*

ATFERO

The Atlantic Ferry Organisation, or ATFERO, came under the control of the British Ministry of Aircraft Production, but the arrangement was short-lived for in June 1941 President Roosevelt informed Winston Churchill that he was prepared to assist with the ferrying of aircraft destined for the United Kingdom. It was, however, a condition that the hand-over must be to a military command instead of a civil authority. It was for this reason that on 20 July 1941 ATFERO became the RAF Ferry Command; Air Chief Marshal Sir Frederick Bowhill, who had been directing RAF Coastal Command in the Battle of the Atlantic, became C-in-C at Montreal. These changes in direction did not affect operations or staff. A mixture of civilian and service personnel continued to work together both in the air and on the ground.

The autumn of 1941 saw the completion of the huge RCAF base at Dorval. RAF Ferry Command

moved out from Montreal on 4 October and this airfield became the hub of the huge organisation under Sir Frederick Bowhill. The flying ranks of the command were still mainly civilian as the RAF could not spare service crews in any numbers. There were something like 100 trained crews at that time, and it was evident that this number would have to be doubled. The shortage of men led to an amazingly daring improvisation.

In Canada, airmen from all over the world were being trained under the huge Commonwealth Joint Air Training Plan. These men were learning everything they would need to know on the operations in Europe and the Middle East. Within a space of one year, after undergoing elementary, secondary and operational training, they became qualified for operations. Sir Frederick suggested that these newly trained crews should be entrusted with the task of delivering operational aircraft from Lend-Lease contracts. The 'one-trippers', as they were called, took on the Atlantic crossing even in winter, when many experts still considered it impracticable.

The Atlantic Ferry Organisation had operated under a number of titles, and under several immediate controls. This was the result of a natural and logical growth. It was the Secretary of State for Air, Sir Archibald Sinclair, who first announced the change of title from Ferry to Transport Command on 11 March 1943 in the House of Commons:

'All transport aircraft which we now possess, or which we shall produce here, or obtain from America, will be used to meet urgent requirements. With these increased numbers of transport squadrons an organisation will be required to control their operations throughout the world. I have, therefore, decided to establish a Royal Air Force Transport Command. To create such a Command sooner would have been to put the cart before the horse. It has not been commanders and staff that we have been short of, but aircraft. Now the Command will come naturally into being through the process of bringing supply and organisation into focus. In addition to controlling the operations of RAF transport squadrons at home, the Command will be responsible for the organisation and control of strategic air routes, for all overseas ferrying, and for the reinforcement moves of squadrons to and between overseas theatres.'

Sir Frederick Bowhill took command of this worldwide organisation and Montreal (Dorval) remained the headquarters for the North and South Atlantic ferry routes. Apart from the steady expansion the changes in command had not affected the flying.

44 Group Gloucester

With the formation of Ferry Command in July 1941, in order to administer the whole business of ferrying Lend-Lease aircraft across the Atlantic, No.44 Group was formed in August at Gloucester to take over from the Overseas Air Movement Control Unit responsibility for all non-operational flights in and out of the United Kingdom, which included transatlantic delivery flights, the preparation and dispatch of aircraft to overseas commands, and the training of ferry aircrews.

During the build-up for Operation 'Torch' – the Allied landing in North Africa – the Group was charged with the dispatch of aircraft to Gibraltar and

a joint operations room with the US Army Air Force was established. Extra briefing parties were set up at the dispatch points and in November 1942 alone 254 RAF and 491 USAAF aircraft were sent to the North African theatre of operations.

On 23 March 1944, No.44 Group was transferred to the control of Transport Command. From April on the function of the Group had changed slightly to include a greatly increased training and ferrying programme. Aircraft of all types from Lend-Lease contracts were ferried to the United Kingdom by various transatlantic routes and dispatched to all theatres of war in increasing numbers. The shorter range aircraft, such as Douglas Dakotas, were dispatched from Portreath, and the heavier, longer range aircraft from St Mawgan, both bases being in Cornwall. Because of the great increase in air transport activities, Operational Training Units were formed within No.44 Group to provide the specially trained crews required for the increasing number of transports operating Lend-Lease-equipped squadrons.

In June 1944 regular scheduled services to Gibraltar, North Africa, Cairo, the Azores, Malta, Colombo, India and Iceland were operated. The air transport operations of the Group continued to expand and in 1944 it was decided to transfer these operations to a separate unit operating under the direct control of Transport Command, and in September operational control of transport services was handed over to No.116 Wing.

Although No.44 Group relinquished scheduled services, the control of aircraft entering and leaving United Kingdom airspace was undertaken by the Group through Overseas Air Control (OAC) located at Prestwick. These two control units were responsible for the air safety of virtually all non-operational aircraft flights which took place directly between the United Kingdom and overseas bases. The lists of passengers on these flights were endless and included Heads of States and political and military leaders of many nations. Even after the end of the war in Europe aircraft from Lend-Lease contracts continued to be ferried to various places, but reduced commitments made the existing ferry organisation uneconomical and No.44 Group was disbanded on 14 August 1946. Just prior to disbandment the last Douglas Dakota for the RAF under Lend-Lease KP231, built at Oklahoma City under Contract No. AC-2032 and delivered from the

The last of nearly 2,000 Lend-Lease Douglas Dakotas for the RAF – KP231 – is seen parked at Dorval, Montreal, where it arrived on 13 June 1945 for processing with No.45 Group at Montreal. It is seen with RAF/RCAF personnel prior to delivery to the United Kingdom where it arrived on 26 June. It served with various operational conversion units until 1949. On 24 January 1950 it went to RAF St Athan as a ground instruction aircraft with the ground trainer serial 6731M. (AP Photo Library).

factory on 13 June 1945, was processed by No.45 Group at Dorval and arrived safely in the United Kingdom on 26 June.

With the formation of RAF Transport Command, a worldwide organisation, Ferry Command became No.45 Group retaining its headquarters at Dorval and responsibility for all Lend-Lease delivery by air. Within the Group No.231 Squadron was re-formed on 7 September 1944 operating from Dorval and equipped with various Lend-Lease types which included Dakotas, Hudsons Liberators and Marauders. It even had a number of Coronado flying boats which were mainly flown from Nassau. With these aircraft it provided a vital airline-type service schedule between the many factories and many points in North America, and Group headquarters.

7. Ferry Routes

In order to deliver aircraft faster than ocean-going cargo ships could carry them, the Allies established a globe-encircling system of air lanes. Hundreds of bombers, transports and long-range fighters were flown daily over these routes on their way to the various theatres of operations, often carrying troops and emergency supplies. In the development of these vital air routes, Lend-Lease was at the forefront.

Ferry crews were initially recruited from BOAC, airlines in Canada and the US, these becoming part of the huge ATFERO organisation. Many were trained at a navigation school which Pan American Airways had set up in Miami, Florida.

Since the spring of 1939 both American and British flying boats had flown transatlantic commercial schedules by way of Bermuda, the Azores and Lisbon, this route being closed to military traf-

fic. Portugal was neutral and naturally would not permit British Lend-Lease warplanes to use its air bases in the Azores or at Lisbon. The only route left was the tough North Atlantic one from Newfoundland to Ireland which had never been flown on a regular schedule. Bases for land planes and the necessary handling facilities needed to be developed from practically nothing before any ferry route could be put into operation. It was necessary to lengthen and hard-surface new runways on the small airfields located at Halifax, Nova Scotia and at Botwood, Newfoundland for the flow of aircraft necessary for the war effort under Lend-Lease. Weather and radio stations, plus repair and supply depots, were built during the winter of 1940–1 under almost unbelievable weather conditions. At the same time weather stations were set up and additional airfields were built on the

Depicted is Catalina GR.IIA VA703 coded 'WQ-M' from No.209 Squadron who operated this Lend-Lease type between 1941/45 including Catalina I AH545 'WQ-Z'. Canadian Vickers built the GR-IIA batch 36 of which went to the RCAF as '9701–9736'. Only 22 went to the RAF including VA703, VA712–732 of which VA719, 721 and 724 were lost on or before delivery flight. (Via Philip Jarrett).

In addition to the 1,694 Liberators supplied to the RAF under Lend-Lease, a large number were handed over to RAF units in the field by the USAAF. Depicted is Liberator III a B-24D-C0 41-1087 seen during April 1942 under test and evaluation at the A&AEE at Boscombe Down in full RAF markings. Records reveal that there were many Liberator transfers to the RAF in both the European and Mediterranean theatre of operations. (Via Philip Jarrett).

North Atlantic stepping-stones of Labrador and Iceland.

By December 1940 work was far enough advanced for the departure of the first three flights of seven bombers each, all Lockheed Hudsons. Shortly afterwards the first Consolidated Catalina flying boats and the first Consolidated Liberator bombers were ferried over this route. The crews had to fight fog, sleet and ice on the way. Records reveal that the first Catalina Mk II delivered from North America to the United Kingdom was ferried on 25 October 1940 by Captain I. G. Ross, a Canadian serving with BOAC. To avoid the dangers of night landings at unfamiliar airports and to minimise the risk of attack by the Luftwaffe, departures were timed so that the aircraft would arrive in the United Kingdom at daybreak. Several B-24 Liberators were converted into transports and assigned to the transatlantic run to fly ferry crews back to North America and to carry emergency supplies on return.

In the spring of 1941 when the responsible agencies found it difficult to recruit a sufficient number of qualified pilots for the ferry routes, General 'Hap' Arnold proposed to lend the assistance of the US Army Air Force. By having US pilots ferry aircraft built on British contracts from the factory to the eastern seaboard port of embarkation it would be possible to have more pilots available for flights across the Atlantic. President Roosevelt readily endorsed the suggestion and as a result the US Army Air Force Ferry Command was established on 29 May 1941 under the command of Col Robert Olds. Lend-Lease funds were used to purchase additional transport aircraft and also to finance the training in the US of British ferry crews. The US War Department immediately prepared estimates of the cost of a ferrying programme that would not only provide for the air delivery of aircraft for the Allies to transatlantic terminals in the western hemisphere, but would in the process create the nucleus of an organisation capable of ferrying aircraft for the US armed forces. On 24 June 1941 the British government filed Lend-Lease Requisition No. 2800 for the total amount of these estimates – $31,646,000. This was the birth of the USAAF Ferry Command, later the Air Transport Command. From 30 June 1941 until Pearl Harbor the US Ferry Command was financed by Lend-Lease funds. More than $60,000,000 was allocated to the US War Department for its expansion during that period.

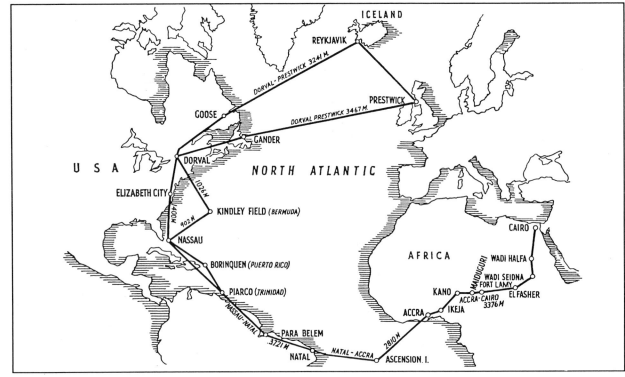

The Atlantic Bridge

Great Circle Routes

Across the top of the world the Great Circle routes, dreamed of by seekers of a north-west passage for four centuries, were now being rapidly realised. Through the silent north, through Greenland and Labrador, lay the paths for express traffic from North America to Europe, the Orient, India and Australia by way of the Atlantic and the Yukon. Work was started by the Americans in Greenland, while in Labrador, in a sandy plateau of muskeg and virgin forest, there was built one of the loneliest, largest and most important of long-distance air bases. It was close to the outlet of Goose River and was therefore given the perfectly complimentary name of Gander.

Goose Bay was discovered in July 1941 and the Newfoundland government agreed to grant a lease of the area to the Canadian government which bore the cost of the construction of the airfield. Never had so vast an undertaking been carried out in the wilds with such precision and speed. Within a month three temporary runways, each about 7,000 feet long, were ready for the largest type of aircraft. The work had gone on by day and night and snow was falling as the runways were being rolled when on 9 December 1941 the first aircraft arrived. This Labrador base was becoming one of the busiest airports in the world. It was positioned at N53°19A', W060°26A' with an elevation above mean sea level (AMSL) of 160 feet.

The Royal Canadian Air Force (RCAF), under whose command the airport came, had carried a great part of the burden and materials into Labrador with the proud record of never having lost an ounce of freight or scratched a wing tip. The RAF ran a scheduled service, or 'milk-run', of freight and passengers from Montreal.

After the winter of 1940 the Canadian government was approached with a request for an airport in the vicinity of Montreal. On flat country some ten miles from the city, adjoining the groups of French-Canadian villages which fringe Lake St Louis, a great airport was planned. This was Montreal airport – Dorval – which later was to house the head-quarters of No.45 Group of RAF Transport Command who were responsible for the delivery of Lend-Lease aircraft to the United Kingdom and beyond.

During the preceding July the United States had

52

sent engineers to Narsarssuak (Narsaruaq) in Greenland for the building of the air base that came to be known as Bluie West One (BW-1) located at N61°10A', W045°26A' with an elevation of 112 feet AMSL. In the following September work began on Bluie West Eight (BW-8), a much more northerly base on the west coast of Greenland. In July 1941 US armed forces had taken over the defence of Iceland, where they improved the airstrips previously occupied by the RAF. In the spring of 1942 the USA built two new airfields near Keflavik, named Meeks and Patterson.

In Scotland, Prestwick had been developed in 1941 from an ordinary airfield into the key transatlantic terminus for democratic Europe, and was to be the final delivery point for Lend-Lease aircraft. It was positioned at N55°30A', W004°35A' with an elevation of sixty-six feet AMSL. The facilities were shared by US Air Transport Command with the aircraft being serviced by civilian personnel, and those intended for delivery to the RAF in the United Kingdom were distributed by the gallant men and women in the dark blue uniforms of the Air Transport Auxiliary (ATA). During 1940 only twenty-six aircraft were ferried across the North Atlantic route: 722 in 1941; 1,163 in 1942; and 1,450 in 1943. The route was open, losses were few, and the air lane was being put to good use by both the RAF and the USAAF.

Middle East Routes

In the spring of 1941, aircraft were needed in a hurry not only in the United Kingdom but also in the Middle East. The problem of ferrying aircraft there was even more difficult than using the transatlantic routes. None of the pre-war commercial airlines from Britain to the Middle East could be used. The only direct route to Egypt remaining in the spring of 1941 was by way of Gibraltar and Malta, but because of the distance between airfields it could only be used by long-range bombers and transports. Eventually these aircraft could not use the route as the airfields on Malta were under constant attack from the Luftwaffe. The air lane through the Mediterranean was cut just as effectively as the sea lane.

The origin of the ferry routes across Africa dates back to the mid-1920s when members of No.45 and 47 Squadrons equipped with Vickers Vimy and Vernon aircraft of the RAF undertook a number of pioneering long-distance flights, the major one being to West Africa. In 1936, British civilian aviators had pioneered an air route westwards from Khartoum in Anglo-Egyptian Sudan 2,250 miles across the continent to Lagos in Nigeria on the Atlantic coast. A year later the service was extended to Accra and Takoradi on the Gold Coast. A few small airstrips had been cut out of the jungles or laid

Three Boeing 314 flying boats were acquired by BOAC from Pan American, purchased for $1.244 million each. Depicted is G-AGBZ ex NC18607 named Bristol which made the first eastbound crossing of the Atlantic from New York to Foynes, Ireland, via Bermuda on 22 May 1941 piloted by Capt. Kelly-Rogers. These three flying boats maintained regular services across the North Atlantic and to West Africa until 1946. (MAP).

out in the desert at locations hundreds of miles from civilisation. It was from these early pioneering flights that the foundation of the routes used during World War Two was laid.

In the early days of the war in the Middle East during 1940–1, a number of aircraft flew up from South Africa, landing at airfields that had been surveyed in the 1920s, checked by the RAF through the years, and that were now proving very valuable. In addition a number of aircraft were assembled at Port Sudan in Anglo-Egyptian Sudan and ferried to the North African front, or the Western Desert as it was called in those early days, via Abara, Wadi Halfa, Luxor, and so into lower Egypt.

When the Mediterranean air lane to the Middle East was severed, an air transport service was established from Britain to Gibraltar which then skirted the west coast of Africa to the Gold Coast. Service on the long over-water route was operated by three large flying boats which Pan American Airways had released and which had been bought for cash. From the Gold Coast to Egypt, a limited service was maintained across Africa by land-based aircraft. Over the African route, RAF pilots in 1941 were flying fighter aircraft brought by ship from the United Kingdom to Takoradi, where a huge assembly plant equipped to assemble 200 aircraft a month had been built. The route saved many, many weeks over the time consumed on the Red Sea run round the Cape of Good Hope, but in the spring of 1941 it was still a primitive affair. Many aircraft were lost on the way, with landing fields little more than emergency strips, with most of the runways being too short for medium bombers.

Control of flying in the early days was vested in the RAF Officer Commanding Khartoum, and later in the Commanding Officer of the Communications Squadron looking after the route. This state of affairs existed until late 1941 when No. 2 Middle East Ferry Control was established to take command of all posts in the Sudan Sector – the majority of staging posts and all flying within that area. A similar control was formed from Takoradi, the main assembly base, to cover West Africa.

Two Aircraft Delivery Units were formed of pilots and other aircrew to ferry the large variety of British and American aircraft from assembly point to the maintenance units near the front line. The main unit was No.2 ADU which was based on a houseboat in Cairo. The aircraft were ferried in convoy with 'mother' aircraft and 'chicks'. The 'mother' aircraft was either a Bristol Blenheim, Douglas Boston, Martin Baltimore, Marauder or Maryland, or sometimes even a Lockheed Lodestar. The route timing depended very much on the weather, but basically it was a day's hop between staging posts. The navigation equipment on the route was very limited and the most one could really hope for were medium-frequency beacons on continuous wave (CW). The main method of navigation was dead reckoning (DR) and local knowledge. The number of aircraft lost through errors of navigation was comparatively few. The 'mother' aircraft always carried a RAF master-navigator.

Takoradi was one of the main bases with an assembly plant built by the RAF on top of red cliffs on the outskirts of the vivid Gold Coast bush. Built early in the war, the existing facilities had to be rapidly extended with new workshops, hangars and runways. Living accommodation had also to keep pace with a staff which by 1942 had been increased to more than 3,000 men. From Takoradi fighters, bombers and transport aircraft were ferried in the many air convoys across Africa to Cairo, and later to points further afield.

Across the waist of Africa, airfields had been cut from the jungle or laid out on the desert as at Kano in Nigeria, one of the most romantic cities in all Africa, built on reddish clay, encompassed by a wall eleven miles in perimeter, and ruled by the Emir from a palace whose grounds covered thirty-three acres. Ferry crews encountered the harmattan, a persistent wind which raised a haze of Sahara dust sometimes to 10,000 feet, often blotting out visibility. Only constant cross-checking with aircraft by radio kept the convoys together. The next leg after Kano was over the jungle before reaching Maiduguri, over territory which was so densely forested as to make a forced landing inconceivable. It was possible to fly direct from Kano to Fort Lamy in French Equatorial Africa, where the aircraft maintenance personnel who refuelled the aircraft only spoke French. Then it was on into Anglo-Egyptian Sudan with stops at El Geneina, El Fasher or El Obeid to the confluence of the White and Blue Niles by Omdurman and Khartoum. El Fasher was the capital of Western Dafurand the governor, Phil Ingleson, was a great friend to the RAF. (One of the added attractions on landing at El Fasher, apart from its excellent breakfasts, was a tame lion which used to

The Lockheed 18-07 Lodestar was acquired for use by BOAC during 1941 and was operated in the Middle East and Africa. Depicted is G-AGCM c/n 2093 Lake Mariut *seen flying over Cairo during the North African campaign in 1942. It was previously NC33617 of Catalina Air Transport. In 1946 G-AGCM was impressed as VR955 in October. (Via Philip Jarrett).*

be handled like a small cat by Tadeuc Milenski, a Polish cavalry lieutenant with the most enormous hands. The lion eventually became too playful and big and was presented to a zoo. At the staging post located at Abeche in Chad, the French commissioner also had a number of lions chained underneath his stilted house.) An additional and slightly more southerly route was founded after the bombing of Fort Lamy, which went south from Maiduguri to Fort Archabault, eastwards to My Ala, north to El Obeid and on as before. The last leg was the magnificent flight down the Nile until the pyramids loomed ahead, followed by the sprawling city of Cairo, and a let-down into Cairo West airfield, or LG224 as it was known to many.

With the creation of a South Atlantic ferry route, more Lend-Lease aircraft of many types flowed into West African bases. The route was Nassau in the Bahamas, Natal in Brazil, then over the ocean to Ascension Island before the final leg into either Takoradi or Accra. The Desert Air Force needed the Martin Marylands and Baltimores, North American Mitchells and the Douglas Bostons and Dakota transports. For these aircraft the southern route was open, their arrival base normally being Accra, a peacetime airfield constructed by the Gold Coast Public Works Department and extended at British government expense to become a vital ferry destination base, with the US government also involved.

Within three months of becoming operational Takoradi dispatched its first aircraft, and within fourteen months more than 1,400 had passed 'up the line', as they called it, to the Middle East. Ferry crews who ferried the assortment of aircraft in convoys to Cairo made their own way back to base at Takoradi utilising a varied assortment of air transport. On 8 October 1941 Pan American Air Ferries equipped with Douglas DC-3 transports established a base at Accra, and thirteen days later a DC-3 took off on the first scheduled flight to Khartoum. By the end of the month, seven DC-3s and thirty pilots were maintaining regular scheduled operations.

Pan American

The United States realised that the only way to ferry more aircraft to Egypt in a hurry was to extend the trans-Africa route into a real, effective air lane, connecting with the South Atlantic route so that bombers could be flown all the way from the US. From Miami, Florida the route went to Brazil by way of British and US airfields in the West Indies. From Natal on the bulge of Brazil there was a 1,800-mile over-water hop to Bathurst in The Gambia where it joined the trans-Africa route.

The logistics required several hundred more experienced ferry pilots, as well as the establishment of a regular transport service to return crews to the US, to carry light emergency freight and to ferry military personnel back and forth across Africa. An enormous amount of equipment was required for building and expanding airfields, setting up emergency fuel depots, plus radio and weather stations. Personnel including ground crews were needed to man and operate the airfields. Airfields on the route from Miami to Natal had already been expanded by Pan American Airways. But there were problems.

At a series of urgent meetings during late May and early June 1941 these problems were discussed between British, Lend-Lease and US Army Air Corps officials. The route was a hazardous one and only a commercial airline with experienced crew could operate it. After consultation with the Civil Aeronautics Authority (CAA) and with representatives of the US commercial airlines, the US War Department chose Pan American Airways, which had been flying a route to Brazil for ten years and one across the Atlantic to Lisbon since 1939.

Juan T. Trippe, president of Pan American, spent many days in conference at the Division of Defense Air Reports and with the US and British representatives. Early in July, the airline entered into a contract with the British to ferry from Miami to Bathurst a few transport and cargo aircraft which were badly needed in the Middle East. On 15 July the British filed a Lend-Lease requisition for the establishment of a permanent ferry service over this route. Twelve days later a Boeing Clipper was on its way across the South Atlantic with a Pan American vice-president and other airline officials on board to survey the route.

Shortly after their report had been received, Pan American signed three contracts with the US War Department: one for the operation of a transport service across the South Atlantic; a second for a transport service across Africa; and a third for the ferrying to Egypt of US-manufactured bombers and fighters assembled at Takoradi, together with the development and operation of the necessary airfields, some of which had problems introduced by nature. The staging post at El Geneina, for instance, was often cut off for three months of the year by rains, and all fuel had to be carried by camel. An allocation of $20,600,000 of Lend-Lease funds was made to cover the expense of the operation.

In the meantime discussions between Brazilian, British and American officials were underway concerning the use of airfields in Brazil, whose government offered its full co-operation and provided a corridor through which US transports and combat aircraft could be flown to Egypt and the Middle East.

At the same time, airfield equipment of all types was assembled in New York to go by ship to Africa. Pan American officials organised items of equipment from airports all over the United States and sent them in pieces to the African jungles. Mayor La Guardia of New York came through with some steam shovels and graders that the city was willing to sell. Other equipment was obtained from many sources, and the first three shipments of this miscellaneous cargo left the US during September.

Once in Africa the material had to be transported inland for hundreds of miles. It was possible to use narrow-gauge railway for a short distance inland from the coast, and personnel managed to drive lorries along jungle and desert trails hardly intended for wheeled vehicles. As much as possible was flown in to its destination, but a great part had to be packed on the backs of native carriers. The country was healthy for neither men nor machine. The worst enemy was malaria, and an anti-malaria mission was sent to fight the mosquitoes and to keep the number of casualties as low as possible. On top of all the other difficulties of distance, jungle communications and a hot climate, ants were also a dangerous enemy. Armies of ants had a habit of invading the airfields and in only a few hours raising ant hills over a foot high that could upset aircraft landing and taking off. Insecticides and equipment had to be sent to Africa to fight ants as well as mosquitoes.

Communications in the bush were primitive and the control tower staff at the staging posts received signals by wireless telegraphy (WT) in Morse giving details and estimated time of arrival (ETA) of the 'hen' and 'chicks' air convoy. On occasions dusk or even night landings were necessary entailing the laying of a 'goose-neck' lighting system involving a series of paraffin-filled 'kettles' with the wick in the neck. This flare path had to be laid and lit shortly prior to the aircraft landing as monkeys from the bush had a habit of stealing them.

On Saturday afternoon, 16 August 1941, President Franklin D. Roosevelt and his party, returning from the Atlantic Charter meeting with Prime Minister Winston Churchill held earlier in the week off the Newfoundland coast, landed at Rockland, Maine. President Roosevelt went directly to Washington DC and, on the following Monday, 19 August, released a statement which described the new trans-African military supply line, to be operated by Pan American Airways for the US War Department, as a practical means of furnishing aid to Britain, Russia and China.

Pan American Airways Africa Ltd was incorporated in Delaware on 15 July 1941. Contracts for both Pan American Air Ferries, incorporated on 24 July 1941, and PAA Africa were signed on 12 August 1941. To help Pan American meet this formidable assignment, pilot personnel newly trained and commissioned at various USAAF advanced training stations were placed on active duty status and released for African service. Civilian maintenance, communication and ground operations personnel were granted draft-board deferments and permission to leave the US for work with PAA Africa. The organisation was granted the necessary supply priorities and transportation privileges, and was furnished with military transport aircraft for route operations. These various factors help to clarify the peculiar position of PAA Africa – a military supply airline operated by civilian personnel which began operations while the United States was nominally at peace and continued operations as part of the strategic military effort of a nation in total war.

The 1941 programme of aid to Britain, Russia, China, and other nations friendly to the Allied cause, as financed by Lend-Lease, resulted in PAA Ferries, based in Miami, Florida, being involved. They entered the African picture principally because their pilots used PAA Africa route facilities in the delivery of military aircraft to the Middle East. In addition PAA Ferries was responsible for a flight and ground training programme, plus a school for navigators. Both RAF and USAAF personnel were trained in this huge programme, and it was also a means of training Pan American personnel who were later assigned to PAA Africa.

Douglas DC-3

The first flight of a PAA Africa aircraft was an air test from Bathurst in The Gambia on 3 October 1941 involving Douglas DC-3 NC33642, a DST-A-207D c/n 4114 acquired by the US government from United Air Lines. The pilot for the air test was Captain Frank Glen. The transport was part of a pool assembled to aid and save the British forces in the Battle of Crete. Unfortunately, Crete had fallen by the time the transports were available. On 4 October NC33642 was flown to Takoradi by operations manager George Kraigher along with two Douglas DC-2 transports scheduled for delivery to the RAF piloted by Captains Poplowski and Blakely. Meanwhile, back at Bathurst, Captain Glen accepted delivery of a second DC-3 transport, NC25643, a DC-3A-228C c/n 2230 from a PAA Ferries crew. On 5 October Glen flew NC25643 to Takoradi, joined the DC-3 and two DC-2s and flew to Accra. On 9 October NC25643 and the DC-2s departed Accra for Maiduguri on what was the first route survey by PAA Africa transports and personnel. The following day they flew to El Fasher and on 11 October to Khartoum where the two Douglas DC-2s were handed over to the RAF.

The DC-3 continued the route survey flight to Cairo, returning to Accra by the same route. Scheduled operations began on 22 October when NC33642 departed Accra for Kano, Maiduguri, El Fasher and Khartoum with Glen as pilot and Furr as co-pilot. The first PAA Africa station was opened on 8 October 1941 at Accra on the Gold Coast, and this was established as headquarters and principal maintenance base. On 19 October the station at Maiduguri was opened, Khartoum the following day and Takoradi on 21 October. By the end of the year PAA Africa had established and manned stations from Bathurst to Cairo over a route distance of nearly 5,000 miles. It must be emphasised that PAA Africa was an entirely isolated entity, separate from the USAAF, BOAC, RAF and PAA Ferries agencies all of which used the trans-African route during the short period of PAA Africa operations. However, PAA

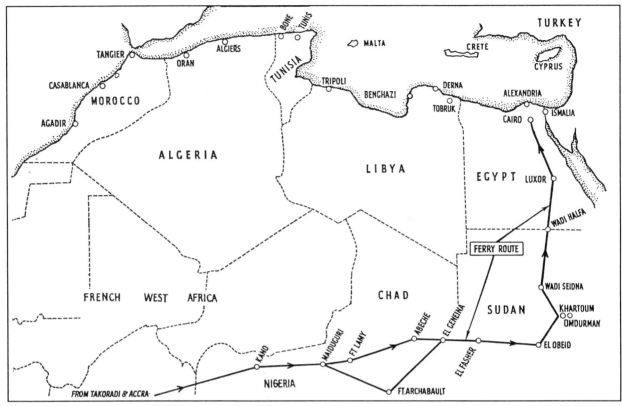

North Africa with ferry routes and major airfields used by the Douglas Dakota

Africa did depend heavily on British help and a friend of the author, Air Commodore Denis F. Rixon, who in 1942 became Officer Commanding Sudan Sector of the aircraft ferry routes, held a meeting with PAA vice-president Franklin Gledhill and assistant operations manager Karl F. Luedar, during their initial survey flight which lasted approximately one month and which actually took place before President Roosevelt's announcement on 19 August.

A White House announcement on 19 August revealed that twelve Douglas DC-3s were assigned immediately, and eight additional transports were promised later. Pan American was able to enlist some experienced commercial flyers as ferry pilots, but many more were needed. The large-scale training programme mentioned earlier commenced at Miami. Hundreds of mechanics, meteorologists, radio operators, surveyors, construction engineers, foremen, ground crews and other personnel were enlisted.

Preparations for personnel destined for Africa was a complex procedure. There were pre-employment checks by the FBI, the State Department, and British Intelligence agencies. A total of 1,855 applicants were examined by PAA doctors between 27 August 1941 and 1 September 1942. Of this number 298 were rejected, about sixteen per cent of applicants. Inoculations were given for smallpox, yellow fever, typhoid-paratyphoid, tetanus and cholera. Native labour was used extensively at the bases, especially at Accra where the native payroll numbered in excess of 5,000 African labourers, mostly unskilled, but well qualified to perform hard work under the hot Gold Coast sun. In addition to Accra, a secondary maintenance depot was located at Khartoum.

US Air Transport Command

During the summer of 1942 there was, in addition to PAA Africa personnel, an increasing number of USAAF personnel engaged in activities connected with the operations. At first these personnel were used in connection with censorship of mail, cargo and passengers. However, on 12 July 1942 the

Africa–Middle East Wing of the huge US Air Transport Command was activated, and Brigadier General Shepler W. Fitzgerald became Wing Commander at Accra, with Col Thomas O. Hardin as deputy commander and chief of operations. When PAA Africa was taken over by the USAAF during late 1942, pilot personnel holding reserve commissions on inactive status were called to active duty. Pilot captains with PAA Africa were granted commissions as captains in the Air Transport Command. It was not unusual to see an airline skipper come down the line from Cairo wearing the flight wings and uniform of PAA Africa, only to return to Cairo a few days later with USAAF captain bars and a military uniform. PAA Africa operations manager George Kruigher, chief pilot Henry C. Kristofferson, and assistant manager John Yeomans all became Lieutenant-Colonels in the USAAF.

The Douglas transports initially operated by PAA Africa were unique in that they were original DC-3s built for US domestic airline use by Eastern, American, United, Penn Central, Canadian Colonial, TWA and even Pan American. Seven DC-3s were in use by October 1941, and eventually a fleet of eleven was operated in civilian markings by PAA Africa, several being acquired within a few weeks of their manufacture at the Santa Monica factory in California. Records show that some were sold to the USAAF, whilst others were sold to the British Purchasing Commission for use by the RAF.

On 18 February 1942 orders were issued to the effect that the trans-Africa service was to become a completely military operation as rapidly as practical. Eleven DC-3s were allotted military serials 42-38250 to 260 to be designated C-48s and C-49s on 14 March 1942, but many had already been transferred to the RAF on 4 March. Newly built USAAF C-53 Skytroopers were assigned to Accra for use on the route and by June 1942 thirty-eight of the Douglas military transports were in use.

Many thousands of aircraft, including those from Lend-Lease contracts for the RAF, had been flown and ferried into action over the trans-Africa route since the summer of 1941, when the huge project was little more than a daring dream. Every type of US-built aircraft had flown the route – fighters and pursuit aircraft from the west coast of Africa or from US aircraft carriers which ferried them to within flying range of the African coast, plus medium and

heavy bombers all the way from Miami. Even the light Douglas A-20s, so much liked by the Russians, made the flight with the addition of auxiliary fuel tanks. Transports carried important loads of air freight.

The US War Department was the first to acknowledge that without joint British development of the ferry route, plus full co-operation from the Brazilian government, the Eighth Army could not have gained in time the air superiority that made possible the victory at El Alamein. The route was used to ferry aircraft to Russia, to the USAAF and RAF in the Middle East, and after the invasion of North Africa for ferrying aircraft to Allied forces in North Africa, Sicily and Italy.

During Rommel's rapid advance towards Alexandria and Cairo, radio signals were received at Accra from Cairo that shell fuses were urgently needed in the Western Desert. Just seven hours after receipt of the signal on 3 July 1942, six DC-3 transports departed Lagos with the shell fuses. The aircraft flew direct to Khartoum for crew change, arriving in Cairo early the following day. The distance by air from Lagos to Cairo via Khartoum was approximately 3,200 miles. By the night of 4 July the fuses were in use in the Western Desert thanks to PAA Africa. There were the odd losses, of course. On 19 April 1942 DC-3 NC18117 crashed on take-off from Khartoum and NC21750 was destroyed by fire also at Khartoum on 10 March 1942.

The unique PAA Africa organisation performed five broad tasks of military air transport operations closely associated with the huge Lend-Lease task. Firstly, it transported military supplies, mail and passengers to and from Cairo, supply centre of the Western Desert war. Secondly, it transported military supplies, mail and passengers to and from India, for delivery to the theatre of operations in Burma and China. Thirdly, it transported military supplies, mail and passengers to and from Tehran in Iran, supply centre for the Russian front. Fourthly, it transported RAF and PAA Ferries pilots and crews who had delivered operational aircraft to the Middle East back to their bases at Accra, Takoradi and Fisherman's Lake. And fifthly, it transported priority mail and passengers from India, Iran and Egypt back to Lagos, Accra and Fisherman's Lake for connection with transatlantic aircraft.

8. United Kingdom Air Depots

Liverpool on the River Mersey was the port at which much of the Lend-Lease material produced in the United States, 'the arsenal of democracy', arrived. During World War One the port had received many aircraft including Handley Page 0/400s built in the US. In 1939 warplanes began to appear on the dock-side in the form of Lockheed Hudsons for the RAF, the initial contract being for 200 (N7205–7404). Lockheed set up an organisation known as Lockheed Overseas Corporation.

Speke airport was the obvious location for Lockheed to assemble and air test the aircraft purchased by the British Purchasing Commission, and on 15 February 1939, on the day the first Hudson arrived at the port by ship, part of the large No.1 hangar was taken over. Operations expanded so quickly that within a week the Air Ministry requested permission to erect a Bellman hangar to provide more space. Later that year a second Bellman was erected. Accidents were few in number in the early days, but a Hudson Mk I N7260 lost part of its tail unit whilst on an acceptance air test on 28 July 1939 killing the American crew of three. This loss was replaced by Hudson R4059.

Although initially established to service the Hudson contract, the Lockheed organisation was ideally placed to handle deliveries of other US aircraft products. This proved interesting as the US manufacturers of aircraft in these early days of World War Two used entirely different tooling, with very little standardisation. Except for powerplants the simplest servicing was impossible without the appropriate tools and spare parts.

By 1940 Lockheed had agreed to assemble and air test Douglas Bostons, this setting a precedent for many other US types. Speke remained the head-quarters of the British Reassembly Division with Lockheed later setting up satellite units at Langford Lodge in Northern Ireland and Renfrew near Glasgow. The organisation came under the control of the Ministry of Aircraft Production (MAP) in May 1940 when the latter was established to take over the procurement responsibility of the Air Ministry. Around this time Lockheed at Speke was designated

No.1 Aircraft Assembly Unit (AAU). A similar unit, No.7 AAU, was located at Hooton Park seven miles south-east of Birkenhead. The pre-war firm of Martin Hearn Ltd assembled Douglas Bostons, North American Harvards and Canadian-built Handley Page Hampdens.

There were a number of RAF Maintenance Units (MU) earmarked for specialisation in Lend-Lease aircraft from North America. No.37 MU was located at RAF Burtonwood and No.29 MU at High Ercall in Shropshire. It must be remembered that these early orders for US-manufactured aircraft types originated pre-war with the British Purchasing Commission, whilst orders for France and Belgium were diverted to the United Kingdom after the invasion of mainland Europe by the Germans. On 22 November 1940 High Ercall's first arrivals were Curtiss Mohawk Mk IV BS731 and BS732. Other Mohawks from this batch of thirteen were delivered to India and South Africa. Many Curtiss Tomahawks and North American Harvards followed, some being assembled at Speke, others arriving in crates.

Two days prior to the bombing of Pearl Harbor, the Ministry of Aircraft Production organised a small display of newly delivered US types. This was evidently a propaganda exercise for the press and local dignitaries showing the extent of US support for Britain's democratic cause. Speke was the venue for the exhibition and the US types on view included North American Mustang Mk I AG349, a Curtiss Kittyhawk, a Douglas Boston, a Bell Airacobra and a Lockheed Hudson. The second production Mustang I AG346 was at Speke during November 1941, and of the batch of 320 aircraft AG345 to 664 some twenty-one were lost at sea during delivery and a further ten were shipped to Russia. The display at Speke included a demonstration showing the different stages of reassembly after shipment across the Atlantic, plus the handling qualities of the various US types. However, the weather was very inclement and British test pilot Mr H. A. Taylor, who was scheduled to demonstrate the Airacobra, did a low flypast after take-off from Hawarden near Chester, and went on to land at

Hooton Park which was closed for runway construction, but apparently he landed safely.

A friend of the author, Charles W. Cain, wrote up the display in the 12 December 1941 issue of *The Aeroplane*, describing the measures taken to preserve the aircraft for the Atlantic sea voyage and their subsequent reassembly on arrival. Great care was taken to prevent corrosion of metal parts by sea water. Wings and tailplanes were removed and packed separately. Fighters were stowed in the hold, and most medium bombers were lashed to the forward and aft well-decks. These were normally types such as the Boston and Hudson when the whole of the fuselage, undercarriage and engines were sprayed with a black composition called Para-al-tone whilst the joints and openings on the aircraft were masked with protective tape. Once in the hangars at Speke a de-greasing process took place involving very hot paraffin to soften the grease

coating, and with the help of a scraper and scrubbing brush the grease was removed. This process took less than half a day, or about forty man hours per aircraft. Personnel from Lockheed and the RAF, including WAAFs, were involved. The aircraft passed from hangar to hangar until finally the radio equipment – both Bendix and TR-9 – plus oxygen equipment was fitted prior to the acceptance air test.

Lockheed Expansion

The Lockheed Overseas Corporation also set up US aircraft assembly facilities at Renfrew, Glasgow and at Sydenham, Belfast, retaining Speke as the headquarters. At Belfast a wharf was built on the edge of the airfield and many aircraft such as Grumman Avengers and Vought-Sikorsky Corsairs for the Royal Navy (FAA) passed through here on delivery. Renfrew received many aircraft for the RAF and RN

Seen parked on the deck of the British merchantman Silversandal *are Republic Thunderbolt fighters for the RAF shipped over from the USA. During a heavy air raid on Liverpool and the docks during the first week of May 1941 the ship was damaged. (Via David J Smith).*

including Bostons and Grumman Wildcats. Many of the Bostons were in sand camouflage, destined for the Middle East.

During 1942–3 the Ministry of Aircraft Production (MAP) built runways at Renfrew. Lockheed Overseas Corporation established a facility to assemble fighters shipped over from the US and unloaded at the King George V dock at Shieldhall. The aircraft were mainly Lockheed Lightnings and North American Mustangs. From December 1943, only partially dismantled aircraft brought over as deck cargo were handled, any crated aircraft being sent direct to one of the Base Air Depots for assembly.

A controversial type, of which 750 were allocated under Lend-Lease, was the Brewster Bermuda aircraft, never flown operationally but which was adapted for target-tug duties. By March 1943 there were 160 of the type in the UK including sixty-three at Speke in various stages of assembly. Meanwhile, No.7 Aircraft Assembly Unit (AAU) at Hooton Park, Cheshire dealt mainly with Bostons, Mustangs and North American Harvards. The first Sikorsky HNS-1 Hoverfly Mk 1 helicopter was assembled and test-flown in 1944.

Many complete aircraft in their protective coatings were carried on the decks of cargo ships and tankers. The latter, with their extensive flat surfaces, were most useful for this purpose and false timber decks were built just to carry aircraft. When the cargo ships reached the River Mersey, the aircraft were unloaded by two converted baggage boats, *Oxton* and *Bebington*, whilst a third vessel was requisitioned as a crane. It is claimed that these three vessels put ashore 11,000 aircraft. Many lesser known Lend-Lease types were assembled at Speke including the Vought-Sikorsky Kingfisher for the Royal Navy, the Fairchild Argus, the Stinson Reliant, the Curtiss Seamew and the Helldiver.

Hundreds of aircraft for the Fleet Air Arm were handled at Speke. The folding wings of types like the Wildcats, Avengers and Corsairs plus the Hellcats made it easy to tow the aircraft from the docks to the airport. After inspection they were flown to RAF maintenance units tasked with naval aircraft reception, or to the air yard located at RNAS Stretton some twelve miles east of Speke. Lockheed received support from other organisations including BOAC engineers in 1940, as well as US Army Air Force and RAF personnel. The RAF resident unit was the Special Servicing Party, American Aircraft (SSPAA).

Burtonwood

Located at Burtonwood was No.37 MU opened on the first day of April 1940, and by April 1941 the unit had no less than 300 aircraft on charge, initially mainly RAF types. It was a normal RAF unit with mainly service personnel with a civilian factory site on the opposite side of the airfield separately organised. This was mainly managed by Fairey Aviation and Bristol Aeroplane Company staff, augmented by personnel from Avions Fairey Belginas, members of the Polish Air Force, and Dutch aircraft technicians. The assembly and modification hangars were dedicated to the preparation of US-manufactured aircraft, many originally ordered and paid for from the United States by the French and Belgian governments. Other aircraft were for the RAF and the Fleet Air Arm.

Crated and deck cargo aircraft arrived by ship at Liverpool docks and the first for assembly was a Glenn Martin 167 Maryland Mk I AR702 on 29 June 1940. This was the first of a batch of fifty (AR702 to 751) of which five – AR708/742/745/746/747 – were lost at sea en route. This Maryland was soon assembled and flown out on 18 July 1940. By 28 January 1941, when Maryland BS776 from a French batch of eighteen (BS760 to 777) was processed, over eighty of the type had passed through Burtonwood.

Photo from the A&AEE Boscombe Down dated 30 July 1941 depicting Bell Airacobra AH573 (P-39D) from the batch of 170 AH570–739 of which approximately 80 only used by the RAF. Remainder going to either USAAF or shipped to Russia after brief RAF service. Some lost en-route. The Air Fighting Development Unit at Duxford received the first Airacobra in July 1941. (Via Philip Jarrett).

The Blackburn Aircraft Company at depots here in the UK and in the USA modified hundreds of Lend-Lease aircraft destined for use by the Royal Navy. Depicted in February 1945 is a Grumman Avenger TR.III (TBM-3) JZ635 seen fitted with underwing rocket projectiles. It is the first of a batch of 112 JZ635–746 and were built by General Motors Corporation at Trenton, New Jersey. (Via Philip Jarrett).

From September 1940 they provided excellent service on photo-reconnaissance operations based on Malta, whilst others found their way to the Western Desert.

Commencing in July 1940 No.37 MU began to receive a naval fighter, the Brewster Buffalo, initially nine followed by a single aircraft in August, and by the end of October thirty-six of these were assembled and tested. A batch of twenty-eight (AS410 to 437) was delivered for RAF and Royal Navy use. The Brewster Model 439 was ordered by the Belgian government and thirty-eight were merged with the British contract, known as Brewster Model 339s. Most of the type were eventually transferred to Admiralty charge and ultimately saw limited action from shore bases in the Mediterranean area. There was a plan to equip the famous US Eagle squadron, No.71, of the RAF based at Church Fenton with the Buffalo, but after brief trials with AS414/416/421 it was concluded that the type was not up to the performance standards needed to enter combat with the Luftwaffe in western Europe, and Hawker Hurricanes were substituted.

In September 1940 came the Curtiss Mohawk, this being the P-36 export version coming from remaining French contracts and known as the Hawk 75A. Burtonwood assembled and air tested twenty examples by January 1941, but the type was not consistently viable for RAF Fighter Command operations, and the 195 Mohawks which had reached the UK by the end of 1940 were all put in reserve at MUs located at Little Rissington, Wroughton, Lossiemouth and Colerne. At the end of 1941 they were sent to the Far East where they proved useful against the Japanese in Burma from January 1942 onwards.

Manufactured by the Brewster Aeronautical Corporation, Johnsville, Bucks County, Pennsylvania, the Lend-Lease Bermuda served in the US Navy as the SB2A-1 and named Buccaneer. This official Air Ministry photo depicts RAF Bermuda FF-444 fitted with twin machine-gun on a mounting in the open rear cockpit. The engine was a single 1,700 hp Wright Cyclone R-2600-8. (Via Philip Jarrett).

Douglas DB-7

One of the most important programmes carried out at Burtonwood during this early period was the extensive modification of the Douglas DB-7 twin-engined light attack bomber which was for a time a revolutionary design featuring a tricycle nosewheel undercarriage. The A-20 was already in service with the US Army Air Corps and the examples which reached the UK in July 1940 were all turned over from uncompleted French contracts. These required many modifications to throttle controls, metricated instrument panels, radio equipment, armament etc. The name Boston was applied to the British DB-7.

These early Bostons were earmarked for extensive were converted; they retained the transparent nose, had a three-man crew and carried out intruder raids on German airfields.

During this period of World War Two, with the blitz in full operation, the pressure to find defensive measures was at its height, resulting in many new innovations in the Douglas Havoc programme at Burtonwood. Among these were the aircraft's carrying of aerial mines in the bomb bay, to be parachuted into the path of oncoming enemy bombers. These were known as Havoc Mk Is (Pandora) or LAM Havocs. Another idea was the powerful searchlight installation fitted in the nose. This led to the emergence of the Havoc Mk Is (Turbinlite), the brainchild of Air Commodore Helmore. They were

Historic photo depicting Sikorsky YR-4B FT-835 ex 42-107936 of the Royal Navy being prepared for flight on MV Daghestan, a British freighter bound for Liverpool to deliver Lend-Lease Hoverfly helicopters. During the rough crossing it was only possible to fly one flight on 16 January 1944 piloted by Cdr Stew Graham USCG, one of the early pioneer helicopter pilots. The Swordfish passing by is 'C3' from 'C' Flight 836 Squadron based on the MV Empire MacColl. (US Navy).

conversion into a night-fighter, later christened Havoc. By late 1940 a number had been converted with a soot-black RDM2 dope finish, and carried a variety of aerials on the nose and wings. This was the radar for air interception, then a closely guarded secret. First off the line was Havoc Mk I BJ464 from a batch of thirty-seven (BJ458 to 501) in December 1940. Fifty examples went through what was known as the famous 'Mary Ann Site' hangar located on the actual Burtonwood airfield. They had solid nose eight-gun armament. On a parallel assembly line were Havoc intruder versions of which thirty-eight intended to illuminate enemy bombers for the benefit of other defending night-fighters. Including all variants, No.37 MU supplied over seventy Turbinlites to the RAF including the later Havoc Mk III and Boston Mk III conversions.

Havoc night-fighters with augmented nose guns and the new radar proved a valuable addition to RAF Fighter Command's night force. When the more powerful Double Cyclone-powered Douglas DB-7A aircraft began to arrive, Burtonwood set up a new Havoc Mk II line involving the installation of an impressive lengthened nose, manufactured by

The Vought-Sikorsky OS2U-3 Kingfisher I supplied under Lend-Lease was a two-seat reconnaissance aircraft, with interchangeable land or sea float undercarriage, and suitable for catapult launch from warships. Depicted is FN678 one of 100 supplied in a photo dated April 1942. Seaplanes were embarked on HMS Canton, Cicilia, Corfu, Emerald, Enterprise, Fidelity, and Rampura. (Via Philip Jarrett).

Martin-Baker, which housed a battery of twelve machine-guns. The aircraft were from yet another French contract of 100, although `one was sunk during transit by ship. Twenty-five were converted, the remaining DB-7As going into Turbinlite configuration. The final variant to appear at Burtonwood was the Boston Mk III which were DB-7s ordered on British contracts. These later performed distinguished work with light day bomber squadrons, as well as in North Africa.

During 1941 early examples of the Martin Baltimore made their appearance, though bulk supplies of this type were mainly shipped to Africa. Designated Baltimore Mk I, the prototype AG685 reached the UK in October 1941 and was taken through trial installation stages at Burtonwood. There was a batch of 400 on order made up of Mk I/II/IIIs with AG710 not delivered, AG750 retained in Canada, thirty-five lost at sea en route and many shipped direct to the Middle East to serve with units of the SAAF.

An unusual US type which was resident at No.37 MU during August 1940 was a number of ex-French Navy, ex-US Navy Curtiss SBC-4 Helldiver biplane dive-bombers, prior to onward dispatch to No.8 MU at Little Rissington. These became the Cleveland Mk Is with five carrying the serials AS467 to 471. Early in 1940 France ordered ninety export versions of the SBC-4. The US Navy released fifty of its aircraft to hasten the French acquisition of the type. These were

Rare photo dated May 1943 depicting Seamew I FN472 for the Royal Navy with US military marks but British camouflage and fin flash. It is doubtful if the second batch of 150 JW550–699s ever reached the Royal Navy. A further 11 aircraft known as Queen Seamews were added, these were converted for use as radio-controlled target drones. However it is known that the Seamew I served at Worthy Down, Hampshire, training wireless telegraphists and air gunners. They were operated by the Fleet Air Arm in Canada up to March 1945. (Via Peter M Bowers).

Stinson Reliant I FL107 of the Royal Navy. Power was by a 290 hp Lycoming R-680 engine and the type was known in the USAAF as the L-12 but only four ex-commercial Reliants saw service. It served with the Royal Navy Ferry Pools as a communications aircraft with FK987 serving at Culham, Oxfordshire; FK960 at Donibristle, Fifeshire; FL163 at Worthy Down, Hampshire; whilst FK940 coded 'R9A' served at Stretton, Lancashire. The Lend-Lease documents quote the Reliant as the AT-19. (Via Peter M Bowers).

returned to the factory for refurbishment and application of French markings, but were later replaced by fifty of the aircraft then under construction for France. When France fell in June 1940 most of the SBC-4s had been loaded on to a French aircraft carrier which was diverted to the island of Martinique where it sat out the war, and eventually the dive-bombers were scrapped. Five not on board

the aircraft carrier reached the UK. These differed from the US Navy SBC-4s in having self-sealing fuel tanks.

At Burtonwood the Boeing B-17C Fortress Mk I bombers which flew the Atlantic by way of Prestwick or Squires Gate, Blackpool received their blue underside paint between May and August 1941. This was in readiness for high-altitude bombing

This official photo dated July 1940 depicts a rather battered Mohawk III AR634, possibly ex French, from the first batch for the RAF AR630–694. The Curtiss Model 75 was an export fighter being ordered and delivered to France commencing in December 1938. Later French orders were taken over by the British Purchasing Commission for use by the RAF. The H75-A5 Cyclone-powered version was assembled in China, later India, and at least six were absorbed into RAF service. Norway, the Netherlands, Iran, Siam and Argentina were some of the customers for this type. (Via Philip Jarrett).

experiments with No.90 Squadron. With the French capitulation, Britain took over fifty Vought-Sikorsky Chesapeake Mk I V-156 B1 dive-bombers, the residue of a French Navy contract, and allotted the RAF serials AL908 to 957. These aircraft were known in the US Navy as Vindicators. They arrived in the UK early in 1941 and were assembled at Burtonwood with fourteen going to No.811 Squadron Fleet Air Arm at Lee-on-Solent on 14 July 1941.

From 1941 onwards several hundred Fairchild Argus light communications aircraft were supplied under Lend-Lease serving with both the RAF and the Air Transport Auxiliary (ATA) ferry units. A number appeared at Burtonwood. A similar type received was the Vultee-Stinson Vigilant delivered to the RAF for trials on Air Observation Post (OAP) duties with the British Army during 1941–2. They

the French were interested. Unfortunately, on 23 January 1939 with a French officer on board the prototype DB-7 crashed killing the Douglas test pilot, John Cable. However, the type was ordered to meet the needs of the Armée de l'Air and a large quantity was built for France, many subsequently going to the RAF to be processed at Burtonwood. Boeing built 240 DB-7B aircraft for the RAF, known as Boston Mk IIIs, and an example, AL452 c/n 2833, was completed on 29 December 1941, the last of a batch of 166 (AL337–452). They were powered by two 1,600 hp Wright GR-2600-A5B-0 Double Cyclone 14 engines. On 9 November 1943 Boardman C. Reed, a friend of the author, flew AL452 for one solo from RAF Honington, Suffolk to HQ 1st Bomb Division Alconbury air base near Huntingdon.

By July 1942 there were no Lend-Lease aircraft with the MU at Burtonwood, which then became the

This Douglas A-20 Havoc AH522 was one of a number modified from the Boston and seen during October 1941 and finished in the non-reflective black known as Special Night Finish RDM 2A. The type was initially referred to as Moonfighter and later Rangers before the name Havoc became widely used. This Havoc came from a batch of 100 DB-7B Boston II aircraft delivered prior to Lend-Lease which were allocated AH430–529. (Via Philip Jarrett).

served in Tunisia, Sicily and Italy and three of the type appeared with No.37 MU in March 1942, possibly from an early batch of four, FR401–404 ex-USAAC 40-262/265. Among the miscellaneous types which appeared were a few Pitcairn Autogiro aircraft.

The French Purchasing Commission in the United States visited most of the aircraft manufacturers, and they had their products demonstrated to the French representatives. One was the Douglas Model DB-7, known in the RAF as the Boston and Havoc, in which

UK centre for the repair of all US-built airframes and engines for the US armed forces and was operated by a private firm called the Burtonwood Repair Depot Limited. The management was shared equally between the Fairey Aviation Company and the Bristol Aeroplane Company.

C. H. Chichester-Smith of Fairey, a former naval aviator was the Controller described as a man of style and elegance. The chief designer was E. O. Tips, the renowned Belgian aircraft designer from Avions Fairey. From Poland came the aerodynamicist

Interesting Martin photo dated 23 January 1942 depicting an early RAF Baltimore which has the US civil registration NXM53 on the rudder. In the USA the type was initially a project designated A-23 Model 187 which was cancelled. Later it became the A-30 Model 187B which covered Lend-Lease aircraft for Britain and Russia. Production for the RAF, which ceased in May 1944, with FW880, reached a total of 1,575. (Via Philip Jarrett).

The Curtiss Cleveland I was the RAF version of the SBC-4 Helldiver two-seat carrier-borne dive-bomber used by the US Navy. Five AS467–471 reached the UK in the summer of 1940 as the residue of 50 handed over to France by the US Navy. Illustrated is AS468 one of the five, assembled at Burtonwood in August 1940 and later delivered to RAF Little Rissington. The type was never used operationally but used for ground instruction training. (Via Philip Jarrett).

68

Rudlicki, whilst another Avions Fairey character was called Godfrey. The Glen Martin Maryland assembly line was supervised by an outstanding ground engineer from de Havillands named Humphreys. John Currie was the flight shed superintendent, a suave Savile Row dresser who charmed all the ladies and, it was alleged, ran his 1930 Red Label Bentley on 100 octane aviation fuel.

On the shop floor were members of the Polish and Belgian air forces, recently escaped from the advancing German armies in Europe, assisted by local skilled and unskilled civilians and including a no-nonsense type called Weedie who once worked for Supermarine with the RAF Schneider Trophy racing seaplanes.

Mention must be made of the odd rare US type which passed through Burtonwood in those early days. These included a single Northrop 8-A5 Nomad Mk I AS974, known as the A-17 with the US armed forces. The example was assembled with No.37 MU in August 1940 and flown to No.20 MU at Aston Down. Some of the A-17s in US service were

Boeing B-17G-DL 42-297109 from a batch of Flying Fortress bombers built by Douglas at Long Beach seen shortly after delivery to the RAF under Lend-Lease as a Fortress III HB766. Records reveal that this bomber was returned to the USAAF. The three pretty girls are possibly part of the reception committee for the crew and aircraft after it arrived at Prestwick. (Via Bruce Robertson).

The British order for 50 V-156-B1 Chesapeakes was the residue from a French contract, and were allocated serials AL908–957. These differed from the French in having four forward-firing guns instead of one and installation of British type arrester gear. First arrived in UK during 1941 and assembled at Burtonwood. The only operational unit was No.811 Squadron at Lee-on-Solent which received 14. Depicted in flight are AL924 'K': AL927 'A' and AL936 'D'. Proved unsuitable so replaced by Swordfish in November 1941. (Peter M Bowers).

Vultee-Stinson Vigilants were delivered to the RAF during 1941/42 for light liaison and artillery spotting duties. During 1943/44 they supported the British Eighth Army in Tunisia, Sicily and Italy. Originally designed by Stinson, the company was later taken over by Consolidated-Vultee, the Vigilant having first flown in 1940 and used by the US Army as the 0-49. Depicted is HL429 carrying (P) markings, the photo taken at the A&AEE Boscombe Down on 20 December 1941. (Via Philip Jarrett).

returned to the factory for re-sale to Britain and France and the serials AS958 to 990 were allotted to the aircraft. Six were lost at sea on delivery, one went to No.37 MU and the rest to the SAAF.

Langford Lodge

The possibilities of an airfield at Langford Lodge in County Antrim were recognised by the Ministry of Aircraft Production officials early in 1941, and work was well advanced when a change of policy came in February 1942. The US government had decided to set up an air depot in Ulster for the repair and servicing of USAAF aircraft. The site was allocated to them and plans were made under Lend-Lease for the UK government, through the MAP, to bear the cost of construction, estimated at £1¼ million, whilst the US government would furnish the specialised equipment.

Sites and facilities were erected for some 2,600 civilian personnel of the Lockheed Overseas Corporation, contracted to run the depot. Being highly secret, Langford Lodge was known as the 'Y' scheme and it was given absolute priority over all other construction in Northern Ireland. It was opened on 15 August 1942 and was renamed HQ 1st US Service Area, Station 597.

During late 1942, in addition to the first USAAF Lockheed P-38 Lightnings which had arrived by sea at Sydenham on 11 November 1942, the depot was busy assembling a number of Brewster Bermuda Mk I dive-bombers for the RAF. Large-scale production

at the Brewster factory at Johnsville, Pennsylvania was assisted by the sale of the Model 340 to the British Purchasing Commission, which ordered 750 in July 1940, the Dutch government ordering 162. After the passage of the Lend-Lease Act on 11 March 1941 and its approval with the signature of President Roosevelt, the US Army Air Corps, which became the USAAF on 20 June 1941, and the US Navy jointly assumed responsibility for the British order. Bermudas FF419 to 868 were ex-USAAF A-34 aircraft, whilst FF869 to 999 and FG100 to 268 were ex-US Navy SB2A-1s. They were not flown operationally, being adapted as target-tugs, with FF457 the prototype. There is no record of deliveries to the UK after FF633, but it is understood a number were diverted to the RAAF and the RCAF.

Scottish Aviation Limited (SAL)

Prestwick in Ayrshire will be remembered chiefly as a transatlantic ferry base and terminal through which were delivered many thousands of US- and Canadian-built aircraft. The Atlantic Ferry Organisation was set up by the Ministry of Aircraft Production and administered by BOAC. It was from Prestwick that the Return Ferry Service was organised with Liberators to fly the ferry crews back to Dorval for more Lend-Lease aircraft. The first aircraft to be ferried across the Atlantic – Lockheed Hudsons – left Gander on 10 November 1940 arriving in Northern Ireland the following day. Thereafter most flights made Prestwick their terminus. A mixture of civilian and service personnel continued to work together both in the air and on the ground.

Scottish Aviation Limited (SAL) received instructions in July 1940 to assemble sixteen US-built aircraft at Abbotsinch, and these were followed by further fighters built by Grumman, Northrop, Chance-Vought and Curtiss, including Tomahawks, Mohawks, Kittyhawks, Kingfishers and Martlets. On 29 November 1940 a RAF Lockheed Hudson arrived at Prestwick instead of Aldergrove in Northern Ireland, and after this Scottish Aviation

took on the responsibility of servicing and modifying all land planes ferried across the Atlantic from North America. On 18 December 1940 Captain E. P. M. Eves inadvertently landed Hudson Mk I T9426 at Prestwick having strayed a little off-track.

At Prestwick, SAL worked principally on Lend-Lease Liberator, Dakota, Mitchell, Hudson and Fortress aircraft. As many as thirty aircraft could arrive overnight. At one time Consolidated were thinking of taking an interest in the company. The first routine delivery through Prestwick arrived there on 10 February 1941; this was Hudson Mk I

After the fall of France in June 1940, the entire contract for the Lockheed Model 322 was taken over by the RAF – 143 Lightning Is and 524 IIs. Following unsatisfactory testing at Boscombe Down and a contract dispute with Lockheed, the RAF refused delivery after receiving only three aircraft. The rest went to the USAAC. This interesting photo depicts two Lightning Is which were never delivered with Lockheed c/n on the nose, making c/n 3097 which would have been AF174 and c/n 3034 the second aircraft AF111. (Via Peter M Bowers).

T9464 flown by Captain R. Allen, Flying Officer Watt and radio operator Mitchell. There was no reception committee, just a handful of personnel including HM Customs from Ayr docks, who at that time constituted the Customs, immigration and security police.

The next ferry flight on 15/16 February involved five Hudsons, no less than four of which turned back due to mechanical problems. This was intended to be the first mass ferry to Prestwick and the next attempt, Ferry Flight No.7 on 20/21 February comprising five aircraft, was almost equally ill-fated. The Hudson carrying a VIP passenger, Sir Frederick Banting, the scientist who discovered insulin, crashed in Newfoundland; the pilot was the sole survivor.

Prestwick was selected as the transatlantic terminal for a number of reasons, and it is a myth that its good weather record was discovered only by chance. Liverpool, to which the Hudsons were delivered after the initial landing in Northern Ireland, was suffering heavy air raids whilst balloons both here and at Belfast added to the hazards at the end of a long and tiring Atlantic crossing. Captain D. F. McIntyre of Scottish Aviation Limited had been pressing for the use of the company's airfield as an Atlantic terminal, stressing its remarkable fog-free record, and it was decided to act on his advice.

A resident unit attracted by Prestwick's weather record since September 1940 was No.4 Ferry Pilots Pool (FPP) of the Air Transport Auxiliary (ATA). This unit found itself in charge of most of the onward ferrying of newly arrived aircraft from North America, a task which continued until the end of World War Two. However, bad weather affecting bases in the south sometimes resulted in a backlog, so it was not uncommon for aircraft to be dispersed alongside public roads around the periphery of the airport. Once the USAAF commenced using Prestwick the terminal was often literally a mass of parked aircraft of many types. Towards the end of 1941, in an effort to disperse aircraft away from such a vulnerable target, a Satellite Landing Ground (SLG) was constructed at Kayshill, Ayrshire, but was abandoned before being put into use. This was possibly due to the Luftwaffe bomber force being otherwise engaged on the Eastern Front, providing a lull in the serious air attacks on Britain.

As mentioned earlier in the book, the LB 30

Liberator was chosen to ferry crews back to Montreal, seven of these converted bombers being acquired. On 4 May 1941 the first east and west-bound flights were made simultaneously between St Hubert, Montreal, and Squires Gate, Blackpool, in each case via Gander. The westbound Liberator was slightly damaged in an air raid whilst parked at Squires Gate, but was soon repaired. Over the next two months there were twenty more flights in each direction. Owing to bad weather in Newfoundland, more than half the westbound flights had been forced to route from the UK direct to Montreal, a distance of 3,100 miles. The two-way route had been firmly established, at least during the summer months, for there was a real test ahead with the ice, snow and gales of the winter. In May 1941 ATFERO came into being which to some was merely a paper exercise as many CPR employees stayed on, expansion continued and ferry operations were not affected.

Towards the end of this period, the UK terminal was changed to Ayr, constructed during 1941. Gradually delivery totals mounted, and on 14 April 1941 the first of thousands of Flying Fortress bombers to fly the Atlantic arrived, namely Fortress Mk I AN534, one of twenty purchased by the British Purchasing Commission. This new fighter base, only a mile from Prestwick, planned for the air defence of Glasgow, had three runways making it ideal as a temporary terminal for four-engined aircraft until the runways at Prestwick were completed. Squires Gate remained a useful alternative and several of the RAF Fortress Mk I bombers flew there direct.

Despite its initial grass surface, some heavy aircraft did use Prestwick, including Fortress Mk I AN529 on 16 April 1941 and Liberator AM912 on 23 April, both first visits by the type. The Return Ferry Service mainly used Ayr during 1941, but the short runways were very difficult for fully loaded Liberators. On 14 August 1941, Liberator AM260 crashed and burned on take-off, killing all twenty-two on board, all but one being aircrew. The sole civilian fatality was the Rt. Hon. Arthur Purvis, a prominent member of the British Purchasing Commission responsible for procuring aircraft and munitions in North America. This disaster came shortly after an accident on 10 August when Liberator AM261 flew into Goat Fell, that dramatic peak which protrudes from the north end of the Isle of Arran, ten miles north-west of Prestwick. The

The first Lockheed Hudson I N7205 first flew on 10 December 1938 and was first of an Air Ministry order for 200 N7205–7404. Lockheed design number was B14L and 1,338 were delivered under the direct purchase scheme. Depicted is N7205 which was tested at A&AEE Boscombe Down, RAE Farnborough and at Martlesham Heath. It was eventually struck off charge on 17 December 1943. A further 1,302 Hudsons were delivered to the RAF under Lend-Lease contracts. (Via Philip Jarrett).

theory was that the slow-climbing aircraft set course in cloud with a following wind. Twenty-two lives were lost including distinguished and irreplaceable aircrew like Captain E. R. B. White and navigator Captain F. D. Badbrook. A further blow was the crash of eastbound Liberator AM915 on the Mull of Kintyre on 1 September 1941.

Flying Boat Bases

A parallel operation with land-based US aircraft commenced with flying boats between Bermuda and the UK. Back in July 1939 the British had purchased a single Consolidated 28-5 commercial version of the Catalina P9630 bearing the nickname

As early as 1936 the US Navy introduced the Catalina into service under the designation PBY-1 with its patrol-bomber squadrons. The Air Ministry ordered one example, designated Consolidated 28-5 for experimental testing with serial P9630. It reached the Marine Aircraft Experimental Establishment at Felixstowe, Suffolk in July 1939. It was sunk during tests in February 1940. At the outbreak of World War 2 an initial order for 30 (PBY-5) was placed, with hundreds more to follow under Lend-Lease. (Via Philip Jarrett).

Guba, after a squall peculiar to New Guinea where the aircraft had operated in 1938. On 25 October 1939, *Guba* took off from Botwood, Newfoundland for Scotland and after sixteen hours and twenty-one minutes in the air it landed at Wig Bay, Stranraer in Dumfries and Galloway.

During January 1941 the base at Darrell's Island on the outskirts of Hamilton, Bermuda opened up with the arrival of seven Catalinas from the US. The first Atlantic crossing from here was memorable because the aircraft, when six hours out of Bermuda, lost both ailerons recovering from a spiral dive caused by a malfunctioning autopilot. The Canadian skipper pressed on and managed to get back on course. After weathering a storm, he succeeded in reaching Milford Haven in Wales having been aloft for twenty-eight hours and fifty minutes.

Some of the Catalinas ferried during 1941 flew the route from Gander Lake to Scotland, the normal destination being Greenock on the Clyde where Scottish Aviation Limited had an out-station overhauling and preparing flying boats for the RAF. The first Catalina arrived on 1 February 1941. Stranraer was available as an alternative, one of its users being Catalina Mk I AH569 on 8 June 1941. In addition to Greenock, Largs in Strathclyde provided a parallel facility operated by Scottish Aviation Limited. By 1943 Largs was acting as a reception base for all Lend-Lease flying boats crossing the Atlantic. Aircraft were moored to the leeward side of Great Cumbrae Island and the crews were ferried to and fro by launch. Largs opened around December 1942 and the Catalinas were normally delivered here. Martin Mariners were also to be seen, including JX110 which departed for Stranraer on 2 February 1944.

During June 1944 a new service was inaugurated by No.45 Group Montreal for the carriage of urgent freight to the UK and the return of ferry crews to Canada. It was operated by huge Consolidated Coronados from No.231 Squadron, formed at Dorval in 1944 from No.45 Group Communications Squadron. It operated twice weekly routing Boucherville–Gander–Largs eastbound and Largs–Reykjavik–Gander–Goose Bay westbound. Coronado Mk I JX501 was one of the planes used for these freight services, and on 25 September 1945 the service was terminated with the departure from Largs of Coronado Mk I JX498.

Wig Bay, Stranraer was the home of the Flying Boat Training Squadron which was allocated one of the first Catalinas for the RAF, W8406, and in June 1941 three US Navy PBY Catalina instructors were attached to the unit. No.57 MU formed here in October 1943, its task being the preparation, modification, repair and storage of Catalinas and the new Martin Mariner, which was just entering service.

Beaumaris, Anglesey was developed as the headquarters of Saunders-Roe from the Isle of Wight, right in the front line of the war in the air. The company had received a contract for the modification of newly delivered Lend-Lease Catalinas so it was vital to find a less vulnerable site to carry out this important task. The Menai Straits east of the suspension bridge were found to be ideal as an alighting area, with deep water up to the bridge a safe haven for mooring in reasonable shelter. A small estate called Friars, one mile from Beaumaris town, was selected as a factory site, and a slipway was built giving access to the water. Over 300 Catalinas passed through here and modifications included the installation of armament, radio equipment, ASV radar and Leigh Light fitting. Some of the Catalinas were ferried across the Atlantic to Largs and then onward to Beaumaris, but most flew direct.

Another Scottish flying boat base handling Lend-Lease aircraft was Oban in Strathclyde which opened in 1933, followed by RAF units from 1937 which in April 1941 operated Catalinas. On 28 July 1941 Catalina Mk I W8416 from No.210 Squadron left Oban via Invergordon for Archangel on a high priority mission. It carried Mr Harry Hopkins, President Roosevelt's personal representative in Europe, and two US Army Air Corps officers. The objective was to obtain for the President at first hand Stalin's thoughts on the current war situation and details of any armament requirements.

On 20 October 1943 No.524 Squadron was formed and equipped with Lend-Lease Martin Mariners to gain experience on the type. The flying logbook of a good friend of the author, the late Ray Gough, reveals that he flew Mariner JX105, a PBM-3C, on 27 October on a test flight from Saro's at Beaumaris, and on 1 November ferried it to Oban. Mariner Mk I JX100 was involved in training, and flying ceased with JX110 on 8 December 1943. The Mariner was found to be unsuitable for RAF service, partly because of its poor single-engine performance. The flying boats were returned to the US, the first one being JX122 which was ferried to Gibraltar on 28 February 1944, followed by JX131 the next day. From Gibraltar the ferry route was Bathurst, The Gambia to Natal and Belem, Brazil; Chaguramas Bay, Trinidad to San Juan, Puerto Rico; then to Banana River, Florida and finally to Norfolk, Virginia, with JX131 arriving on 3 March 1944. Mariner JX106 was ferried to Wig Bay on 26 February 1944.

Lend-Lease was then at its peak so Ray Gough was seconded to Elizabeth City, North Carolina, a reception base for RAF Catalinas. On 28 March 1944 he test-flew a Boeing-built PB2B-1 Catalina JX365, and on 10 April ferried JX341 to Largs via Bermuda and Dartmouth, Nova Scotia where he arrived safely on 16 April.

Transatlantic Control

On 15 August 1941, in order to supervise the North Atlantic ferry routes, Transatlantic Air Control was set up at Prestwick in Powbank Mill on the edge of the airport. On 21 October a move to Redbrae took place for TAC which would monitor the movement of all aircraft within a range of about 1,000 miles. The unit had direct links with its opposite numbers in Iceland and Newfoundland. The early flights across the Atlantic had been monitored by the Overseas Air Movement Control Unit at Gloucester. In August 1941 No.44 Group RAF Ferry Command was formed at Gloucester to take over from the OAMCU responsibility for all non-operational flights in and out of UK airspace, the preparation and dispatch of aircraft

to overseas commands, and the training of ferry aircrews.

Meanwhile Lend-Lease deliveries were on the increase, with sixty Hudsons arriving during the second half of August 1941, and many Catalinas using the Gander Lake to Greenock ferry route. On 11 November 1941 the Curtiss CW 20 G-AGDI c/n 101 41-21041, a type similar to the C-46 Commando, flew from Gander to Prestwick for evaluation by BOAC. It was scrapped in October 1943. By the end of 1941, a total of 722 aircraft had been ferried over to the UK. Some carried a few passengers and all were loaded with spares and other vital supplies.

Losses were inevitable. On 27 April 1941 Hudson AE577 hit a hill near Dundalk after take-off from Baldonnel near Dublin. This was a particularly sad end to the flight as the crew had safely negotiated the Atlantic crossing, becoming lost on the final stages and landing in Eire from where they were allowed to continue. On 15 April 1942 Hudson Mk IIIA FH263 flew halfway across the Atlantic with one engine out and crash-landed at Blackrod, County Donegal with only two gallons of fuel left.

On 24 June 1942 a milestone was passed when a Lend-Lease Lockheed Ventura landed at Prestwick, making the 1,000th safe delivery to the UK. Mitchells and Bostons were now appearing and the first two Bostons were delivered by air on 12 October 1942, all previous examples for the RAF being shipped by sea. The first British westbound flight took place on 29 October 1942 with BOAC Liberator G-AGCD ex-AM259, which eight days earlier had flown to

Official photo of Mariner GR.I JX-103 dated October 1943 beached at Oban, the home base of No.524 Squadron which operated the type between 20 October and 7 December 1943. This flying boat JX-103 later became a trials aircraft receiving the suffix to the serial so becoming JX-103/G. The aircraft was ferried back to the USA by 524 Squadron crews, most of whom returned with Catalinas. (Via AP Publications).

Moscow. The onset of winter took its toll. On 18 December 1942 a Catalina went missing between Bermuda and Largs, and on 8 December a Boston failed to arrive after transmitting an SOS. On the same day a Boston reached landfall but was lost above thick overcast. The crew eventually baled out and the bomber crashed in a field in Suffolk.

Civil Contractors

At Hooton Park, Cheshire, the pre-war firm of Martin Hearn Limited became known as No.7 Aircraft Assembly Unit which, as its name suggests, assembled Lend-Lease Bostons and Harvards in a hangar complex on the south-east corner of the airfield. At Walsall in the Midlands, Helliwells had constructed a factory in 1938 at the airport and obtained servicing contracts mainly for Lend-Lease North American Harvard training aircraft. The company also serviced Douglas Boston light bombers which had Free French markings. Due to the grass airfield being too small for test-flying of the Boston, this was done at RAF Perton on the outskirts of Wolverhampton. At Weston-super-Mare in Somerset the resident Western Airways repaired Lend-Lease Curtiss Tomahawks under contract with the Central Repair Organisation.

The Operational Record Book (ORB) for RAF Shawbury in Shropshire mentions North American using D1 hangar. This was the home of No.27 MU. Also located in Shropshire was RAF High Ercall, home of No.29 MU, and the following details were extracted from the unit's ORB. The MU was formed on 1 October 1940 to deal with the flood of US-built aircraft deliveries. The first two aircraft appeared on 22 November 1940, Curtiss Mohawks BS731/2, both departing on 2 January 1941. On 26 November 1940 Harvard N7162 was delivered by air, followed three days later by Tomahawk Mk I AH752. Harvard Mk II BJ412 arrived on 8 December, departing on 4 January 1941, whilst Tomahawk AH751 also arrived. On 10 December Harvard Mk II BJ410 was delivered and went out on 4 January. Four Harvards arrived on 29 December – P5827, P5875, N7083 and N7804, the latter crashing on landing. Records show that on 31 December 1940 the unit had in store two Mohawks, five Harvard Mk Is, two Harvard Mk IIs and three Tomahawks.

By mid-1943 Lend-Lease Dakotas were being ferried over in large numbers in preparation for the build-up leading to the airborne assault on Europe on D-Day, 6 June 1944. Crews from RAF Squadrons flew up to Prestwick to pick up newly arrived transports, one being from No.271 Squadron, then based at Doncaster in Yorkshire. On 8 February 1944 Jimmy Edwards flew from Doncaster to Prestwick in FZ633, and three days later flew back in FZ641, returning with FZ615, and on 21 February ferrying back FZ667. At Doncaster the new transports were checked, brought up to date with any modifications and the installation of British VHF radio sets. On 24 February the Squadron with its Dakotas moved south to its newly constructed base at Down Ampney. The first Dakota for the RAF under Lend-Lease, FD768, was finished at the Long Beach factory in California on 9 January 1943, the second – FD769 – arriving at Prestwick on 11 February.

Among the notable events in 1944 was the arrival on 22 May of the 15,000th aircraft controlled by TAC at Prestwick. On 10 June a VIP Douglas C-54 Skymaster, EW999, flew direct from Dorval to Northolt, Middlesex. It was a C-54B ex-43-17126 and a gift for Prime Minister Winston Churchill. The RAF total of aircraft delivered for February 1944 alone was 191. It must be mentioned that delivery of USAAF aircraft for this month was probably double the RAF total.

On 13 December 1944 three Catalinas from Bermuda failed to arrive at Largs because of bad weather. Catalina Mk IVB JX590 arrived off Portstewart, Northern Ireland, landed, took off again and landed at Ballantrae, north of Stranraer. It was towed to Wig Bay but was damaged on the way. Another Mk IVB, JX603, alighted at Wig Bay but was damaged taxiing and JX597 bent a wingtip float in Girvan harbour.

Towards the end of World War Two some Lend-Lease aircraft found a haven in neutral territory such as Eire, having either been lost or caught short of fuel. The civil flying boat terminal at Foynes had two Catalinas land, JX330 and JX422, on 9 March and 5 September 1944 respectively. The Mk IVB JX330 was built by Boeing in Canada and had been airborne for twenty-six hours from Bermuda. Both were re-fuelled and allowed to continue. North American Mitchell Mk II FW235 was not so fortunate, being written-off in a forced landing in County Mayo on 31 January 1944. The crew were unhurt. On 10 February 1945 Liberator Mk VIII KK295 became lost while inbound to Prestwick from Dorval and force-

Nearly 2,000 C-47 Dakota transports were supplied to the RAF under Lend-Lease with many more to the Allies, also under Lend-Lease. Depicted at Oklahoma City awaiting a ferry flight are C-47 Skytrains for the USAAF plus an RAF Dakota KK131, one for Russia and one for China. The RAF Dakota arrived in the UK after its ferry flight across the Atlantic on 28 November 1944 being allocated to No.1 Parachute Training School (PTS) at Ringway on 2 January 1945. It went to No.271 Squadron on 17 November 1945 and took part in the Berlin Airlift in 1948 being based at Oakington. It was eventually broken up at Brooklands on 10 February 1950. (Douglas).

landed on a beach in Donegal. Two other total losses near the end of the war included Mitchell Mk III KJ751 on 3 January 1945. It had sent out an SOS indicating the starboard engine was out. Dakota Mk IV KK194 was lost on 1 February 1945.

Civilian Repair Organisation

To cope with the huge influx of aircraft, including Lend-Lease types, requiring repair and modification during World War Two, a unique organisation, the huge and efficient Civilian Repair Organisation (CRO), was brought into being. Aircraft casualties soon exceeded the usual RAF capacity to repair them. The major aircraft manufacturers in the UK were already working flat out to produce new machines, so there was no organisation available to cope with the rapid influx of battle-torn and accident-damaged aircraft.

A solution was needed rapidly, so attention was turned to the previously untapped civilian sector of the British aircraft industry. Numerous small companies had the necessary expertise and often the capacity available. Many of these became part of a national UK scheme known as the CRO. During the course of World War Two numerous firms helped it return thousands of bent and battered airframes back to active service, and carried out modifications to many more.

A whole volume would be required to cover the task of the CRO, but the county of Leicestershire is an excellent example of the nationwide work of the CRO. Around Loughborough, Airwork Limited worked on Lend-Lease Douglas Bostons and Havocs; Brush & Willowbrook Coachworks rebuilt Handley Page Hampdens early on in the conflict; Taylorcraft (England) Limited at Rearsby dealt with large numbers of Hawker Hurricanes, Typhoons and de Havilland Tiger Moths; and at Desford, some six-and-a-half miles west-south-west of Leicester, the aircraft manufacturer Reid & Sigrist worked on the Boulton & Paul Defiant. The company was also contracted to work on the Bell P-39 Airacobra, but because the aircraft was considered unsuitable for RAF requirements, the small numbers received did not warrant setting up a repair line.

However, Reid & Sigrist signed a contract to repair and modify North American B-25 Mitchell medium bombers. The first of these arrived at Desford on 9 April 1943 when FL189 and FL671 came in from the A&AEE at Boscombe Down, Wiltshire. During 1943 only a further sixteen more of the type were processed at Desford, but the situation was to change dramatically during 1944 with the Allied invasion of Europe. During the first six months of 1944 Reid & Sigrist received thirty-two Mitchells, and by the end of the year the total had reached seventy-two. Naturally a number of the B-25s which required repairs had their injuries attributed to flying accidents, but it was enemy action which accounted for the majority. On one such occasion, the company benefited from no less than eight complete airframes damaged as a result of enemy action. Raids by Luftwaffe fighter and fighter-bombers on airfields of the 2nd Allied Tactical Air Force in Europe resulted in many casualties to aircraft dispersed. There were six RAF squadrons operating the Mitchell.

Examples of Mitchells arriving at Desford for treatment included FV903, FW202, FW225 and KJ586 from 180 Squadron and FV982 and FW252 from 98 Squadron. Two others were FV961 and HD382. By the end of hostilities in Europe a large number of damaged Mitchells accumulated at Desford were classified as unworthy of repair. Surveys resulted in many being re-classified as Category E for scrap, and so they were struck off charge (SOC).

It is recorded that eight Mitchells were processed during June 1945, with no more arrivals until 22 October when FR209, destined to be the last of the type, was flown in from the Empire Central Flying School (ECFS) at Hullavington. The end of an interesting era came on 16 November when FV973 and FW225 left Reid & Sigrist at Desford for storage with 12 Maintenance Unit at Kirkbride, whilst FR209 was returned to the ECFS. This Mitchell was used on a variety of tasks serving with the RAF into the early 1950s, and being equipped at one time as a flying laboratory. Along with FR208, FR209 was a North American B-25G model, ex-USAAF 42-64822 and 42-64823 respectively. The type was named after General William 'Billy' Mitchell, pioneer of US military aviation.

Final Deliveries

Despite victory being in sight, delivery totals of Lend-Lease aircraft were still high. In March 1945 Prestwick received 242 aircraft which included 106 Canadian-built Mosquitos. By July the figure had shrunk to 120, of which forty-five were Dakotas. In August 1945 ten Canso flying boats flown by Soviet Navy crews landed at Prestwick from Elizabeth City, North Carolina. They went on to Kolberg in the USSR. Five more followed in September. Also during August forty-one RAF Liberators returned to the UK from No.111 OTU in Nassau.

The wind-down of the huge ferry operation was well illustrated by a mere eight deliveries in September 1945, comprising four Dakotas, three Canadian-built Mosquitos and a lone Canadian-built Lancaster. On 31 October 1945 No.4 Ferry Pilots Pool closed down. It is natural that the total numbers recorded of aircraft delivered across the Atlantic, north and south, by Ferry Command and its antecedents conflict, dependent on what source one refers to, as also do the aircraft losses. I would like to quote a figure of 9,340 aircraft ferried, the casualties totalling 162 civil aircrew and 158 service personnel lost.

9. Montreal and Beyond

When the first ugly strains of World War Two fell upon the ears of RAF Coastal Command it was very short of modern aircraft, with only one Lockheed Hudson squadron out of thirteen land-based squadrons. For practically the whole of the first year of the war when the Battle of the Atlantic was causing a heavy loss of shipping, Coastal Command could not provide any consistent air cover over the convey route. The aircraft in the single Hudson squadron were the first arrivals in the United Kingdom of those ordered for the RAF by the British Purchasing Commission in June 1938 by Lord Swindon, the Secretary of State for Air. The initial order for 200 Hudsons, commencing with N7205, was delivered between April 1939 and January 1940. They provoked a storm of controversy in Britain at the time as many felt it was wrong to order aircraft for the RAF other than those designed and built by the industry at home. In the event, the decision proved a wise one, as the Hudson filled an important gap in Coastal Command and made a great contribution to the harrying of the menacing U-boat from the air in the early stages of the war.

When World War Two started it was the Ministry

Appropriately marked with a Donald Duck cartoon and description, the documents for yet another Lockheed Hudson for the RAF are handed over to the civilian ferry pilot at Gander, Newfoundland on 10 November 1940. The Hudson was the first US-built aircraft to see operational service with the RAF. It was initially ordered by the British Purchasing Commission in June 1938, the initial order being for 200 which aroused controversy in Britain at the time, many feeling that the RAF should have a home built type. (Via Bruce Robertson).

of Aircraft Production that ordered and processed US purchases and arranged delivery to RAF air depots in the United Kingdom. It took a long time to persuade the authorities that the idea of ferrying the badly needed Hudsons by air was the right one. Apparently it was a director of a firm of London export merchants, Mr Oakes-White of Hunt & Holditch Ltd, who wrote to Lord Beaverbrook, the Minister of Aircraft Production, proposing a convoy system whereby each group of Hudsons would be escorted by a flying boat. The scheme was turned down, but the letter did bring the suggestion of an air ferry into the open. Mr Yost, the Lockheed representative in London, persuaded his superiors to have long-range kits designed for the Hudson and even proposed that the factory engage personnel to ferry the aircraft. This was also turned down.

The British air attaché in Washington DC was Group Captain George Pirie, who discussed the air ferry idea with the British Purchasing Commission and involved Mr Woods-Humphrey, former managing director of Imperial Airways, then resident in the US. He had directed North Atlantic survey flights during 1937. It was Morris Wilson, Canadian representative of the British Purchasing Commission, who persuaded the chairman of the Canadian Pacific Railway to provide office space in Montreal. Col Burchall, former general manager of Imperial Airways, went to Montreal in charge and six pilots, all with Atlantic Division experience, became involved. These were Captains Bennett, Page, Powell, Ross, Store and Wilcockson, who first discussed the availability of the Hudson aircraft for the Atlantic ferry flight. Captain Bennett and Page visited the Lockheed factory at Burbank to test-fly the Hudson and check on fuel consumption and performance necessary for the long ferry flight. It was arranged for two Hudson Mk II aircraft to be used for training, to be flown back to Montreal.

Recruiting for pilots commenced and a wide variety of types presented themselves ranging from airline pilots and flying instructors to bush pilots from the far north, all very experienced. When accepted they went to St Hubert near Montreal for a flight check, and a monthly figure of $C1,000 for pilots was considered, with lower scales for other aircrew categories and ground staff. Initially there was a problem obtaining wireless operators, this being overcome when the Canadian Department of Transport released volunteers from their radio

stations. Skilled navigators were also difficult to find, but BOAC released five experienced pilot/navigators – Captains Eves, Stewart, Allen, Wilson and Andrews. Ground and later flight engineers also initially caused a problem. The Hudsons had Wright engines and engineers detached from the Canadian Wright Corporation assisted, whilst the aircraft's radio equipment was serviced by the Canadian Marconi Company. When the first Consolidated Liberators arrived powered by Pratt & Whitney engines and different radio equipment, the maintenance contract was transferred.

The ferry plan was that the Hudsons would leave Montreal singly and assemble at Hatties Camp, Gander for group departure. The flight to Gander was 950 miles, mostly over inhospitable terrain. Captain Bennett had devised a constant airspeed cruise procedure for the Mk III Hudsons with periodical compass course changes to keep on the chosen track and to allow for the forecast winds. The weather forecast was split into zones, and at the departing briefing all crews noted the drift allowance to be made for forecast winds in each zone. This partial pre-computed system when put to the hard test on the actual ferry flights was a notable success. The scheme was to have a group leader with the highest possible qualifications as a pilot with a first-class navigator's licence, a deputy in another aircraft, and a total of seven aircraft per group.

The first group of seven aircraft departed on the night of 10 November 1940, the second group was dispatched on 29 November, and the third group on 17 December. History was made on 11 November when the first transatlantic delivery flight of the first group of seven Lockheed Hudsons arrived at Aldergrove in Northern Ireland from Botwood, Newfoundland. The leader was Captain D. C. T. Bennett and the crossing was completed in around nine-and-a-half hours. They took off for Speke airport, Liverpool the following day.

First Catalina

The Battle of the Atlantic called for a long-range seaplane type to operate over ocean convoys and carry out submarine hunts. Consolidated PBY Catalinas could be conveniently delivered from the US assembly lines to Bermuda some 700 miles from the mainland of North America and approximately 3,400 miles from the United Kingdom.

The success of the Catalina with the US Navy attracted the attention of the Air Ministry as early as 1938, the first reaching the UK in July 1939 for experiments. During World War 2 Boeing in Canada built the PB2B-2 Catalina and Canso mostly for Lend-Lease to the Allies including the RAF. Depicted is Catalina VI JX632 marked PB2B-2 on the fin ex US Navy BuNo.44250. Only a few were delivered to the RAF, others going to the RAAF. (Via Peter M Bowers).

The success of the Catalina with the US Navy attracted the attention of the Air Ministry, which ordered one example (P9630) for experimental testing. This aircraft, known as Model 28-5, was ferried across the Atlantic and reached Felixstowe, Suffolk, the home of the Marine Aircraft Experimental Establishment, in July 1939. It crashed on landing at Dumbarton and sank on 10 February 1940.

With the outbreak of World War Two an initial order of thirty was placed for the equivalent of the US Navy PBY-5, known in the RAF as the Catalina Mk I. The British Purchasing Commission increased the order to 109, and the first, W8405, was ferried to the UK under the command of Flight Lieutenant Fleming on loan from Coastal Command. Due to inclement weather the aileron controls were damaged and problems were experienced with ice.

Air Chief Marshal Sir Frederick W Bowhill, GBE KCB CMG DSO, took over RAF Ferry Command on 18 July 1941 and continued with RAF Transport Command until 15 February 1945. He is seen here at his desk in Montreal, Canada. (CAN 788).

However, the flight was completed safely in twenty-eight hours, landing at Greenock in the Firth of Clyde. By May 1941 some fifty-one Catalinas had been ferried from Bermuda.

On 15 July 1941 ATFERO became RAF Ferry Command and Air Chief Marshal Sir Frederick Bowhill, previously head of RAF Coastal Command, flew out that month as Air Officer Commanding of Ferry Command, which took over control from the Ministry of Aircraft Production. Senior Air Staff Officer (SASO) of the Command was Group Captain Griffith 'Taffy' Powell who remained in charge of operations until victory in Europe was secured.

When Ferry Command was created the ferry delivery score was 331 aircraft to the UK plus nine to Australia via the Pacific ferry route. Of these, Montreal had dispatched 278, mainly Lockheed Hudsons, of which four had been lost, and Bermuda had contributed fifty-seven Catalinas all safely delivered. There was a brief pause in deliveries into Montreal while the recently established US Air Transport Command was getting organised. In 1941 the RAF Ferry Command was concentrating strictly on North Atlantic flights using the land plane route through Gander and the Catalina route via Bermuda to the Clyde. Within a year the South Atlantic ferry route was in full operation, with the battle in North Africa requiring US built aircraft of all types.

A mid-Atlantic route was added with long-range deliveries to India until Singapore was lost, forcing a crossing of the Pacific to get to Australasia. In mid-1941 Catalina deliveries were speeded up by routing as many as possible via Boucherville on the St Lawrence river just outside Montreal and then via the lake at Gander, which being adjacent to the airport was able to utilise the main control and weather forecasting facilities. This was a long haul for the Catalina, which had been delivered from the Consolidated factory at San Diego, California to Elizabeth City, North Carolina, and then to Bermuda. Urgent freight was put on board Catalinas ferried via the Gander lake route.

New Bases

The British and Canadian governments had been well aware of the potential shortcomings of Gander as it gained a prominent position in Atlantic Lend-Lease ferry deliveries. In June 1941 the RCAF sent a photo detachment and a survey party from the Department of Mines & Resources to Labrador to investigate reports of a fog-free and fairly benign area alongside the North West river where it enters Melville Sound. The sheltered inland area was spared the cold and turbulence of the coast with a near perfect airport site next to a deep water anchorage, with ample deposits of gravel and all the timber required.

Prompted by the Ministry of National Defence, the Canadian Department of Transport placed a construction contract and the first laden ship reached the Goose Bay anchorage in September. The supply ships helped to get a wharf constructed, a road and then a three-runway layout with such speed that on 3 December a ski-equipped aircraft of Quebec Airways was the first aircraft to land, with the first military type from the RCAF arriving six days later. It was not long before sixty aircraft a month transited through Goose en route to the UK, and by the year ending 30 September 1945 the airfield turned round 25,000 aircraft of the RAF, RCAF, USAAF and various return ferry services. The opening of Goose Bay was the opportunity to send short-range aircraft to the UK via Reykjavik, Iceland, a route established in 1942.

Surveys of the Greenland coastline had been carried out by United States agencies, partly as patrols exercised to safeguard their frontier out to 26°W. They also wanted to establish landing strips and bases for ferry purposes. They constructed the Bluie West bases, of which BW-1 was the first at the southern tip of Greenland followed by BW-8 high up on the west coast just above the Arctic Circle and near the settlement of Sondre Stromfjord with an elevation of 165 feet above mean sea level. They also built BW-3 on the east coast near Angmagssalik, but it was BW-1 which was utilised by Lend-Lease ferry aircraft as it provided a refuelling point for the short-range aircraft through Dorval, Goose Bay, BW-1, Reykjavik to Prestwick. All the sectors were of near equal length at less than 800 nautical miles. The RAF organisation was geared to a figure of 300 Lend-Lease land planes per month, which was occasionally reached, though rarely in winter.

It is of interest to record that in terms of numbers when it was formed, RAF Ferry Command, for all the imposing nature of its name, had only just over 900 staff of which 500 were aircrew. This latter total included loans of 167 RAF personnel made up of seventy-nine pilots, sixty-nine engineers and twenty-four radio operators. Air Vice-Marshal Marix was an administrator, Group Captain Deane the Ferry Command accountant, and Squadron Leader Maynard a station adjutant. A few other officers and clerks were on the staff, including cypher specialists. They were all commissioned members of the WAAF and were under the command of Squadron Officer Lady Bowhill.

A training plan was established which proved to be slow, for although conversion to the Lockheed Hudson was not time-consuming or difficult, all service personnel lacked instrument flying experi-

trippers'. This meant more training, and in April 1942 alone 2,500 hours of training with the 'one-trippers' were accomplished. It produced sixty pilots and forty co-pilots.

Lend-Lease aircraft destined for the RAF were delivered to Montreal by USAAF crews, and on arrival at Dorval became RAF property officially. On any one day 100 aircraft of various types could be parked on the airfield, of which a number were normally engaged on training, a dozen or so on acceptance air test and the rest in various stages of being prepared for ferry on Lend-Lease delivery.

The Consolidated Liberator was a remarkable design not started until 1939, was in service by the middle of 1941 and was withdrawn from Allied use almost overnight in 1945. More were built during World War 2 than any other single type of US aircraft. Depicted at the huge RAF maintenance unit located at Cawnpore, India, at the end of World War 2 are rows and rows of surplus RAF Liberator bombers. The front aircraft is a Ford, Willow Run, Michigan built B-24L Liberator VI KL611 'W for Whisky' from No.357 Squadron. (Via Philip J Moyes).

ence and had never been exposed to radio range work. The situation changed in 1942 when the first aircrew products of the Empire Air Training Scheme emerged from their schools in Canada and the US. These graduations occurred at a time when the projected delivery rate involved more ferry crews than Dorval had. Some 200 personnel were absorbed in the flying boat operation, so Ferry Command had barely a hundred complete crews to deliver a target of 300 aircraft a month. A plan worked out in 1942 enabled products of the Empire Air Training Scheme to ferry Lend-Lease aircraft to the UK as 'one-

Liberator Ferry

The task of RAF Ferry Command was to deliver aircraft safely to the UK in a fit state for war service; then came the task of getting ferry aircrew back to Canada. In the early days of Lend-Lease the return cycle for ferry crews was as long as six weeks, allowing for the waiting time of Atlantic ship sailings. There was a great need for a return air service.

At the commencement of air deliveries, Mr A. S. Dismore, the former secretary of Imperial Airways, had been employed by Lord Beaverbrook in his Ministry of Aircraft Production in London to act as liaison officer with the Montreal headquarters. Lord Beaverbrook persuaded the Air Ministry to turn over six Consolidated Liberator bombers for use on an Atlantic passenger service. Three of these were already in the UK and the rest in Canada. They were hastily converted by stripping out all armament and by sealing the bomb bay doors. A wooden floor was fitted in the bomb bay and another wooden floor went in the tail behind the entry door underneath the fuselage. A fairly simple passengers' oxygen system was fitted with twenty individual masks. Sleeping bags, pillows and rugs made up the luxury fittings and all the passengers wore full flying kit – sidcot suits, overboots, gloves and leather helmets – as the heating in the Liberator was not good.

Because of a contract exchange, the first of the long line of production Liberators to be rolled out were the six Consolidated LB-30As, ex-USAAF YB-24s, for the RAF, all of which were accepted in December 1940. Lacking self-sealing tanks but possessing great range these aircraft, AM258 to 263, were employed on the transatlantic Return Ferry Service. Initially operated by BOAC, three of these Liberators had been issued with temporary civil registrations – AM259 G-AGCD, AM262 G-AGHG and AM263 G-AGDS. The first westbound flight left Prestwick on 4 May 1941. The early development of the service with BOAC crews was tested severely by a series of fatal crashes in 1941 with three Liberator accidents causing the death of forty-seven returning aircrew as well as distinguished passengers.

On 13 August 1941 when President Roosevelt and Prime Minister Churchill were concluding their conference at Placentia Bay, Newfoundland on the battleship *Prince of Wales*, it became necessary for them to send for Lord Beaverbrook and a great English public servant Mr Arthur Purvis, who was head of the British Purchasing Commission in the US but who was in England at that time. They departed the UK for Newfoundland in separate Return Ferry Service Liberators, both with loads of returning aircrew from Prestwick. The Liberator with Lord Beaverbrook on board made a successful crossing, but the other with Mr Purvis and twelve ferry aircrew on board flew into the Mull of Kintyre shortly after take-off and all were killed.

Early US Types

Dorval eventually delivered 661 Lockheed Hudsons

and 1,749 Consolidated Liberators, but parallel in time with the latter type were the B-17 Flying Fortress bombers. Twenty of these were part of the 1,480 aircraft of a wide variety ordered from the US before the Lend-Lease Bill was passed. Many were small or short-range aircraft not suitable for delivery by air, although a number of Hudsons had been delivered as deck cargo by sea. The cost of these pre-Lend-Lease purchases was quoted at £202 million. Most of the aircraft lacked radio and armament.

During December 1940 thirty RAF aircrew assembled at RAF Uxbridge, Middlesex, and on New Year's Eve arrived by ship at Halifax, Nova Scotia and reported to ATFERO at Montreal. They had been drawn from various Coastal Command squadrons and were to commence training for the acceptance of the first RAF Boeing B-17C Fortress Mk I. A number of the aircrew went to TWA headquarters in Kansas City, the airline then operating the four-engined Boeing Stratoliner, thought to have had some similarities with the Fortress. After some casual flying with TWA they joined the rest of the party at the USAAF base located at March Field, California, and all became attached to the 93rd Bomb Squadron of the 19th Bombardment Group for training on the B-17C bomber. In the RAF group were Flight Lieutenants Biddell, Ross and Clarke and Flying Officer Franklin, a navigator. One of the Fortress delivery pilots was Paddy Uprichard.

Apparently the first twenty Fortress Mk Is for the RAF (AN518 to 537) were late in delivery from the Boeing factory at Seattle, had been completed during late 1940, and were flown in US Army Air Corps markings to McChord Field, Tacoma in Washington State. On 11 February 1941 Boardman C. Reed flew in B-17C 40-2055 c/n 2056 which had been completed by Boeing on 23 September 1940. The thirty-minute flight was from McChord to Boeing Field where the aircraft was given RAF markings and became AM537, later AN537.

On 12 February 1941 Boardman Reed was fortunate to obtain a forty-minute flight in RAF Fortress Mk I AM531, later AN531, when it was ferried from Boeing Field back to McChord. It was ex-40-2076 c/n 2077 completed by Boeing on 15 November 1940. All twenty aircraft had an overall silver finish and were powered by four 1,200 hp Wright R-1830-73 Cyclone engines. These were pre-Lend-Lease aircraft on a cash order, and in order to avoid sales tax the hand-over to RAF crews took place at Portland, Oregon.

A total of 20 Boeing B-17C Flying Fortress I bombers were transferred from the US Army Air Corps for use by the RAF. This photo depicts most of the consignment with RAF markings applied but the wrong prefix to the serials which were AN518–537 not AM. The bombers were bought by the British Purchasing Commission as Boeing Model 299Ts. The first one AN534 departed Gander on 13 April 1941 arriving at Prestwick after a flight of 8 hrs 49 mins. (Via Philip Jarrett).

The first batch of six was flown to Wright Field in Dayton, Ohio where they were camouflaged prior to flying to Montreal for delivery. Due to inclement weather conditions the bombers were diverted to Floyd Bennett Field in Brooklyn, New York, then a US Navy and US Coast Guard air station. The second batch of RAF bombers, and even some RAF Liberators, was ferried to the UK from this useful base.

The first RAF Fortress MK I AN521 left Gander for the ferry flight across the Atlantic on 14 April 1941 carrying Major Walshe of the US Army Air Corps who was to advise the RAF on the operation of the new bomber. It made the transatlantic crossing in a record time of eight hours and twenty-six minutes, eventually arriving at No.37 MU Burtonwood. It was ex-B-17C 40-2052 and the twenty had been bought by the British Purchasing Commission as Boeing Model 299Ts.

If the Lockheed Hudson was one of the best liked and most reliable aircraft the RAF operated, its stable companion the Lockheed Ventura was just the opposite. It was a hefty companion of the Hudson, being some 8,000 lb heavier when loaded. It was fitted with the more powerful Pratt & Whitney Double Wasp GR-2800 SIA4-G engines with large paddle-blade propellers to absorb the extra power. It was employed as a bomber and on anti-submarine and reconnaissance duties, but it had a very high fuel consumption and was difficult for a young, newly trained pilot to handle on take-off owing to the abnormal torque. The original British contract was for 675 Ventura Mk I and Mk II aircraft, the first (AE658) making its maiden flight on 31 July 1941. Deliveries to the RAF for March 1941 did not in fact commence until the summer of 1942, and deliveries ceased altogether with the 349th aircraft. Of the first batch (AE658 to 845) forty-two went to the RCAF and eighty-two to the SAAF, while sixteen crashed on delivery.

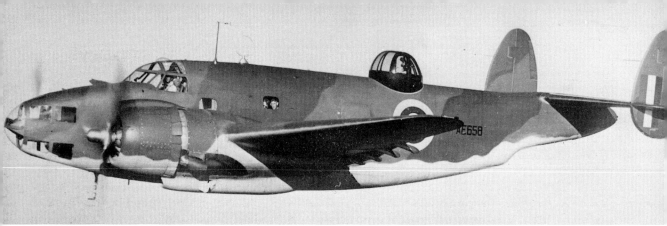

A contract was placed for the Lockheed Model 37, a military version of the Lodestar, in the summer of 1940, its design incorporating all the experience gained with the earlier Hudson. Depicted is the first Ventura of a British contract for 675, AE658 which made its maiden flight on 31 July 1941. This order came from the British Purchasing Commission and Lend-Lease orders followed. Deliveries for the RAF commenced in the summer of 1942 and the type was used by the USAAF as the B-34 and the US Navy as the PV-1. (AP Publications).

As already mentioned, the Douglas DB-7 Boston had been ordered pre-war by the French Purchasing Commission and the Belgians, and it was from these contracts that the RAF took delivery via the British Purchasing Commission. Sixteen (AE457 to 472) were from the Belgian contract, of which AE461 was returned to the USAAF and AE471 to the Royal Navy. The first Boston Mk III (DB-7B), W8252, was shipped to the UK during the summer of 1941 and approximately 780 of the Boston Mk IIIs were delivered, ending with AL907. Some 200 Mk IIIAs followed. Many were ferried to North Africa and the Middle East, and this versatile type did well in Sicily and in the Italian campaign.

A Lend-Lease type used exclusively in the Mediterranean theatre of operations was the Martin B-26 Marauder of which just over 500 were delivered. It was able to carry a larger bomb load than the Boston, but did not have a good reputation for handling characteristics, reputedly landing 'hot' and needing careful attention. It was very unforgiving and caused many accidents during training. Five Marauder Mk IAs crashed before delivery – FK368/369/372/379/380. It is reputed that some seventy were retained in the UK for use by RAF Bomber Command.

Numerically the North American B-25 Mitchell should have been mentioned first, and was a type well liked by Ferry Command crews. It could carry nearly the same bomb load as the B-26 Marauder. Only three of the Lend-Lease order for twenty-three Mk Is arrived in the UK – FK161/162/165 – while FK168 went to Canada, FK178 crashed before delivery and the rest went to equip No.111 Operational Training Unit (OTU) based in Nassau. By the time the Mk II and Mk III had been delivered

some 900 plus of the type were on RAF inventory.

Prior to the airfield at Nassau in the Bahamas being ready for use by Lend-Lease deliveries via the South Atlantic route, Ferry Command set up a temporary base at Nashville, Tennessee under Wing Commander P. Maxwell RAF and a pool of aircrew, most of them civilians, under Captain Siple who transferred from Dorval. (Incidentally the new airfield at Nassau was called Windsor Field as the Governor of the Bahamas at this time was the former King Edward VIII, the Duke of Windsor.) The move to Nassau took place in February 1943, this base being to the South Atlantic ferry route what Dorval was to the North Atlantic.

Another Lend-Lease US type which was ferried for exclusive use in the Mediterranean was the Martin Baltimore, a type produced from the outset to British requirements. A development of the Maryland, it differed in having the more powerful 1,660 hp Wright Double-Row Cyclone GR-2600-A5B engines giving improved performance. It had a deepened fuselage allowing direct access between crew members; in the Maryland crew members had been separated by transverse bulkheads. The first Baltimore flew on 14 June 1941 and was designated Mk I. The prototype, AG685, reached the UK in October 1941 for trial installation at Burtonwood. Production for the RAF ceased in May 1944 (with FW880) with a reputed 1,575 being produced and 1,000 ferried to the Middle East. Of the production block AG685 to AH184 covering 400 Mk I/II/III aircraft, AG710 was not delivered, AG750 went to Canada, and thirty-five were lost at sea on delivery, while a number went to SAAF units in the Middle East. The type was the main day and night light bomber in the North Africa offensive and in the subsequent Allied advance through Italy. To increase the range Ferry Command had to fit an underslung belly tank which was in a very vulnerable position when it came to an undercarriage failure. Subsequently several aircraft were lost for this reason.

Some 435 Catalinas were ferried across the Atlantic for Allied air forces serving in all theatres of operations including a number which were ferried to Russia. During 1942 nine Catalinas were ferried to Australia with help from the RAAF due to shortage of aircrew within Ferry Command. These flights had a return cycle of about two months. Most of these

also not many virtues, and the type was used for return ferry flights from Iceland and Scotland to Montreal and also across the South Atlantic. It could carry eighteen passengers and only a few were delivered to RAF Coastal Command, used mainly for supply and troop movements. Some thirty-two are listed with serials JX470 to 501, deliveries including JX470/1/2/486/490/494/5/6/8 and JX501. The rest were retained by the US Navy.

From time to time RAF Ferry Command handled small numbers of odd types for delivery which included fifteen Douglas C-54 Skymasters similar to the VIP transport presented to Winston Churchill by

This excellent air to air profile of B-26A Marauder I FK111 is dated 26 November 1942 and was evaluated at the A&AEE Boscombe Down. Only a few of the type were delivered to the UK, many being ferried direct to the Middle East theatre of operations. (Via Philip Jarrett).

versatile flying boats were ferried using a variation of the North Atlantic route, either direct from Bermuda or via Boucherville. Additional Catalinas were manufactured in Canada in 1941 by Canadian Vickers at their plant in Cartierville, and by the Boeing factory in Vancouver. Some became known by the RCAF as the Canso, and thirty-seven were delivered via the Pacific route.

The twin-engined PBM Mariner was a latecomer to the flying boat scene. It had an excellent performance and was faster and more agile than the lumbering Catalina, but lacked the long range. Some 137 of the type were delivered to the RAF and arrangements were made with the US Navy in San Juan, Puerto Rico and at Corcorite in Trinidad to provide extra staging posts for them. On the ferry route to Gibraltar a stop was made at Bathurst in The Gambia.

A rather late arrival to US flying boat Lend-Lease deliveries was the large four-engined Consolidated PB2Y-3B Coronado. Apparently it had no vices, but

the United States. They set up a unique RAF airline service with 'B' Flight of No.232 Squadron moving out from the UK to Palam, Delhi, India in July 1945. Later a regular route was flown with the type from Ratmalana in Ceylon, the Cocos Islands, which was No.129 Staging Post, and Perth and Sydney in Australia. Some twenty-two Lend-Lease Skymasters are listed (KL977 to 999) of which KL987 was not delivered. A smaller transport from the US was fifteen Lockheed Lodestars, a passenger aircraft reputed to have been destined for the Royal Norwegian Air Force. A contract was signed for 140 Douglas A-26 Invaders (KL690 to 829) but only KL690/1 were delivered, the remainder going to the US Navy.

Ad Hoc Routes

Goose Bay, Labrador was put to full use by Ferry Command in the spring of 1942, enabling aircraft to fly a shorter range route via Reykjavik supplementary to the old main line route via Gander, Newfoundland to Prestwick direct. The Hudsons, Liberators and Fortresses were normally ferried through Gander, but Dakotas, Bostons, Venturas and the much-loved Mitchells took the shorter route. By the summer of 1942 some excellent totals were being built up. A forecast of US aircraft availabilities made it clear that Ferry Command would be required to do even better, as there was a growing requirement for Ferry Command to deliver aircraft nearer the pressure points of theatres of operations.

Both light and medium bombers were urgently needed in North Africa to stem the German advance. The Desert Air Force supporting the Eighth Army was under pressure. Normally aircraft could be ferried from the UK to North Africa, but as more territory fell into enemy hands only transit flights at night could be attempted. The Middle East was reinforced by the South Atlantic route and West Africa on the back door route to Cairo. Nashville, Tennessee, mentioned earlier, was a convenient assembly point for Lend-Lease aircraft, and the fairly short sector to West Palm Beach was a good resting place before the long passage down the Caribbean Islands to Piarco, Trinidad, which was a Fleet Air Arm station. Thereafter it was on to Belem and Natal before the 1,400-mile leg to Ascension Island.

Some fifty Marauders and Mitchells were flown to Accra and thence to the battle area by making ad hoc arrangements with the RAF at Trinidad, with the government in Brazil, with Pan American Airways and with a number of embryo US Army Air Force bases still under construction. Pan American Ferries was busy delivering aircraft under contract to the US War Department and it must be recorded that it had

operated a pre-war flying boat route from Miami through the Caribbean to British Guiana and on to Belem and Natal in Brazil. They had staff and handling facilities in Brazil, the airport at Ascension Island was being built and Pan American Africa had their bases in West Africa. There was no shortage of assistance if required, but there was a need for clarification of route development. On the first day of December 1942 a conference was held in the Pentagon in Washington DC attended by RAF Ferry Command, US Air Transport Command and the British Air Commission. There were observers present from the British Embassy as the Caribbean and West Africa were areas of British influence, if not sovereignty. General George, Commanding General of US Air Transport Command, and his Chief of Staff, Colonel Cyrus R. Smith, on temporary loan from American Airlines, were present. Sir George Cribbett was the spokesman for the RAF. He had full UK government and treasury authority to make deals, particularly on Ascension Island and West Africa.

Following this meeting a joint communiqué was issued and signed. It declared that:

1. The RAF would have full rights on the South Atlantic route when ferrying American-built aircraft allocated to the RAF.
2. The US Air Transport Command would deliver such aircraft to the RAF at Nassau in the Bahamas in the same way as they delivered North Atlantic aircraft to Montreal.
3. The point of entry for Nassau would be Morrison Field at West Palm Beach where there would be RAF liaison staff for filter control purposes.
4. The point of entry in West Africa would be Accra.
5. The US authorities would house RAF personnel

This North American Mitchell TT.IV HD326 (B-25D) coded 'ML-G' was one of many RAF Lend-Lease aircraft retained for use in Canada. It is ex B-25D 43-3797 and is equipped as a target tug being brightly coloured for identification with yellow/black stripes. It served for some years after World War 2. (Via Peter M Bowers).

The Baltimore was procured from the outset to British requirements and was a development of the earlier Maryland, but was powered by the more powerful 1,660hp Wright Cyclone GR-2600-A5B engines. The first flew on 14 June 1941 and the prototype was AG685 which reached Burtonwood in October. The early I, II, III models were direct purchase, the IIIA, IV and V being Lend-Lease. This official Martin photo is heavily censored but shows the lines of the RAF Baltimore to good effect. (Via Peter M Bowers).

where necessary. This applied both to our permanent staff and transient aircrew.

6. The Air Transport Command of the USAAF would undertake to provide return ferry service arrangements for 100 crews a month from Accra to West Palm Beach.

This made Ferry Command's presence on the route much easier, dispensing with the earlier temporary arrangements, but there were still many items to co-ordinate. For instance, under the Roosevelt–Churchill agreement, South America was in the US sphere of influence and Britain was constrained from asking direct permission from the Brazilian authorities for her representatives at Belem and Natal. General George arranged lodger-unit status on all US-manned airfields.

In many ways, however, the Pentagon agreement outlined arrangements for the future rather than the present. Ferry Command was also transiting aircraft over the route. Nassau was by no means ready, and General George did not have the capacity available to get 100 ferry crews a month back from West

Africa, or even half that number. Ferry Command was having to fly reinforcements for the Desert Air Force all the way to Cairo, then after delivery the crews had to make their own way back to Accra or Takoradi, often difficult but nevertheless interesting.

Although Ascension Island was a British dependency, the airfield itself, known as Wideawake, was constructed by the US government during World War Two as a staging post for aircraft flying between Brazil and Africa. Prior to 1939, and until the runway had been carved out of the volcanic rock, the island's commercial and maritime importance had relied on its wireless relay station. It was, and still is, the principal breeding ground of the sooty tern, or wideawake. From Belem it was a long 1,400-mile leg to Ascension, a volcanic peak only nine miles long protruding from the vastness of the South Atlantic. However, it had Green Mountain rising to nearly 3,000 feet at its summit. A powerful radio beacon assisted navigation and radio silence was less important in this area. There are no records of RAF aircraft going astray for navigation reasons.

Emergency Ferry

The long retreat in the Western Desert left the Eighth Army short of vitally needed anti-tank ammunition. Winston Churchill said every field gun should have armour-piercing tracer shot so that every mobile gun would become an anti-tank gun. As a consequence this special ammunition was used at a high rate, resulting in a shortage, and as it was available in the US, Ferry Command received urgent instructions in June 1942 to arrange a massive airlift via the South Atlantic ferry route to Cairo.

Fourteen Liberator bombers were taken off the delivery line and seventy aircrew, including thirteen of the most experienced captains, all civilians, were detailed for the emergency. The ammunition was loaded at Mitchell Field, Long Island, New York after arriving from the factory by train, as it was expected to be shipped by sea. Ferry Command picked up the vital cargo at Miami. After safely delivering the ammunition the airlift continued with other urgently needed equipment and spares, not only for supply to the Eighth Army, but also to West Africa, to Takoradi and Apapa near Lagos, where short-range fighter aircraft were being re-assembled after shipment by sea.

There were some extraordinary feats accomplished. One Liberator B III FL918 piloted by Captain Norman Williams made four crossings of the South Atlantic from Brazil to West Africa in three days and sixteen hours. To accomplish this, Williams and his crew of four flew 11,500 miles in eighty-eight hours at an average speed of 135 mph, including all refuelling and rest stops. During this epic sequence they had breakfast at Ascension Island four mornings running.

The Liberators used in the emergency departed Dorval in groups between 28 June and 9 July, and all had temporary wooden floors fitted in the bomb bays. The crews and aircraft were as follows:

Ferry Command Liberators

FK214 Captain A. J. Lilly; F. W. Baillie; Sgt Fulton RAF:, G. L. Johnson; C. B. Swaney.

FK227 Captain L. Bisson; W. C. Ross: Sgt Griffith RAF: A. M. King; D. McKay.

FK243 Captain J. Bradley; R. Parkinson; Sgt Archer RAF; H. Gorman; W. C. Harris.

FL908 Captain C. A. Rector; J. Devine; Sgt Eberhart RAF; H. McKercher; D. Delworth.

FL909 Captain T. Livermore; G. S. Tobin; Pilot Officer Hyland RCAF; H. G. Filtness; A. D. White.

FL911 Squadron Leader W. Biddell; F. Hawthorne; J. C. Glover; A. V. Atkinson; J. Affleck.

FL912 Captain W. Davidson; G. Bliss; Pilot Officer Lacombe RCAF; J. M. Shrewe; J. H. Sursfield.

FL913 Captain H. Herndon; H. Chouteau; Sgt Taylor RAF; G. C. Lane; M. Andrews.

FL914 Captain R. M. Lloyd; B. Watt; L. A. Tanner; G. McPherson; Flying Officer Farr RCAF.

FL915 Captain G. Horsum; B. M. Merrill; Pilot Officer Sharke RCAF; D. Ewart; G. Woodward.

FL917 Captain E. W. Hightower; R. G. Johns; Sgt Shaw RAF; W. D. Erdeley; J. W. McGuinness.

FL918 Captain N. Williams; J. H. O'Neill; Pilot Officer Palser RCAF; D. Jervis; I. M. Wilson.

FL922 Captain N. Tooker; G. E. Barnes; Sgt Andrews RAF; A. C. Coote; W. A. Lewis.

Temporary civil registrations were given to FL909 (G-AGFN); FL915 (G-AGFO); FL917 (G-AGFP); and FL918 (G-AGFR).

Of the crews listed, the co-pilot was also a civilian, and the third crew member was the navigator, a service product of the Empire Air Training Scheme in Canada. Most of the Liberators stayed on the South Atlantic return ferry service and were based at Nassau, remaining in service for the rest of the war. Four of the aircraft had temporary civil registrations allocated.

Normally the eastbound flight carried freight from what became known as the United Nations Air Transport Depot in Miami, and brought eighteen Ferry Command aircrew back. It was inevitable that some of these hastily converted Liberators would be adopted by their aircrew and become recognised on the route by names like *Swagman*, *Highball*, *Spitball* and *Magic Carpet*, the latter being for two years almost the private property of Captain Don Teel.

The most famous of all the Liberator bombers pressed into passenger service was Liberator Mk II AL504, taken off the delivery line in the summer of 1942 for an assignment in the UK to fly Lord Louis Mountbatten on his appointment as Chief of Combined Operations. Group Captain 'Taffy' Powell flew the aircraft and received permission to name the Liberator *Commando*. During the following months this aircraft flew Winston Churchill

Seen after conversion is AL504, one of the original Consolidated LB-30 transport version of the Liberator bomber. It was christened Commando *becoming the personal transporter of Prime Minister Winston S Churchill, who flew in it to many of his World War 2 conferences world-wide. Modification included a longer fuselage and a large single fin and rudder. It disappeared during a flight over the Southern Atlantic during May 1945. (IWM).*

and his chiefs of staff on many important diplomatic missions to Cairo, Moscow, Tehran and Chungking.

The personal pilot selected for Winston Churchill was Captain Bill Vanderkloot from the US who had been with Ferry Command for a year, having been recruited by the Clayton-Knight organisation in Washington DC. He was well qualified as a navigator and had experienced a great deal of instrument flying, having made a study of let-down and radio procedures for UK airspace, especially for approaches to Prestwick, the Atlantic ferry terminal. He had already flown *Commando* carrying Canadian government ministers to Prestwick and London and had flown to Bathurst with Lord Swinton, minister resident in West Africa. The Liberator carried two first-class flight engineers, Affleck and Williams.

All of Winston Churchill's flights in *Commando* are described in his *History of the Second World War Vol. IV* from which the following extract is taken.

'It became urgently necessary for me to go to the Middle East and settle decisive questions on the spot. It was at first accepted that this journey would be by Gibraltar and Takoradi and thence across Central Africa to Cairo involving five or even six days' flying.

As this would carry me through tropical and malarious regions a whole series of protective injections was prescribed. Some of these would take ten days to give their immunity and involved considerable discomfort and even inactivity . . .

However, at this juncture there arrived in England a young American pilot, Captain Vanderkloot, who had just flown from the United States in the aeroplane *Commando*, a Liberator plane from which the bomb racks had been removed and some sort of passenger accommodation substituted. This machine was certainly capable of flying along the route prescribed with good margins in hand at all stages.

Portal, the Chief of the Air Staff, saw this pilot and cross-examined him about *Commando*. Vanderkloot, who had already flown about a million miles, asked why it was necessary to fly all the way round by Takoradi, Kano, Fort Lamy, El Obeid etc. He said he could make one bound from Gibraltar to Cairo, flying from Gibraltar eastwards in the afternoon, turning sharply south across Spanish or Vichy territory as dusk fell and then proceeding eastwards until he struck the Nile about Assiout when a turn northwards would bring us, in another hour or so, to the Cairo landing ground north-west of the pyramids. This altered the whole picture. I could be in Cairo in two days without any trouble about Central African bugs and the inoculations against them.'

Apparently Portal was impressed with Vanderkloot and on 3 August 1942 *Commando* departed RAF Lyneham, Wiltshire with Winston

Churchill and his staff flying to Gibraltar, Cairo, Tehran and Moscow, returning to the UK on 24 August. In January 1943 the Liberator took Churchill to Casablanca, Cairo, Adana and Tripoli.

During 1944 *Commando* was returned to the Consolidated Modification Centre in Tucson, Arizona where it was extensively modified, including a fuselage stretch and the fitting of a single fin and rudder. Since Winston Churchill's last flight in *Commando* was on 7 February 1943 he never flew in the aircraft in the new configuration. It was used on special missions and Group Captain 'Taffy' Powell flew it across the Pacific on the first regular service flight to Sydney. In the hands of Wing Commander W. Biddell and Squadron Leader Rees, it did two circumnavigations of the globe, but unfortunately that same crew and AL504 were lost over the Atlantic in March 1945.

Whilst *Commando* was being modified the US government kindly donated a Douglas C-54B ex-43-17126, Skymaster EW999, to the RAF for VIP use by Winston Churchill. It was converted at Dorval and ferried to RAF Northolt, Middlesex by 'Taffy' Powell. Built at the Santa Monica factory it was delivered on 3 June 1944, and with effect from 19 November was on the strength of the Metropolitan Comm Squadron for use by the VIP Flight of No.246 Squadron as from 22 February 1945. On 5 November 1945 it was back at Dorval awaiting its return to the US.

Special Flights and Milk-Runs

Within Ferry Command, special flights, return ferries and milk-runs absorbed a lot of aircraft and aircrew, the latter often being in short supply. A milk-run from Dorval, Gander and Goose was virtually an airline operation, shared with the RCAF, and initially operated by a Ventura, and later with the ubiquitous Dakota. A similar service was the round-the-island circuit in the Caribbean which originated at Nassau, stopping as required at the various island territories and terminating in Trinidad. An aircrew shuttle was operated between Nassau and Willow Grove near Philadelphia in Pennsylvania. Ferry Command collected Lend-Lease Venturas from the Lockheed factory, these being urgently needed in North Africa, but which the USAAF could not deliver as their aircrew position was possibly worse than the RAF. After the airlift with ammunition to

Cairo, the South Atlantic return ferry became permanent and had to be reinforced by Coronado flying boats in order to accommodate the volume of aircrew. A Lend-Lease aid programme to the USSR was underway and the Coronado was impressed to bring Ferry Command safety aircrew back from Iceland, leaving the Russians to continue on their own.

By early 1945, despite Lend-Lease deliveries slowing down, the return ferry capacity was found to be inadequate and the combined efforts of the BOAC Return Ferry, the Canadian Government Transatlantic Service and that of the RCAF proved inadequate for the passenger and mail loads. Eight additional Coronados were put on a supplementary ferry service between Boucherville near Montreal and Largs, Scotland during the summer of 1945. The unit was in the charge of Flight Lieutenant Hughie Green who had lots of hours on the Catalina and who had assisted with the delivery of five Cats for the Russians, acting as safety captain.

After Singapore was lost in 1942, Lend-Lease aircraft for the Far East and Australia had to go via the Pacific. Initially it was normal to fly the ferry aircrew back via the US Air Transport Command or the US Naval Air Transport Service (NATS), but by 1943 these organisations had no spare passenger capacity. The Air Ministry gave approval for Ferry Command to operate a return ferry service across the Pacific, and two return services a week between San Diego, California and Sydney, Australia became established. The route was San Diego, Honolulu, Canton Island, Fiji, Auckland and Sydney, using Liberators.

During October 1943 the Portuguese government, in spite of their neutrality, agreed that the Azores could be used by the aircraft of Ferry Command, and a staging post was established there. Subsequently an RAF detachment was based at Lagens to handle a flow of seventy Lend-Lease aircraft a month plus 130 by the USAAF. Later other airfields in the Azores, such as Lajes, were brought into use and an RAF Dakota took passengers and freight on a shuttle around the islands.

In May 1943 a high level meeting between Winston Churchill and President Roosevelt was moved from Washington DC to Gibraltar under the codename 'Watson'. This involved the BOAC flying boat, a Boeing 314A G-AGBZ *Bristol*, Return Ferry Service Liberators AL514 and AL258, and Ferry

Command Liberators AL504, AL578 and AL593.

The US government released a number of Catalinas to the USSR in May 1944 and Ferry Command was requested to provide safety crews for the first batch of forty-eight for the delivery flight from Elizabeth City, North Carolina to Reykjavik, Iceland. From here they flew to Murmansk alone. A second batch of ninety Catalinas sold to the USSR was destined for Baku on the Caspian Sea. They were ferried to Lake Habbaniyah near Baghdad via San Juan in Puerto Rico, Trinidad, Belem, Natal, across the Atlantic to Bathurst, Port Lyautey in Morocco, Djerba, and Kasfareet in Egypt. Sixty were ferried by this route; the remaining thirty were taken by the Russians direct from the San Diego factory to Great Falls, Montana, over Canada to Alaska and across the Bering Sea to Markovo in Russia.

On the morning of 25 April 1944 Liberator Mk VI EW148, destined for delivery to India from Dorval and piloted by Flight Lieutenant Burzinski, pre-war pilot with the Polish airline LOT with 12,000 hours' flying behind him, took off with a cloud base of 300 feet, intermittent light drizzle and visibility of three miles. The Liberator hit a building in downtown Montreal shortly after take-off. The crew of five were killed plus ten civilians.

Some 42,850 aircrew had been employed by Ferry Command during World War Two, and the accident record was seventy-four aircraft out of 9,442 successful deliveries out of the 9,516 planned. The Lockheed Hudson suffered worst, with the Martin Baltimore next with twelve broken, followed by ten Douglas Bostons and nine Liberators. The organisation under various titles lost less than one per cent of the Lend-Lease aircraft handed over for delivery.

Transport Command

This new command embraced all forms of military support and communications, including the delivery of Lend-Lease aircraft. Sir Frederick Bowhill left Dorval to take over the new organisation and the old Ferry Command became No.45 (Atlantic Transport) Group with no change of task or responsibility. It was later just plain No.45 Group, and unique in that it still had a civilian core. The group was eventually divided into three wings: No.112, which covered the North Atlantic operations from Dorval; No.113, which did the same for the South Atlantic from Nassau; and No.280 Wing covering

the Pacific operation. The en route airfields, large and small, became numbered staging posts, twenty-five in all. Bermuda, with its large staff, became No.80, Lagens in the Azores No.74, and even the minuscule unit on Ascension Island became No.90 Staging Post.

During June 1945 the South Atlantic route was closed for Lend-Lease delivery aircraft and the Dakotas waiting to go to Africa, the Middle East and beyond were ferried by the mid-Atlantic route. The South Atlantic return ferry service was reduced to once a week until the last of the ferry aircrew had been airlifted back to Canada. All training at Dorval ceased in May 1945 and was handed over as the responsibility of No.313 Flying Training Unit (FTU) at North Bay. The flying boat base on the St Lawrence near Montreal was closed at the end of October 1945. Air Vice-Marshal Marix RAF took over command at No.45 Group, and 'Taffy' Powell was promoted to Air Commodore.

Delivery of nearly 2,000 Lend-Lease Dakotas from the factories of the Douglas Aircraft Company located in Long Beach and Oklahoma City was nearing completion, one of the last to arrive being Dakota Mk IV KP231 completed at Oklahoma City on 12 June 1945, ferried to Montreal the following day and to the UK on 26 June. The very last Dakota was KP279, which arrived at Montreal on 2 July 1945 and was retained by No.45 Group, finally arriving in the UK on 1 February 1946.

In September 1945 the resident No.231 Squadron at Dorval was detached to Bermuda for Coronado operations and it was finally disbanded on 15 January 1946. It had re-formed at Dorval on 8 September 1944 from the No.45 Group Communications Squadron and operated a wide variety of Ferry Command Lend-Lease types including Dakota Mk IV KP276, the Liberator Mk IX JT983, Hudson Mk VI FK540 and Coronado Mk I JX501, the latter operating from Bermuda.

Lend-Lease had been a vital weapon for victory, a measure of war involving a huge programme into which the United Nations pooled their economic resources in the search for success. As Lend-Lease drew to a close the personnel of the Atlantic Ferry Organisation (ATFERO) March to July 1941, Royal Air Force Ferry Command, July 1941 to April 1943, and RAF Transport Command No.45 Group, April 1943 to December 1945, had every reason to be proud of their outstanding achievements.

10. Men and Machines

The first detachments of the survivors of Dunkirk came ashore at Dover on 29 May 1940. With the fall of France and the almost desperate situation in the United Kingdom, the British Purchasing Commission in the US took immediate steps to place large orders for aircraft and to take over aircraft contracts placed by the Belgian, French and Dutch governments by their equivalent of the BPC. Since the US was officially neutral, with an active German embassy functioning in Washington DC and consulates in other US cities, there was little chance of keeping any BPC orders secret, and so 'black-out-blocks' regarding serials were dispensed with and aircraft numbered consecutively.

With the victorious Germans poised to invade Britain's shores at any time, the somewhat bewildered leaders turned their thoughts to the defence of the island and ways of hitting back at the German tanks and troops once they had come ashore. What was needed was the equivalent of the Junkers Ju 87 'Stuka' dive-bomber.

Fortunately for Britain there appeared on the scene the dynamic shape of Lord Beaverbrook, the Canadian press baron, hastily introduced into the wartime government to cut through red tape and get vitally needed aircraft delivered in large quantities. He was appointed by Winston Churchill to get the job done as Minister of Aircraft Production. Despite resistance from some quarters Beaverbrook insisted on getting dive-bombers for the RAF. In California a small but innovative go-ahead company, the Vultee Aircraft Corporation, was discovered and on their drawing-board was the very aircraft sought after by both Beaverbrook and Britain. The aircraft was the Vultee Vengeance and the original cockpit layout was designed in conjunction with RAF pilots for ease and accessibility of operational functions. Unfortunately the US military found it did not fit their specifications and altered much of it, to the detriment of the Vengeance.

The Vultee V-72 was originally conceived as a result of negotiations with the French government. A series of visits took place from 1938 onwards by a mission from the French Air Force which was urgently seeking new designs to supplement France's ailing aircraft inventory. Having learned the hard way from the success of the Junkers Ju 87s in Spain during the civil war, an order was placed for 300 dive-bombers powered by Wright 2600 engines, with delivery of the first three aircraft due in October 1940 and the last seventy of the order by September 1941.

With the fall of France and thus the rapid exit of their only dive-bomber customer, it was lucky for Vultee that this tragedy coincided with the arrival of the British Purchasing Commission seeking the same type of aircraft that was incorporated in the V-72 Vengeance. After some haggling in government quarters, an initial contract was signed on 3 July 1940 by Mr Henry Self on behalf of the BPC of 15 Broad Street, New York for 200 Vultee Model 72 dive-bombers less engines, propellers, propeller governors, starters, generators, control boxes, radios, armament and spare parts, exclusive of tyres and tubes. Due to the critical situation in Europe the contract called for quick deliveries, with the first aircraft to be ready by January 1941. The contract price was quoted as $14,202,200 for the aircraft and $2,840,440 for the spares, giving a total contract price for the 200 aircraft of $17,042,640.

Under order A557 there were two prototypes, AF745 and AF746. A further 200 Vultee dive-bombers were ordered on 26 September 1940 and final deliveries of the Vengeance to the RAF are quoted at over 1,000. A problem developed with the 1,700 hp Wright Double Row Cyclone GR-2600-A5B-5 engine, and this added to other problems which included the all-up weight. At one time the BPC, later the British Air Commission, considered cancelling the project. Shortly before the US government passed the historic Lend-Lease Act, orders for the Vengeance were as follows:

100 aircraft – 2 December 1940 – Vultee – Contract A557

200 aircraft – 25 February 1941 – Northrop – Contract A1555

300 aircraft – 9 April 1941 – Vultee – Contract BSC145

A Northrop-built Vultee V-72 Vengeance I AN899 from the British contract AN838–999 seen with fuselage complete and painted plus RAF roundel and serial number applied. The factory was located at Hawthorne near Los Angeles. The Vengeance first flew in July 1941. (Northrop via Peter C Smith).

100 aircraft – 17 June 1941 – Vultee – Contract BSC2647

200 aircraft – 17 June 1941 – Northrop – Contract BSC2648

With the USAAF designation A-31, the Vengeance order totalled 700 under direct purchase for Britain and 600 under Lend-Lease.

The first aircraft did not fly until July 1941, quoted as AN838, this requiring many modifications to be incorporated including a revised fin and rudder plus dive brakes on the top surface of the wing. It was quite evident that delays in delivery to the RAF were to be expected. During 1941 the Air Ministry dispatched a team of experts including pilots to the US to conduct what was called accelerated service tests on new aircraft the RAF were expecting under Lend-Lease.

Wing Commander Mike Crosley was in the team which was seconded initially to North American to flight-test the Mustang. This was not merely a British version of an existing US type, but was designed from the outset to satisfy RAF requirements.

Following a visit by the BPC, North American commenced design of the Mustang in April 1940. The first prototype was built in just over 100 days, a record achievement, and the maiden flight took place in September 1940. North American received a large contract from Britain. The first production Mustang I, AG345, flew for the first time on 1 May 1941 with the first aircraft arriving in the UK during November 1941. The first batch, AG345 to 664 (320), suffered a loss of twenty-one at sea during delivery and ten were shipped to Russia.

Wing Commander Crosley, after completion of 100 hours of flight-testing the Mustang, transferred to Vultee to flight-test over 90 hours on the Vengeance. Meanwhile Beaverbrook had phoned Morris Wilson, his representative in the US who responded the next day by secret telegram to the effect that 'the designing of the new Brewster [presumably this referred to the Brewster Bermuda] and Vultee dive-bombers in specific response to this need must take time. Moreover the progress of the designs has inevitably been delayed by the incorporation of successive modifications to meet developments of air technique in the interval.' A report to the Air Ministry dated 3 May 1941 noted, 'Flight tests on prototype Vengeance airplane have revealed faults in design. Present delivery schedule cannot be assumed to hold.'

A strike at the Vultee company in July 1941 did not help much, losing the company many of their most able staff. On 29 August 1941, the two V-72 prototypes were flown to the Vultee plant at Nashville and the Northrop plant at Hawthorne in order to give new workers their first glimpse of the dive-bomber they were employed to construct. Based at the Northrop plant near Los Angeles at this time was Mr C. V. J. Childs in charge of British Air Commission personnel, and he was quoted as saying, 'In working on this bomber we have embodied not only the advances in design developed by Vultee engineers, but we have used every bit of experience gained through the use of dive-bombers in the war.'

Even as late as May 1942 and possibly after, the BAC was sending letters of amendment to both Northrop and Vultee. On 28 May 1942 letter No.43 stated that, 'It is hereby agreed that Vengeance Airplane RAF Serial No.AN868 shall be retained at your plant as resident airplane until delivery of the last airplane off the contract unless otherwise agreed, for the purpose of development tests and verification of the functioning of accessories and equipment.' This aircraft was from a batch of 500 dive-bombers AN538 to AP137. In addition to AN868, AN993 was similarly retained in the US, while AN670 crashed prior to delivery. A total of nine aircraft were lost at sea while en route to India, and fifteen were shipped from Los Angeles direct to Sydney for the RAAF.

As late as 1944 problems with the Vengeance were being investigated. Records reveal that the National Advisory Committee for Aeronautics (NACA) at the Lewis Research Center in Cleveland took Vengeance EZ887 from a batch of 200 for the RAF (EZ800 to 999) in July 1944, the type apparently experiencing R-3350 mixture distribution problems. It remained with NACA until July 1945. Vengeance AF782 from a batch of 200 (AF745 to 944) was delivered to NACA at Lewis in July 1944 for R-3350 ground tests and instrumentation development, departing in June 1945. Both were listed in NACA records as YA-31C aircraft.

When the United States entered World War Two she was forced to take stock of her own armaments and, like the French in 1939 and the British in 1940, she found herself in dire need of almost everything. The Army Air Corps had no dive-bombers designed for land-based operations. Envious eyes were turned to British dive-bombers being produced in US factories, and thus ready to hand. On 16 January 1942, the USAAF gave Vultee a letter of intent for the acquisition of 400 A-31 Vengeance dive-bombers, but since British contracts covered all possible production for the rest of 1942 there was very little hope of any aircraft until 1943. This problem was solved by what became known as the Arnold–Portal agreement under which a certain proportion of British production in the US was turned over to the USAAF. (General H. H. Arnold was Chief of the US Army Air Force and Lord Portal was Minister of Works and Chairman of the Materials Committee.)

Colonel J. J. Llewellyn at the Ministry of Aircraft Production was to write a scathing letter to Sir Archibald Sinclair, Secretary of State for Air, on 28 May 1942: 'We were about to get deliveries when Pearl Harbor occurred. The US Air Corps thereupon seized about 200 Vengeances and 192 Bermudas. The Arnold–Portal agreement increased the number of those which we surrendered, and sanctioned the seizure from our orders of 300 Vengeance dive-bombers; 158 of these were ex-contracts for which we had paid hard cash and 142 were Lend-Lease.' Various sources indicate that aircraft repossessed included 243 which had been ordered on the British cash contract, and were in consequence known in the USAAF as V-72s rather than A-31s. Seven aircraft were taken in January 1942, sixteen in February, and eventually a total of 300.

Douglas Commercial Transports

The first Douglas DC-2 transports for the RAF were allocated to 31 Squadron based in India, the aircraft arriving at the docks at Karachi as deck cargo with both wings removed and the undercarriage down. They were slung off the merchant ships and towed from the dock area to nearby RAF Drigh Road for assembly and air test. Ropes were rigged from the undercarriage axle, one airman controlling the brakes in the cockpit. They were towed via the main road through Karachi and over the desert to the airfield. Here the sticky tape and protective covering was removed from the DC-2s, wings replaced and then after a successful air test the new transports for the RAF were flown to Lahore, home base of the vintage 31 Squadron.

This was May 1941, and on 16 May four DC-2s equipped 'B' Flight and were involved in flying reinforcements to Shaibah in the Middle East as a detachment. Four more DC-2s were taken over from Pan American Airways Africa civil pilots at Shaibah. Three more Douglas transports came from the British Purchasing Commission (BPC) via US agent Cox & Stephens.

On 19 August 1941, President Franklin D. Roosevelt released the statement describing the new trans-African military supply lifeline to be operated by Pan American Airways for the US War Department; projected route operations were to include transport services and the ferrying of operational aircraft to the Middle East. The programme was to be financed under the provisions of the Lend-Lease Act, passed by Congress in March 1941.

By August 1941, the Mediterranean was in fact an Axis lake, closed to British shipping. Supplies for the Middle East had to be transported by ship around the Cape of Good Hope, and up the East African coast to Red Sea ports. A quicker alternative was by water to West African ports like Freetown, Takoradi and Lagos, then by aircraft across Africa to Khartoum and Cairo. But a serious deficiency in transport aircraft made it impossible for Britain to utilise this sea-air route to good effect. It was this situation in August 1941 which made US assistance in developing the trans-African route essential to the continuation of Allied resistance. Under the combined operations of Pan American Airways, British Overseas Airways Corporation and the Royal Air Force, this airline route became a great supply artery to Cairo and the Western Desert, to Russia via the Tehran gateway, and to China by way of India and over the 'hump'.

During February 1941 an RAF master-navigator, Flying Officer J. I. Parry, arrived in Takoradi for ferry duties involving the delivery of both British and US aircraft, the latter being Lend-Lease types with the destination Cairo. The procedure, known as the 'hen

In January 1940 North American undertook to design a new fighter to British requirements taking into account early lessons from aerial combat over Europe. The company accepted a 120-day limit for construction of a prototype with an in-line engine and the then standard British armament of eight machine-guns. The first production Mustang I AG345 is depicted which first flew late in 1941 after the British Purchasing Commission placed contracts. (Peter M Bowers).

and chick' delivery, comprised a lead twin-engine type with the master-navigator on board accompanied by six or more single-engine fighter aircraft. Once the gaggle of aircraft had been delivered safely the aircrew were left to their own devices to get back to base at Takoradi. Authorisation was given to use the Pan American Africa Douglas DC-3 aircraft. Occasionally a lift was available on a BOAC Short Empire Class flying boat from Cairo as far as Khartoum.

During January and February 1942 the return flight to base involved three DC-3s which later were to be handed over to the RAF. The first was a DC-3-277D NC33655 c/n 4118 built by Douglas at Santa Monica on 5 May 1941. It was delivered to American Airlines and on 9 July to Pan American Africa. Still in Africa it became a C-49H 42-38251 with US Air Transport Command on 14 March 1942. During July the British Purchasing Commission acquired the DC-3 for the RAF and it was flown to the Air Reinforcement Centre at Karachi, becoming MA943 on 1 August and delivered to 31 Squadron eight days later. A plan for it to go to BOAC as G-AGEN was cancelled. The second DC-3 was NC33653 c/n 4116, delivered to American Airlines on 5 May 1941 and bought by the US government on 9 July. By October 1941 it was overseas with Pan American Africa and on 1 May 1942 it became MA925 with the RAF. The third Douglas DC-3 used for returning RAF ferry crews from Cairo to Takoradi during early 1942 was NC16094 c/n 1915 delivered to Eastern Airlines on 18 December 1936, going to Pan American Africa in October 1941. On 1 April 1942 it became LR231, going to 117 Squadron on 15 April. Reports indicate that when it went to 31 Squadron later in the month it was still carrying the US registration NC16094. On 6 May this transport was destroyed by the Japanese during a bombing raid at Mytikyina in Burma.

In the flying logbook of Warrant Officer Edward James Ledwidge RAF the long route back to Takoradi from Heliopolis, Cairo is recorded with flight times. These flights took place during August 1942 and by this time the US Air Transport Command had taken over the Pan American Africa task and the transports were Douglas C-47 Skytrains and C-53 Skytroopers. This RAF ferry pilot was employed in the delivery of Bristol Beaufighters to bases near Cairo such as Fayum Road and Kilo 17, which was Cairo itself. In July Beaufighter X7760

was delivered to Fayum Road and the return flight was in Douglas C-53-DO 42-47377 c/n 7319, hardly a month old as it was delivered from Santa Monica on 29 June. Beaufighter X8132 was delivered to Kilo 17 mid-August, return flight courtesy of the US Army Air Force, and Beaufighter EL296 was ferried to Kilo 17 in October. The time taken was anything up to twenty hours, dependent on the number of landings for refuelling required.

Normal flight time for the trip back to base was twenty-four hours, an example being as follows: Heliopolis to Luxor (2.45); Luxor to Wadi Saidna (4.20); Wadi Saidna to El Fasher (3.10); El Fasher to El Geneina (1.15); El Geneina to Maiduguri (3.35); night stop, Maiduguri to Kano (2.00); Kano to Lagos (2.55); Lagos to Accra (2.00); Accra to Takoradi (1.00).

Atlantic Ferry

RAF pilot Stanley Norris completed his captain's course in Canada at North Bay, Ontario during July and August 1942 making his first flights in Lend-Lease aircraft on familiarisation and general instructions in Hudson VI 896, 927 and 938. He also flew in North American B-25 Mitchell II FL180 as second pilot. This came from a batch of fifty five, FL164 to 218, of which FL209 crashed during transit in Canada. His first Atlantic ferry flight was on 10 December 1942 in a Hudson VI from Dorval to Prestwick. Back in Canada he flew Ventura II AJ604 and 703 on 14 March 1943 delivering freight from Dorval to Goose Bay, Labrador. On 24 March Hudson VI FK656 from a batch of 433 was delivered from Dorval to Prestwick.

After a period back at North Bay, Norris returned to Dorval in October 1943 for training on the Martin A-30 Baltimore using FW566, 546 and 750. These were from a batch of A-30A Baltimore Vs numbering 600, FW281 to 880. From this batch he ferried FW533 from Nassau in the Bahamas to Puerto Rico, the next leg being to Belem in Brazil to prepare for the Atlantic delivery to Accra in West Africa. However, on take-off from Belem the port engine failed resulting in a crash-landing. The crew were flown back to Nassau in Consolidated Liberator GRV BZ718.

A posting to 45 group at Montreal followed in January 1944 after flight training on Lend-Lease Dakotas 580, 593 and 679. This training was for a ferry flight from Dorval to Prestwick in Dakota FZ636 which took place between 30 January and 3 February. On arrival in the UK came a posting to 512 Squadron at Hendon, which was busy glider towing in preparation for D-Day. During April 1944 Norris flew Dakota FZ569 from Hendon to India carrying twelve passengers. En route on 16 April to Habbaniya, Iraq they became lost in a storm and made a forced landing in the Syrian desert. After a few difficulties with local Bedouin tribesmen they managed to take-off and fly to Palmyra in Syria, a Free French Air Force base. Here the Dakota was checked over, flight-tested and flew on to Karachi, the destination. On arrival back in the UK Norris was posted to 271 Squadron at Down Ampney, taking part in D-Day operations.

Another RAF ferry pilot was Harry Chatfield, who made a total of seven Atlantic crossings with Lend-Lease aircraft, two on the northern route and five on the southern. His first North Atlantic ferry flight involved Hudson VI FK604, one from a batch of 433, FK381 to 813. The first pilot was Captain Nagurney and the route was Dorval, Gander and so on to Prestwick. The second ferry flight involved Dakota FZ647 from 30 January to 3 February 1944, the route being Gander, Bluie West 1, Reykjavik, and Prestwick. The five south Atlantic deliveries involving the Martin A-30 Baltimore were all flights originating in Nassau. The route to Accra in West Africa varied and could be via Piarco, Borinquen in Puerto Rico or Georgetown in Trinidad. Harry spent his 21st birthday flying in Baltimore V FW455 between Ascension Island and Accra. On return to the UK he flew Dakota FZ647 from Prestwick to Doncaster to join 271 Squadron during February 1944, later flying FZ647 to Broadwell to join 512 Squadron.

Flying Boats

A Lend-Lease serial batch JX100 to 132 covering thirty-three aircraft was reserved for Martin Mariner I flying boats, these being quoted as PBM-3B. Five, including JX101, 120, 126, 128 and 130, were not delivered. On 20 October 1943 524 Squadron was formed at Oban for the sole purpose of obtaining operational experience with the Mariner. The type was not adopted for RAF service and the Squadron was disbanded on 7 December 1943. The Squadron operated eight aircraft and had six qualified crews,

and these crews were involved in returning the aircraft to the US.

Flight Lieutenant R. E. Gough RAF was a highly qualified flying boat pilot and his flying logbook reveals that on 27 October 1943 he test-flew Mariner PBM-3C JX105 at the Saro base at Beaumaris, Anglesey and on 1 November he flew the Mariner to Oban. After flying ceased, JX106 was ferried to Wig Bay and the first Mariner to be returned to the US was JX122 which staged as far as Gibraltar on 28 February 1944, with JX131 ferried to Gibraltar the following day. The route for the Mariners after Gibraltar was Bathurst (West Africa), Natal and Belem (Brazil), Chaguramas Bay (Trinidad), San Juan (Puerto Rico), Banana River (Florida) and Norfolk, Virginia, the journey taking up to five days.

After delivering JX131 to the US Navy at Norfolk, Ray Gough went to Elizabeth City, North Carolina where Lend-Lease Catalina flying boats were being readied for their ferry flight. On 28 March 1944 Ray did a test flight on a Boeing (Canada)-built PB2B-1 Catalina, JX365. On 10 April he ferried a PB2B-1, JX341, back to the UK routing via Bermuda and Dartmouth, Nova Scotia, arriving at Largs in Scotland on 16 April.

NA-73 Mustang

During 1940 the British gave North American Aviation just 120 days to produce a fighter prototype which met their requirements. The National Advisory Committee for Aeronautics (NACA) at Langley, Virginia helped the company to flight-test its prototype NA-73, to be known as P-51 Mustang, this being the first aircraft to employ the NACA laminar flow aerofoil. On 27 December 1941 the North American XP-51 41-38, ex-RAF AG348, arrived at Langley where it remained until it finally departed on 14 December 1942.

North American received a large contract from the British Purchasing Commission and the first production Mustang I, AG345, made its first flight on 1 May 1941, with the first aircraft arriving in the UK on November 1941. A serial Lend-Lease aircraft block AG345 to 664 was reserved for 320 aircraft of which twenty-one were lost at sea on delivery and ten were re-shipped to Russia.

Mention has already been made of Lend-Lease aircraft for the RAF which for some reason were retained for use by the USAAF or even by the US

Navy. In many cases the aircraft retained the allocated RAF serial whilst in US service.

From the batch of 375 Lockheed Ventura II aircraft with serial allocation AJ163 to 537, only forty-one reached RAF service. A total of 108, AJ235 to 442, went to the USAAF and twenty-six, AJ511 to 537, to the US Navy, whilst others went to the RCAF and SAAF with some lost while being ferried. The historical records for the US Coast Guard air station located at Port Angeles in Washington State reveal that on 24 September 1943 a US Army Air Force Lockheed B-34 Ventura bomber with RAF serial AJ405 had landed at the base for training. It crashed on take-off with the loss of five USAAF personnel; in addition two were seriously burned and two had minor injuries and burns. The aircraft which was based at nearby Paine Field, was a complete loss.

Likewise, from the batch of 240 Douglas Boston III aircraft with serial allocation AL263 to 502, only thirty-six aircraft reached the RAF. Twenty-eight were shipped direct to Russia – AL265/267/281/282/287/292/294/295/297/298 /300/303 to 316/320/321/322. Many others went to the US Army Air Force. A good friend of the author, Boardman C. Reed, a Boeing B-17 bomber pilot with the US 8th Air Force here in the UK, had the opportunity to fly a Douglas Boston III, AL452, on 9 November 1943. Despite being Douglas-designed it was a Boeing-built bomber c/n 2833 completed on 29 December 1941 at the Seattle factory. It was powered by two Wright 1,600 hp GR-2600-A5B-0 Double-Cyclone 14 engines and had British camouflage. Flight was one hour duration from Honington, Suffolk to Alconbury near Huntingdon, headquarters of the US 1st Bomb Division.

Earlier, on 17 February 1942, Boardman had over two hours' co-pilot time in a Consolidated 32-MF Liberator II, AL634 c/n 132, built on 26 December 1941, from Pendleton Field, Oregon.

British interest in the Liberator was firmly established by spring 1940 and before the end of the year the British Purchasing Commission was seeking permission to negotiate, in addition to smaller orders already placed, contracts that would run Lend-Lease Liberator deliveries into many thousands. While events soon overtook these plans, the groundwork had been laid to establish the UK as a major user of the aircraft. This policy reached fruition under the Lend-Lease programme.

Under Lend-Lease, Britain received 1,865

Liberator bombers and twenty-four Liberator transports. Canada received eighty-eight B-24s and Australia 275. In addition the RAF and RAAF received a total of fifty-five B-24s as operational theatre transfers, and the RAF also acquired twenty-six RY-3 transports. Adding these to the 112 LB-30As, Liberator Is and IIs that Britain acquired as a result of pre-Lend-Lease agreements, this gives a grand total of 2,445 Liberator-type aircraft in RAF service. Sixty B-24J RAF Liberators were held in Canada under the huge British Commonwealth Air Training Plan.

All Lend-Lease deliveries of Liberators, until the last three months of 1943, went directly to the UK except for eight aircraft that were handed over in North Africa. From October 1943 on, however, the majority of deliveries were made to locations in theatres outside the UK. The South African Air Force had two operational squadrons equipped with RAF

Lend-Lease-supplied Liberators. They were formed in spring 1944.

Atlantic Ferry Tow

A ferry flight of an unusual nature which must be mentioned is that involving two products of Lend-Lease: a Waco CG-4A Hadrian glider, FR579, fully laden with vaccines destined for the USSR plus urgent radio, aircraft and motor parts, which was towed across the North Atlantic by a Douglas Dakota Mk I, FD900, of RAF Transport Command in June 1943. The flight from Dorval, Montreal to Prestwick was completed in stages totalling twenty-eight hours' flying time to cover 3,500 miles. It was

an experimental flight, the first of its kind, and no special emphasis was laid on the accomplishment. The project was considered too hazardous and was not repeated, although it provided useful information regarding the possibilities of an Atlantic air train service. The captain of the glider, named *Voodoo*, was Squadron Leader R. G. Seys RAF with Squadron Leader P. M. Gobeil RCAF as co-pilot. The Dakota tug was captained by Flight Lieutenant W. S. Longhurst, a Canadian, and Flight Lieutenant C. W. H. Thomson, a New Zealander, both serving in the RAF. Mr H. G. Wightman was the radio officer and Pilot Officer R. H. Wormington the flight engineer.

The CG-4A was designed by the Waco Aircraft

The RAF formed a Glider Pick-up Flight at Ibsley, near Ringwood, Hampshire after World War 2, equipped with Lend-Lease Dakotas modified for glider-tug 'snatch' operations using Lend-Lease Waco CG-4A Hadrian gliders. The system was demonstrated to the public at the RAF Display held at RAE Farnborough in 1950 as seen in this photo. Despite its RAF marks the Hadrian glider still retains its USAAF serial 42-74521 being a CG-4A-CM built by Commonwealth Aircraft of Kansas City. (AP Photo Library).

Company of Troy, Ohio, had a wing span of eighty-three feet and eight inches and was built by many sub-contractors, including a piano manufacturer in New York. The freight load was one-and-a-half tons. For the flight it was equipped with rubber dinghies, the ordinary ocean emergency equipment carried by bombers and transports crossing the Atlantic, and flotation gear. The steel attachments were designed to take a pull of 20,000 lb. Loading and unloading were carried out through a hinged nose which opened and closed with a jawlike action.

The Dakota was built at Long Beach under Lend-Lease contract AC-20669, and as FD900 was delivered to the RAF on 14 June 1943. Modifications to the Dakota tug included special tanks for extra fuel, made so that they could be jettisoned intact with their fuel content, should the need arise; petrol could not be jettisoned loose, as it would spray back on the glider and atmospheric electricity would ignite it. The emergency drill for the Hadrian glider, in case of being forced down in the sea, was to be a routine procedure between pilot and co-pilot. The first essential manoeuvre was to cut the fuselage open, and through the hole the freight and the two pilots would go, so that the flotation apparatus would function. The glider and tug were in two-way communication by radio, but this was switched off most of the time to preserve the life of the batteries. When the Dakota pilot wished to speak to the glider pilot he waggled his wings.

The flight set up a world record for total distance for a glider carrying freight. The non-stop record flight had already been established by Squadron Leader Seys, who began actual experiments for the Atlantic crossing six months beforehand. All trials were made with the glider fully loaded, and some of the worst weather known in North America for fifty years was met during the experiments. Once the glider force-landed in deep snow during a blizzard in mountainous country sixty miles from Montreal. The first major achievement was a triangular course flight from Montreal and return by way of Newfoundland and Labrador. The last stage of this flight, a distance of 820 miles, set up a record for a fully laden glider with freight, beating the US record of 670 miles. Longer flights followed. On one, south from Canada, 1,177 statute miles were covered non-stop at an average speed of 150 mph. This flight provided the final data required for the Atlantic crossing venture.

On the journey from Montreal to the UK, conditions were mainly favourable, except on the first leg when progress was extremely slow due to head-winds. After the first three hours the pair had reached 9,000 feet in an attempt to get over the cloud tops. At 13,000 feet it was decided to descend through cloud to 1,500 feet.

The Hadrian glider had to be flown all the time as there was no automatic pilot. The pilot could not afford to take his eyes off the Dakota tug, nor the tow-rope if they were flying in cloud. The physical strain was considerable. Concentration became almost hypnotic. There was no heating system in the glider. Out of the sun, in cloud or a snowstorm, the outside temperature could drop as low as thirty degrees below zero. At one time there was snow inside the Waco glider, yet in clear sunshine the glider cockpit was as hot as a glasshouse.

Departure from Dorval, Montreal was on 24 June 1943 and there were no incidents. Landings at Goose Bay in Labrador, Bluie West One in Greenland and Reykjavik, Iceland were good and without mishap, except that once the tow-rope had to be spliced before take-off, and on another occasion the coupling was damaged by being dropped on a rack. It had to be straightened and re-welded. Precisely on ETA, the Waco Hadrian Mk I glider and Dakota Mk I tug circled Prestwick for the final landing on 1 July 1943.

Unfortunately, RAF Transport Command never propounded the advantages of towing a load inside a glider instead of carrying it inside a transport aircraft like the Dakota with long-range fuel tanks fitted. The Dakota FD900 survived until 21 March 1945 when it was involved in an accident while parked at Lagens on the Azores where it was based with a detachment of 45 Group from Dorval, Montreal. After its record-breaking tow across the Atlantic it served with 512, 511, 525 and 575 Squadrons.

In 1943 at least a dozen Royal Egyptian Air Force pilots had volunteered for service with RAF Ferry Command, becoming involved in ferrying Lend-Lease RAF aircraft across Africa. One of these, Flying Officer Mahmud Rafai, lost his life when the Mustang he was flying crashed near Algiers, while two others, Flight Lieutenant Ali Zeitun and Flying Officer Said Huisain Sabit, were killed ferrying a Baltimore.

11. The Aftermath of Lend-Lease

When the Lend-Lease Act was passed on 11 March 1941 by Congress it stipulated that the aircraft remained the property of the United States and must be returned at the end of World War Two. This stipulation was extended to Russia when the Russo-German alliance fell apart.

To account for Lend-Lease material, US field commissioners were established in various theatres of operations, and after the cessation of hostilities all US-owned material was offered back to Britain. Aircraft lost in accidents and by enemy action had been noted and it was the responsibility of the appropriate field commissioner to decide on the disposal of surviving Lend-Lease aircraft.

The first problem they met with was when they were offered several thousand Kittyhawks, Mustangs, Bostons, Marauders and Baltimores which had accumulated in the many RAF maintenance units scattered around the globe. In Egypt there was No.102 MU at Abusueir, No.103 at Aboukir, No.107 at Kasfareet. In India there was No.301 at Drigh Road, Karachi, No.308 at Allahabad and No.320 also located at Drigh Road; No. 390 was at Seletar, Singapore. Here in the United Kingdom No.5 was at Kemble, No.8 Little Rissington, No.12 Kirkbride, No.13 Henlow, No.22 Silloth, No.33 Lyneham, and No.44 Edzell. RAF Dakotas were in storage after World War Two at Little Rissington, Silloth and Kirkbride.

The last thing the USAAF wanted was an addition to the tens of thousands of war surplus aircraft already crowding their storage facilities set up in all theatres. Many were placed in storage facilities located in the US. The US field commissioners waived their right of return and so for a few years after World War Two thousands of Lend-Lease aircraft crowded the maintenance units, many awaiting disposal to the scrap merchant. Naturally the supply line for aircraft spares dried up immediately after the war, and there were only a very few US Lend-Lease types which could remain operational in the absence of equivalent British-built post-war types.

Two Lend-Lease types falling into the surplus category included the Dakota and the Harvard, the Douglas transport being easy to dispose of to the many early post-war emerging airlines. RAF Transport Command Dakota squadrons were disbanded, only to be resuscitated for the Berlin Airlift in 1948. Many Dakotas were returned to US ownership and given to NATO countries, and to the post-war USAF in Europe. It must be remembered that the RAF under Lend-Lease took approximately one-fifth of the total Douglas production, some 2,000 transports.

On Sunday, 3 August 1947 the approximate number of Lend-Lease aircraft held by No.107 Kasfareet, Egypt included 150 Baltimores, 120 Marauders, fifty Venturas, twelve Dakotas, twelve Mustangs, ten Thunderbolts, five Lockheed 18s, one Kittyhawk III (P-40M) FR862, one Expeditor KJ493, one Hellcat JX818, one Boston AL729 and one Maryland AR738. By 13 August, ten days later, the dump consisted of the following aircraft: sixty-nine Marauders, fifteen Venturas, four Baltimores, three Mustangs, three Thunderbolts, two Kittyhawks and twenty Dakotas.

During 1947, a large number of surplus RAF aircraft including Dakotas was assembled in the Far East and transferred to the Royal Indian Air Force. When the country became divided into India and Pakistan separate air forces were established equipped with aircraft that had been used by the RAF. As the Dakotas came under Lend-Lease jurisdiction the governments had to purchase them from the US Field Commission, both India and Pakistan being involved.

Despite there being victory in Europe and Allied success in the Far East, Lend-Lease aircraft were still being delivered at a high tempo. Records show that Dakota IV KP279 was the last of the type, having been constructed at Oklahoma City, delivered via the USAAF on 30 June 1945, served with RAF at Montreal with 45 Group on 2 July, but not being ferried to the UK until 1 February 1946. It was the last of the batch KP208 to 279 (72), some being delivered to the RCAF and others to the Far East. Next in line came the serial batch KP308 to 328

(21), a small batch of North American NA-108 Mitchell III bombers, equivalent to the B-25J. Finally the serial batch KP329 to KV300 was reserved for Lend-Lease aircraft, type unspecified, and not taken up.

A great deal of planning for the possibility of having to invade Japan had been done by Lord Louis Mountbatten, the Supreme Allied Commander of the huge South-East Asia Command (SEAC), and his staff. However, at midnight on 14 August 1945 President Harry S. Truman announced the unconditional surrender of Japan. Huge stockpiles of Lend-Lease material were already in temporary storage in India. Hundreds of new Waco CG-4A Hadrian gliders for the RAF had already been assembled from their crates and stored in open areas in the Punjab, whilst a larger glider, the Waco CG-13, had been evaluated here in the UK with odd ones for the RAF positioned in India. Many RAF Bomber Command squadrons and aircrew found themselves being converted to Lend-Lease types such as the Dakota and Liberator to be employed on trooping to the Far East. Other personnel were posted direct to the many RAF and two RCAF Dakota squadrons employed in Air Command South-East Asia (ACSEA). Mountbatten had indicated he required more Dakota squadrons to tow the Waco gliders if it became necessary to invade Japan. It was even thought that he was prepared to use British Army aircrew, if necessary to be trained to fly Dakotas as well as gliders. The existing Far East Dakota squadron crews had all done airborne forces training at No.3 Parachute Training School located at Chaklala. As early as 3 December 1944 Exercise 'Pongo 1' had been held involving airborne forces, whilst at the same time 53 Glider Course was in progress at Fatehjang.

Even with the war over there were still heavy commitments for such Lend-Lease aircraft as the Dakota. The many PoWs had to be airlifted to the UK and eventually home, whilst Europe had to be sorted out in conjunction with the US and the USSR. Based at Croydon was 147 Squadron equipped with a large fleet of Dakotas which flew a regular service to Europe. The aircraft were marked 'CMV' indicating the main route which was Croydon–Munich–Vienna. British Overseas Airways Corporation was still operating a huge fleet of Lend-Lease Dakotas acquired during 1943 which had operated in dual markings as required, RAF markings or a civil regis-

tration, the crews wearing one of two types of uniforms accordingly.

Whilst the RAF Lend-Lease Liberator bombers from ACSEA were being assembled for disposal in the maintenance units, Operation 'Mastiff' began from Singapore with one Dakota squadron flying ninety sorties in three weeks on various tasks including airlifting PoWs and dropping rice to starved native outposts abandoned by the Japanese. In November 1945 detachments were sent to Batavia in the Dutch East Indies, one squadron suffering the loss of two Dakotas in unfortunate circumstances: one was shot down by the Indonesians while in the circuit to land at Soerabaya, and another which crashed in Batavia was discovered later with the crew and passengers butchered.

Skymaster

A latecomer to Lend-Lease was the Douglas C-54 Skymaster four-engined transport received in only small numbers and not entering RAF service until 1945. However, one Douglas C-54B-1-DO c/n 18326 ex-43-17126 was transferred to the RAF as EW999 for use by Winston Churchill. It was delivered during the autumn of 1944 and operated by the VIP Flight of 246 Squadron. It was returned to the US during late 1945.

Twenty-two Douglas C-54D Skymaster transports were delivered to the RAF commencing in February 1945 with the Lend-Lease serial allocation KL977 to 986, KL988 to 999. They served with both 232 and 246 Squadrons, 1332 Heavy Conversion Unit, No.1 Ferry Unit and with ACSEA. During March 1946 these transports were returned to Norfolk, Virginia to continue valued service with both the US Navy and the US Marine Corps.

In June 1945 'B' Flight of 232 Squadron formed up at RAF Holmesley South moving to Palam, Delhi, India in July with a further move to Ratmalana, Ceylon in August, moving again to Negombo when the airfield was made ready. A regular RAF Transport Command route was established from Ceylon to the Cocos Islands, then to Perth in western Australia, and finally Sydney.

It is of interest to note that 'B' Flight of 246 Squadron was equipped with a number of Lend-Lease Consolidated C-87 single fin and rudder Liberator types known in the RAF as Liberator VIIs. Twenty-seven were initially earmarked for the RAF

A single Douglas C-54B-1-DO 43-17126 c/n 18326 was supplied under Lend-Lease for the personal use of the British Prime Minister, Winston S Churchill. It is depicted with its USAAF serial still on the fin and EW-999 on the fuselage. Twenty-two other C-54D model Skymasters were supplied to the RAF, these being returned to the US Navy and Marine Corps after World War 2. (AP Photo Library).

but only twenty-four were delivered, EW611 to 634, with ex-USAAF serials 44-39219 to 44-39226, 44-39236, 44-39237, 44-39248 to 44-39261. On 19 July 1945 EW631 crashed after take-off from Sydney and was destroyed killing all on board.

On the night of Thursday, 19 July 1945 Liberator VII EW631 bound for Momote on Manus Island mistakenly taxied out to Runway 16 at Mascot, Sydney before being redirected to Runway 22. After nearly fifteen minutes of engine checks, EW631 entered the runway and rolled approximately 1,100 yards before becoming airborne. It never climbed above forty feet and thereafter lost height, its starboard wing first clipping a pine tree eighteen feet above the ground before crashing only 2,100 feet from the upwind threshold. The Liberator was totally destroyed killing all twelve on board. The transport had only 584 airframe hours and a few days earlier had brought the Chief of Staff, RAF Transport Command to Sydney for a high-level conference. The pilot was Squadron Leader John Rayner RAF. The aircraft was ex-Consolidated C-87-CF 44-39258 using radio callsign 'VMYCB', and was on the strength of No.1315 Flight based at Mascot. It was part of No.300 Group RAF Transport

Command established to provide air transport support for the operation of the British Pacific Fleet, and was equipped with Lend-Lease aircraft which included Beech C-45 Expeditors, Douglas Dakotas and Consolidated Liberators.

After World War Two the RAF held on to Lend-Lease types which had served well, a criterion applying to the Consolidated Catalina patrol bomber. The Air Ministry had ordered one example, P9630 designated Consolidated Model 28-5, for experimental purposes and this arrived at the Marine Aircraft Experimental Establishment at Felixstowe, Suffolk in July 1939. Between 22 April 1946 and 13 October 1947 Ray Gough, a friend of the author who had served on RAF flying boats during World War Two, was one of the civilian test pilots based with 57 Maintenance Unit located at Wig Bay. Aircraft held by the MU included Short Sunderlands and Seafords plus a number of Lend-Lease Consolidated Catalina aircraft. These included a number in the batch JX200 to 437 (238) which were IVA JX218/222/248/261 plus two, IVB JX378/381, built by Boeing (Canada). Two more IVB Catalinas were from the batch JX570 to 662 (93) and included JX578 which was ex-US Navy Bu. No.08218 and JX590.

Reverse Lend-Lease

As late as 1954 the British government decided to return 100 of the Lend-Lease Dakotas held in storage as a gift to the US. These transports were held in open storage at 12 Maintenance Unit at Kirkbride, Cumberland, at 8 MU at Little Rissington, Gloucestershire and at 22 MU at Silloth, Cumberland. The USAF Military Adviser & Assistance Group (MAAG) office in London drew up Contract No.61 (514) – 799 which was awarded to Field Aircraft Services, one of a number of British companies that over many years had specialised in Douglas DC-3 type transports both civil and military, and which had facilities for the overhaul of the Pratt & Whitney R-1830-90 Twin Wasp engines.

Many of the Dakota transports involved in the contract and held in outdoor storage were just hulks. All were transported by road after being dismantled to Tollerton airfield near Nottingham for a rebuild, and in many cases it took parts from other Dakotas to make one complete and flyable one. The rebuild often took many months to complete. For example, KN572 arrived from 12 MU Kirkbride on 1 December 1954 and departed as a new aircraft on 10 January 1956, resplendent in USAF livery as 44-76862. It was later handed over to the West German Air Force.

This was a very unique situation involving Lend-Lease aircraft and many of the Dakotas had not flown since participating in the humanitarian Berlin Airlift in 1948. After being returned to the safe custody of the US Air Forces in Europe (USAFE) over twenty were handed over to the post-war German Air Force, a handful went to the Armée de l'Air in France, whilst others served on with USAF transport elements here in Europe. It was an excellent example of Lend-Lease.

On a smaller scale the North American Harvard extended its life into the post-war training period with the RAF. Prior to Lend-Lease British contracts reached 1,100 aircraft, and total deliveries to British Commonwealth Air Forces exceeded 5,000. By 1945 few examples of the early Harvard I remained in RAF service, the main variant in the post-war Flying Training Command being the Harvard IIB. Today at the Aircraft & Armament Evaluation Establishment at Boscombe Down, Wiltshire, two Harvards, FT375 and KF183, are still in regular use for various airborne tasks such as photography. Both of these training aircraft were built by Noorduyn in Canada, FT375 coming from a batch of 700 and KF183 from a batch of nearly 1,000 Harvards.

Fleet Air Arm

The Fleet Air Arm played an increasingly important part in the Battle of the Atlantic in 1943 with the introduction into service of escort carriers and aircraft obtained under Lend-Lease from the US. Records reveal that no less than thirty-eight escort carriers, all but five launched in 1942–3, were supplied. One went to the Royal Canadian Navy. After World War Two all the escort carriers were returned to the US, the last one at the end of 1946.

In the Atlantic the gap in air cover was completely closed when RAF Coastal Command acquired very long-range Lend-Lease Fortress and Liberator aircraft. The Fleet Air Arm had by this time no less than forty escort carriers which it operated until the end of World War Two, and was operating some 800 US aircraft likewise obtained under Lend-Lease.

When Japan capitulated on 14 August 1945 the British fleet was steaming 100 miles from the enemy mainland, with many of its carrier aircraft airborne ready to attack Tokyo. They were recalled and dropped their bombs in the sea prior to landing. Aircraft types included Lend-Lease Corsairs, Hellcats and Avengers. The fleet was part of the proposed 'Tiger Force' which was to include over 600 FAA aircraft operating from carriers of the British Pacific Fleet.

With the conflict over, the British Pacific Fleet rested on its laurels in Sydney, Australia before loading on board its escort carriers surplus-to-requirements Lend-Lease aircraft for dumping out at sea. They were first stripped of all useful parts and equipment, and it is recorded that more than 300 carrier aircraft, nominally valued at £6 million, were loaded on board escort carriers such as HMS *Pioneer*. Newsreel photos shown shortly after the end of World War Two captured Fleet Air Arm aircraft being dumped overboard as the escort carriers navigated the Suez Canal on their way home to Blighty.

Appendix A

Lend-Lease Aircraft: A to Z

This listing in a chronological A to Z by type order includes all the known aircraft supplied to the United Kingdom (RAF and RN) between 1938 and 1945. Not all contract details are known for the direct cash purchase by the British Purchasing Commission, or for those aircraft taken over from the Allies – France, Belgium, Greece and the Netherlands. Most details of Lend-Lease orders are included and are extracted from the then 'Confidential' document 'RAF Serials Assigned for Lend-Lease Aircraft' dated 18 November 1944 and published by the Planning and Airframe Supply of the British Air Commission, Washington DC. It states that as far as is practicable wasted serials, resulting from cancelled allocations or changed aircraft assignments, have been deleted from the list but a considerable number are retained in order to avoid unduly broken sequences. US serials are provided where they correspond to the RAF serials in numerical order as given. There is the odd discrepancy, which is surely acceptable involving such a massive aircraft listing. Many aircraft were retained by the USAAF for some reason, and USAAF aircraft were loaned for use by the RAF as required in various theatres of operations. Impressments have been included only if involving a Lend-Lease aircraft type. There were many other aircraft impressed into service during World War Two.

Name	Manufacturer	US Designation
AIRACOBRA (see Caribou)	Bell	P-39C
AIRACOMET	Bell	YP-59A
ARGUS	Fairchild	C-61, A, K
AVENGER (see Tarpon)	Grumman	TBF-1B, C TBM-1,3,4
BALTIMORE	Martin	A-30
BERMUDA	Brewster	A-34, SB2A
BOSTON	Douglas	A-20
BUFFALO	Brewster	F2A
CARIBOU (see Airacobra)	Bell	P-39C
CATALINA	Consolidated	PBY-5, A,B, PB2B-1
CHESAPEAKE	Vought	SB2U
CLEVELAND	Curtiss	SBG, SBC-4
COMMANDO	Curtiss	C-46/C-55
CORNELL	Fairchild	PT-26A,B
CORONADO	Consolidated	PB2Y-3B,C
CORSAIR	Vought	F4U-, F3A, FG-1
CRANE	Cessna	AT-17A
CUB	Piper	L-4
DAKOTA	Douglas	C-47, A,B, C-53
DAUNTLESS	Douglas	SBD-5
DC-2/DC-3	Douglas	C-32A, C-49 series
ELECTRA	Lockheed	Model 10 & 12
EXPEDITER	Beechcraft	C-45, B,F
FLYING FORTRESS	Boeing	B-17C, E,F,G
GANNET (see Hellcat)	Grumman	–
GOOSE	Grumman	JRF-5, 6B
GOSLING (see Widgeon)	Grumman	J4F-2
HADRIAN	Waco	CG-4A glider
HARVARD	North American	AT-6C,D, AT-16, SNJ-4
HAVOC	Douglas	A-20
HELLCAT	Grumman	F6F-3,5,5N
HELLDIVER	Curtiss	SBW-1B
HOVERFLY I	Sikorsky	YR-4, R4B
HOVERFLY II	Sikorsky	R-6A
HUDSON	Lockheed	A-28A, A-29,A
INVADER	Douglas	A-26
KAYDET	Stearman	PT-27
KINGCOBRA	Bell	P-63A
KINGFISHER	Vought	OS2U
KITTYHAWK	Curtiss	P-40E-1, F, K-1, M, L

LEND-LEASE AIRCRAFT IN WORLD WAR II

LIBERATOR	Consolidated	B-24D,J,L, C-87, RY-3
LIGHTNING	Lockheed	P-38
LODESTAR	Lockheed	C-59, C-60
MARAUDER	Martin	B-26A,C,F,G
MARINER	Martin	PBM-3B, C
MARTLET (see Wildcat)	Grumman	F4F-3, 4B, FM-1, 2
MARYLAND	Martin	A-22
MITCHELL	North American	B-25C,D,J
MOHAWK	Curtiss	P-36
MUSTANG	North American	A-36, P-51A,B,C,D,F,G,H,K
NAVIGATOR	Beechcraft	AT-7B
NOMAD	Northrop	A-17
NORSEMAN	Noorduyn	C-64
RELIANT	Stinson	SR-9D/AT-A
SEAMEW	Curtiss	SO3C-2C
SEAMEW DRONE	Curtiss	SO3C-1K
SENTINEL	Stinson	L-5, B
SKYMASTER	Douglas	C-54, D
TARPON (see Avenger)	Grumman	TBF-1B
THUNDERBOLT	Republic	P-47B,D
TIGERCAT	Grumman	F7F-
TIGER MOTH	De Havilland (Canada)	PT-24
TOMAHAWK	Curtiss	P-40 series
TRAVELLER	Beechcraft	C-43, GB-2
VANGUARD	Vultee	P-66
VENGEANCE	Vultee	A-31, A-35
VENTURA	Lockheed	B-34, PV-1
VIGILANT	Vultee	AT-1G, O-49, A
WIDGEON	Grumman	J4F-2
WILDCAT (see Martlet)	Grumman	F4F-3, 4B, FM-1, 2

Miscellaneous
  Waco (Ford-built) CG-13A glider
  Pitcairn Autogyro PA-34A
  Monocoupe Universal Moulded Product L-7A

Ref. No. L1–3
CONFIDENTIAL

RAF SERIALS ASSIGNED FOR
LEND-LEASE AIRCRAFT

N.B. *This is a listing of RAF serial assignments and should not be construed to represent either actual or anticipated receipts of aircraft.*

As far as practicable wasted serials, resulting from cancelled allocations or changed aircraft assignments, have been deleted from the list but a considerable number are retained in order to avoid unduly broken sequences.

U.S. serials are provided where they correspond to the RAF serials in numerical order as given.

PLANNING AND AIRFRAME SUPPLY
BRITISH AIR COMMISSION
WASHINGTON, D.C.
NOV. 18, 1944

A batch of 121 Bell Model 14 Airacobra Mk.I fighters, allocated RAF serials AP264–384 were taken over by the USAAC, later USAAF, although twelve were lost at sea whilst in transit and twenty were shipped to Russia. Depicted in US markings is AP375 named "ONE FOR THE ROAD". (AP Photo Library).

AIRACOBRA   Bell Model 12

Mark No.	US Desig.	Company	Requisition	Contract	RAF Serials	US Serials
I	P-39	Bell			AH570–739(170)	
I	P-39	Bell			AP264–384(121)	
I	P-39	Bell			BW100–183(84)	
I	P-39	Bell			BX135–434(300)	
	P-39C	Bell	1681	AC-13383	DS173–175(3)	40-2981/2983/2984

AP264–384 Taken over by USAAF less twelve lost at sea in transit, plus twenty shipped to Russia.

BW100–183 Delivered but many handed over to USAAF, others shipped to Russia. BW114 to RAF.

BX135–434 Majority taken over by USAAF, others shipped to Russia. At least seventeen lost at sea.

DS173–175 Three ex-USAAF to UK for evaluation.

Only about eighty used by RAF, remainder taken over by USAAF or shipped to Russia either after RAF service or direct. Known Russian shipment
AH570/1/5/7/586/599/604/5/6/7/8/610/3/5/6/7/8/9/620/2/3/4/5/6/7/8/630/1/2/3/4/5/6/8/9/640/1/2/3/4/5/6/7/9/650/2/3 /4/5/8/9/660/2/3/4/5/6/7/8/9/670/1/3/4/5/6/7/8/9/680–692/4/5/7/9/700/2–12/14–731/33/4/9.

Non-standard designation P-400 used by USAAF. One source quotes Caribou as name.

AIRACOMET Bell Model 27

Mark No.	US Desig.	Company	Requisition	Contract	RAF Serials	US Serials
	YP-59A	Bell	41017	None	None	42-108773

Listed under 'miscellaneous' in the Lend-Lease document and as 'Experimental'. Possibly evaluation by the RAF.

A batch of 25 Fairchild 24W Argus Mk.I (C-61) HM164–188 were delivered to the RAF and the Air Transport Auxiliary as replacements for EV700–724. Argus HM172 was loaned back to the USAAF. The aircraft had the c/n 208–232 ex USAAF 41-38764–38788. Depicted is HM167 carrying (P) markings and US ex 41-38767 and was tested by the A&AEE Boscombe Down. Photo is dated 25 November 1941. (Via Philip Jarrett).

LEND-LEASE AIRCRAFT IN WORLD WAR II

ARGUS Fairchild
Model 24W-41, 24W-41A, 24R. (Mk.I, II, III respectively)

Mark No.	US Desig.	Company	Requisition	Contract	RAF Serials	US Serials
I	C-61	Fairchild	2130	DA-173	HM164–188(25) EV725–811(87)	41-38764–38863(100) 42-13572–13583(12)
I	C-61		5884, 7202	DA-915	FK313-361(49)	
II	C-61A		7202, 40517		FS500–660(161) FZ719–828(110)	42-32117–32165(49)
			2130	AC-28355	HB551–643(93)	4314824–14916(93)
III	C-61K		7202	AC-28355	HB664–758(115) HB760(1)	43-14918–15032(115) 43-14917(1)
III	C-61K		7202	AC-1679	KK379–568(190)	44-83036–83225(190)

HM164–188 originally allocated serials EV700–724. HM172 loaned back to USAAF.

EV755, 756, 758, 760, 761, 766 lost at sea in transit. FS513 to Yugoslav Air Force.

FZ719–828 mainly delivered to Middle East. KK522–567 to Canada.

FS628 based at Tezgoam, India, 5 September 1944.

AVENGER Grumman Model G-40. Initially allocated the name TARPON. Renamed AVENGER on 13 January 1944.

Mark No.	US Desig.	Company	Requisition	Contract	RAF Serials	US Serials
I	TBF-1B/C	Grumman	N-6	LL 91367	JZ100-300(201)	
I	TBF-1B/C		2851	LL 91367	FN750–949(200)	
					FN750	ex BuNo. 00616
					FN751–753	ex 00620–00622
					FN754–755	ex 00625–00629
					FN756–770	ex 06277–06291
					FN771–785	ex 06387–06401
II	TBM-1	Gen. Motors	N-901	NOs-98837	JZ301–526(226)	
					JZ301–330	ex 24766–24795
					JZ331–360	ex 24876–24905
					JZ361–390	ex 25076–25105
					JZ421–440	ex 25336–25355
					JZ441–460	ex 25446–25465
					JZ461–480	ex 25556–25575
					JZ481–500	ex 25676–25695
					JZ501–526	ex 16967–16992
II	TBM-1		N-901	NOa(S)228	JZ527–634(108)	

This Grumman Avenger 1 (TBF-1) FN765 ex US Navy BuNo.06286 was from a batch of 200 for the Royal Navy FN750–949 delivered under Lend-Lease and manufactured by Grumman at Bethpage, New York. Other RN Avengers, the name incidentally being originally Tarpon, were built by General Motors Corporation, Eastern Aircraft Division, Trenton, New Jersey. (Grumman Corporation).

Mark No.	US Desig.	Company	Requisition	Contract	RAF Serials	US Serials
					JZ527–549	ex 45570–45592
					JZ550–572	ex 45843–45865
					JZ573–595	ex 46141–46163
					JZ596–618	ex 73136–73158
					JZ619–626	ex 73359–73366
					JZ627–634	ex 73467–73474
III	TBM-3		N-947	NOa(S)228	JZ635–746(112)	
					JZ651–658	ex 68328–68335
					JZ659–666	ex 68632–68639
					JZ667–680	ex 69140–69153
					JZ681–694	ex 69479–69492
					JZ721–733	ex 53171–53183
					JZ734–746	ex 53509–53521
					KE430–479(50)	
					KE430–479	ex 91229–91278
					KE480–539(60)	
					KE480–509	ex 91479–91508
IV	TBM-4		N-947	NOa(S)228	KE540–609(70)	Cancelled
I	TBF-1	Grumman		Not known	JT773 (1)	

AVENGER

In 1942, the General Motors Corporation, Eastern Aircraft Division, of Trenton, New Jersey, provided a second source for Avengers, due to growing production requirements. The version was designated TMB-1/3/4. The Grumman Aircraft Engineering Corporation located at Bethpage, Long Island, New York built the TBF- version of the Avenger. Most Avenger squadrons of the Fleet Air Arm operating in the Pacific theatre of operations, formed up in the USA and equipped with Avengers straight off the production lines. Some were modified before delivery by Blackburn Aircraft Limited who had a modification plant at Roosevelt Field, New York.

BALTIMORE Martin Model 187B

Mark No.	US Desig.	Company	Requisition	Contract	RAF Serials	US Serials
I	A-30	Martin			AG685–734(50)	None
II					AG735–834(100)	None
III					AG835–999(165)	None
					AH100–184(85)	None
IIIA					FA100–380(281)	41-27682–27962
IV	A-30A				FA381–674(294)	41-27963–28256
V					FW281–880(600)	43-8438–9037

Mk I to Mk III were direct purchase aircraft, whilst the IIIA and IV were Lend-Lease.

Mk VI designation was reserved for a Coastal Command version of the Mk V which was not proceeded with. A single Baltimore V was transferred to the US Navy as Bu.No.09804 and it may have been FW880 known to have been operated by the US Navy.

AG685–AH184 AG710 not delivered, 750 retained in Canada. AG685, 686, 775, 791, 844, 845, 849, 855, 859, 867, 868, 872, 874, 883, 888–891, 895, 897, 908, 969–973, 985–990, 993, 996, 997, total of thirty-five lost at sea in transit. Many shipped direct to the Middle East to serve with SAAF units.

FA100–674 FA102–104, 106, 111, 117, 120, 125, 128, 135, 140, 155, 174, 177, 198, 205, 213, 214, 218, 243, 330, 334, 340, 354, 363, 487 crashed before delivery. FA385, 435, 466 to Royal Navy.
FA415, 420, 432, 439, 464, 472, 503, 504, 553, 560, 592, 607, 630 to Italian Air Force. Main delivery to Middle East, with some to SAAF and Royal Hellenic Air Force squadrons under RAF command. FA187 to RCAF.

FW281–880 FW288, 323, 337, 409, 511, 664 crashed before delivery. FW326, 352, 356, 365, 456, 527, 746 to Royal Navy. Transfers from RAF to French, Italian and Turkish Air Forces.

FA163 completed 102 operational flights with RAF over Tunisia, Sicily and Italy.

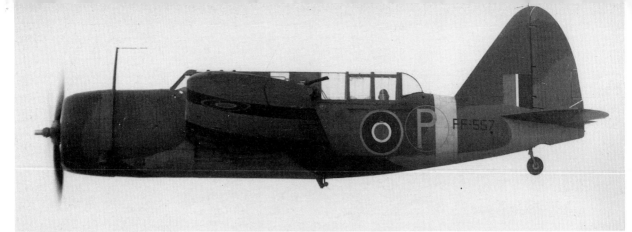

Many of the Lend-Lease Brewster Bermuda I dive-bombers delivered to the RAF were converted as target-tugs. Depicted is the prototype Bermuda TT.1 FF-557 seen with striped under surface including the wings and carrying a (P) marking. It was fully evaluated at the A&AEE Boscombe Down and the photo is dated 12 February 1943. (Via Bruce Robertson).

BERMUDA Brewster Model 340

Mark No.	US Desig.	Company	Requisition	Contract	RAF Serials	US Serials
I	A-34	Brewster			FF419–868 (450)	
I	SB2A-1	Brewster			FF869–999 (131)	
I	SB2A-1	Brewster			FG100–268 (269)	

Many conversions to target-tugs of which FF457 was the prototype. Main deliveries to the UK but no record after FF633. FF568/718/732 went to the RCAF in 1943. Produced at Brewsters Johnsville, Bucks County, Pennsylvania factory. Purchased by British Purchasing Commission.

BOSTON Douglas DB-7. DB-7A. DB-7B.

Mark No.	US Desig.	Company	Requisition	Contract	RAF Serials	US Serials
I		Douglas	Ex-Belgian contract		AE457–472(16)	
I			Ex-French contract		AX848–851(4)	
I			Ex-French contract		AX920–975(56)	
I			Ex-French contract		BB890–912(23)	
I			Ex-French contract		BD110–127(18)	
I			Ex-French Air Force		DK274–277(4)	
II			Ex-French contract		AH430–529(100)	
II					AH740 (1)	
II					AW392–414(23)	
II					AX910–918(9)	
III					W8252–8401(150)	
III					Z2155–2304(150)	
III		Boeing			AL263–336(74)	
III		Boeing			AL337–502(166)	
III		Douglas			AL668–907(240)	
III			Ex-Soviet Air Force		HK869–892(24)	
			Ex-Soviet Air Force		HK894–903(10)	
III			Ex-Soviet Air Force		HK912, HK918(2)	
III			Ex-Soviet Air Force		HK921–924(4)	
III			Ex-Soviet Air Force		HK934, HK935(2)	
III			Ex-Soviet Air Force		HK960–972(13)	
IIIA	A-20C				BZ196–352(157)	

Impressive factory line-up at the Douglas plant located at El Segundo showing completed RAF Boston III aircraft awaiting delivery. They include W8262, 8253, 8258 and 8257 from a batch of 150 W8252–8401 and designated Douglas DB-7B's. The Boston was also manufactured at Long Beach and Santa Monica by Douglas. The first Boston IIIs were shipped to the UK during the summer of 1941. Many were converted from bomber to intruder versions. (Via Philip Jarrett).

Mark No.	US Desig.	Company	Requisition	Contract	RAF Serials	US Serials
IIIA	A-20C	Douglas			BZ355–378(24)	
IIIA	A-20C				BZ381–399(19)	
IV	A-20G				BZ400–568(169)	
V	A-20H				BZ580–669(90)	

BOSTON

Many converted to Havoc configuration with Turbinlite or Long Aerial Mine modification.

AE457–472 AE461 to USAAF, 471 to Royal Navy. *BB890–912* BB891, 896 to USAAF, 902 trainer version, 906 to Royal Navy. *BD110–127* BD121, 122 to Royal Navy. *DK274–277* all arrived in damaged condition so scrapped. *AH430–529* Ten transferred to USAAF. AH430 crashed in US. *AH740* replacement aircraft. *AW392–414* AW394, 400, 403 transferred to USAAF. *AX910–918* French order. AX913 fitted as Turbinlite and with Long Aerial Mine and later transferred to USAAF. *W8252–8401* W8311 not delivered. W8252, 8270, 8316 lost in transit. W8255, 8274, 8280, 8282, 8300, 8309, 8328, 8341, 8352, 8364, 8369, 8392, 8393, 8396 to Royal Navy. *Z2155–2304* Z2169, 2184, 2270 to Royal Navy. Z2268, 2272 not delivered. Z2200, 2250, 2268–2272 to USAAF. *AL263–502* AL265, 267, 281, 282, 287, 292, 294, 295, 297, 298, 300, 303–316, 318–320 shipped direct US to Russia. Many to USAAF. Only thirty-six reached the RAF. *AL668–907* Total of seventy-four to USAAF, forty shipped to Russia. A number of Mk III non-standard aircraft were released by the Russian Commission at Abadan for use by the RAF in the Middle East (Western Desert) in exchange for Spitfires. These included **HK869–892, 894-903, 912, 921–924, 934, 935, 960–972.** HK918 to Royal Navy. *BZ196–669* BZ647 crashed in US before delivery. BZ588–590, 593, 597, 601, 602, 663, 666, 669 held in Canada. Some transfers to the USAAF retained RAF serial, examples AX922, AH438, 454, AL381-398, 442-452, 672, 722, 808. AL672 to RCAF, c/n 3604 returned to RAF. Mk IIIA BZ385 ex-42–33184 RCAF; Mk IV BZ410 RCAF.

BUFFALO Brewster Model 339 and 439

Mark No.	US Desig.	Company	Requisition	Contract	RAF Serials	US Serials
I	F2A-2	Brewster			W8131–8250(120)	
I	F2A-2	Brewster			AN168–217(50)	
I	F2A-3	Brewster	Ex-Belgian contract		AS410–437(28)	
I	F2A-2	Brewster			AX811–820(10)	
I	F2A-2	Brewster			BB450(1)	

Mainly shipped direct from US to Singapore. Used by RAF and RN.

AS410 batch included aircraft from Belgian contract. BB450 to RN in September 1940.

W8131 ex-US civil NX147B.

The RAF version of the Brewster Model 339 corresponded to the US Navy F2A-2 and was named Buffalo. A later version of the Model 439 was ordered by the Belgian government but never delivered. Twenty-eight of these were merged with the original British Purchasing Commission contract and allocated serials AS410–437. Shipped to the UK in July 1940 the fighters were assembled at Burtonwood. At least 15 were in use by Royal Navy squadrons. Depicted is an excellent air-to-air photo of AS417. (Via Philip Jarrett).

CARIBOU Bell Model 12. See P-39 Airacobra

This Catalina GR.IIIA (PBY-5A) FP-533 ex US Navy BuNo.05006 was delivered under Lend-Lease in April 1942 initially serving with No.199 Squadron based on Lough Erne. It later went to No.330 (Norwegian) Squadron, then to No.4 and No.131 OTU. It was struck-off-charge on 3 August 1944. It was from a batch of 12 FP525–536 with FP534 being transferred to the US Navy in the United Kingdom. (Via Bruce Robertson).

CATALINA Consolidated Model 28

Mark No.	US Desig.	Company	Requisition	Contract	RAF Serials	US Serials
	PBY-5	Consolidated			P9630(1)	
					PBY-3 AM258(1)	
I					W8405–8434(30)	
					Z2134–2153(20)	
					AH530–569(40)	
					AJ154–162(9)	
IB	PBY-5B		148	LL 88477	FP100–249(150)	None
			7952	LL 88477	FP250–324(125)	None
II	PBY-5				AM264–269(6)	
IIA	PBY-5				VA701–736(36)	
					VA737–750(14)	Cancelled
III	PBY-5A		10772	N-77713	FP525–533(9)	04985–04990(6)
					FP535–536(2)	05004–05006(3)
						05010, 05012(2)
IVA	PBY-5		N-8	LL 91876	JX200–269(70)	None
					JX570–585(16)	08117(1)
					JV925–361(11)	08211–08225(15)
						08532–08534(3)
						08542–08549(8)
IVB	PB2B-1	Boeing	N-8	NOa(S)1735	JX270–344(75)	None
					JX345–349(5)	72992–72996(5)
					JX350–361(12)	73001–73012(12)
					JX362–373(12)	73017–73028(12)
					JX374–383(10)	73033–73042(10)
					JX384–389(6)	73049–73054(6)
					JX390–423(34)	73061–73094(34)
					JX424–437(14)	73099–73112(14)
IVB	PB2B-1		N-8	NOa(S)782	JX586–599(14)	44188–44201(14)
					JX600–610(11)	44206–44216(11)
					JX611–613(3)	44217–44219(3)
					JX614–617(4)	44224–44227(4)

VI	PB2B-2	Boeing	JX618–627(10)	44228–44237(10)
			JX628–662(35)	44246–44280(35)
			JZ828–841(14)	44281–44294(14)
			JZ842–859(18)	44295–44312(18)

Mk III FP534 transferred to US Navy in United Kingdom as Bu.No. 05008.

RCAF Mk I W8430–8432: Z2134, 2136–2140, DP202.

    Mk IB FP290–297

    Mk IVA JX206, 207, 209, 211–213, 217, 219. JX571, 572, 579, 580.

CATALINA

Model 28 flying boat. Following the evaluation of a Model 28-5 (PBY-5) in July 1939 with the serial P9630, orders were placed by the British Purchasing Commission for 109 aircraft to be designated Catalina I. These were basically PBY-5s with six 0.303 inch guns – one in the bow, four in two beam blisters, and one aft of the hull step. Power was by two 1,200 hp Wright R-1830-SIC3-G engines. The Mk IA was the first Canso model for the RCAF, fourteen being delivered. The Mk IB was the Lend-Lease PBY-5B. The Mk II was similar to the Mk I but did differ in equipment. The Mk IIA was similar but built in Canada. The Mk IIIA was a PBY-5A variant for use on the North Atlantic Ferry Service. Other Lend-Lease models were the Mk IVA (PBY-5), Mk IVB (PB2B-1) and Mk VI (PB2B-2), whilst the Mk V designation was reserved for the PBN–1 but not taken up. A few Mk IVB were converted for air-sea rescue duties as the ASR IVB. The RAF also took delivery of an early Model 28-3 (PBY-3) ex-US civil NC777, allocated the serial AM258, later SM706. Several Catalinas were handed over to BOAC.

P9630 delivered to UK in July 1939 and sunk during testing in February 1940.

AH530–569 AH534 to RAAF. AH543 interned in Portugal. AH563 to BOAC as G-AGDA.

AM258 ex-NC777 *Guba*. Serial allocated in error, to SM706.

FP100–324 Delivered to Scottish Aviation at Prestwick, then to Saunders Roe at Beaumaris, Anglesey for processing for RAF service.

    FP128, 130, 132, 137, 156–158, 166–170, 186–190, 196–200, 206–208, 210, 216–220 not delivered. FP135, 138 lost in transit.

    FP221 became G-AGFL, 244 became G-AGFM for BOAC.

    FP325 (not listed) lost on operations 21 September 1942. Duplicates Anson series.

VA701–750 built by Canadian Vickers. Thirty-six for RCAF '9701–9736' ex-RAF VA701–736. Following to RAAF VA701, 702, 708 (A24–25), 710 (A24–22), 711 (A24–26), 717 (A24–27), 730 (A24–23), 733 (A24–24), 734 (A24–19), 735 (A24–20), 736 (A24–21). Only twenty-two to RAF. VA719, 721, 724 lost on or before delivery. VA737–750 cancelled.

JX200–437 JX200–269 built by Consolidated of which JX228, 230–237 diverted to RNZAF. JX270–437 built by Boeing, Canada. JX287 to BOAC as G-AGKS.

JX570–662 JX575 to G-AGID, 577 to G-AGIE with BOAC. JX628, 629, 632, 634, 635, were delivered to the RAF, majority of remainder to RAAF.

JZ828–859 No records of delivery to RAF. Fourteen to RAAF. Listed in some records as cancelled order.

Early Catalina delivery flights

25 Oct 1940 First Catalina, AM262, delivered from North America to United Kingdom. Captain-navigator I. G. Ross, a Canadian with BOAC. Remainder of crew unknown.

17 Jan 1941 First Catalina AM269 delivery from Bermuda to United Kingdom. Captain-navigator Flt Lt G. Fleming, a Canadian with the RAF; co-pilot Jim Meikle RAF; radio operators F. C. Ayre, R. H. T. Hodgson, both Canadian civilians; flight engineers Latimer and Clark seconded from the Royal Navy Fleet Air Arm.

17 Jan 1941 First Catalina AM264 delivery from Halifax, Nova Scotia. Captain-navigator Flt Lt W. Gautrey RAF; co-pilot D. Gentry, an American civilian; radio operators E. L. Hagger ex-Imperial Airways, A. F. Stark ex-Department of Transport; flight engineer Leading Aircraftman W. Riley RAF.

2 Feb 1941 Second Catalina AM265 delivery out of Halifax, Nova Scotia. Captain-navigator L. L. 'Slim' Jones, a Canadian in the RAF; co-pilot J. Weber, an American civilian; radio operators Glover and Whitney, Canadian civilians; flight engineer Stewart, RAF.

5 Feb 1941 Second Catalina AM266 out of Bermuda. Captain C. Pangborn, an American civilian. Remainder of crew unknown.

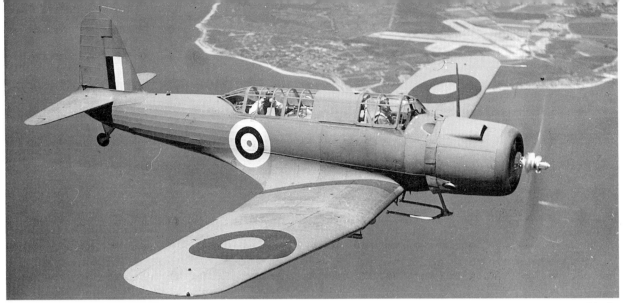

The Vought-Sikorsky Division of the United Aircraft Corporation, based at Stratford in Connecticut, were responsible for production of the carrier-based scout and dive-bomber designated SB2U- and named Vindicator with the US Navy and Chesapeake with the British Fleet Air Arm. Depicted is a British marked Chesapeake seen on flight test from the Vought factory. Despite the markings it still awaits its serial number (Via Philip Jarrett).

CHESAPEAKE Vought-Sikorsky Model V-156B-1

Mark No.	US Desig.	Company	Requisition	Contract	RAF Serials	US Serials
I	SB2U-3	Vought-Sikorsky			AL908–957(50)	

Assembled at Burtonwood Aircraft Repair Depot in 1941. Delivered to the Royal Navy at Lee-on-Solent. Residue of a French contract. Relegated to training duties with the Fleet Air Arm.

CLEVELAND Curtiss CW-77

Mark No.	US Desig.	Company	Requisition	Contract	RAF Serials	US Serials
Mk I	SBC-4	Curtiss			AS467–471(5)	NXC48/49/51/53/54

From a French order of ninety export versions of which fifty were ex-US Navy including the five listed which went to the RAF. Unsuitable for combat and became instructional airframes.

It is most unusual to see RAF aircraft flying after the allocation of a ground instruction serial as seen on Curtiss Cleveland I 2669M ex AS469 in flight after delivery to RAF Little Rissington. They were assembled at Burtonwood during the summer of 1940. Three of the five supplied to the RAF received 'M' serials – AS467 2668M: AS469 2669M and AS470 2785M. (Via Ray Sturtivant).

An unusual Lend-Lease acquisition was a single Curtiss Model CW-20A transport which was the prototype of the military Commando transport used by the USAAF in June 1941. It was priced at $361,556 and designated C-55 41-21041. It was returned to Curtiss and sold to BOAC in September 1941 being registered G-AGDI and named St Louis.

COMMANDO Curtiss CW-20

Mark No.	US Desig.	Company	Requisition	Contract	RAF Serials	US Serials
	C-46/C-55	Curtiss	2991	AC-15802	G-AGDI(1)	41-21041

Sold to British Overseas Airways Corporation in September 1941 and named *St Louis*. Scrapped in United Kingdom 29 October 1943.

CORNELL Fairchild M-62A, M-62A-3

Mark No.	US Desig.	Company	Requisition	Contract	RAF Serials	US Serials
I	PT-26	Fairchild	5472	DA-802	FH651–999(349) FJ650–700(51)	42-14299–14498(200) 42-15330–15529(200)
I	PT-26	Fairchild	5472	AC-41303	EW341–610(270)	44-19288–19557(270)
II	PT-26A	Fleet	40043	AC-30110	FV100–516(417)	42-65585–66001(417)
II	PT-26A	Fleet	40043	AC-30109	FW881–980(100)	42-71247–71346(100)
II	PT-26A	Fleet	65/40/4093	AC-239	FV517–734(218) FX100–197(98) FW981–999(19)	None None None
II	PT-26B	Fleet	45000	AC-40057	FZ198–427(230) FZ699–718(20)	43-36248–36497(250)

Notes: Supplied to Canada, India, S. Rhodesia and South Africa. FZ699–718 (20) to Norway via RCAF. FW990–997 (8) returned to USAAF. FH681/779/954 crashed before delivery. All to Canada except FH651/710/1/2/3/4/766/7/8/9/770. FJ650–700 ex-USAAF to Canada, 852 PT-26A and 250 PT-26B built in Canada by Fleet. FV661–734 taken over by RCAF. Deliveries to Canada and India.

Retained in Canada with RCAF EW341–490, FH652–999, FJ650–699, FV653, 661–734, FX166–197.

RCAF Mk I EW341–490, FH652–680, 682–709, 715–778, 780–953, 955–999, FJ650–699.

MkII FV653, 661–734, FX166–197.

Notes: EW341–490 c/n T4-4400–T4-4549, FH652 c/n T42-4001 ex-42-14300, FV653 c/n 1021, FV661–734 c/n 1029–1102, FX166–197 c/n FA997–FA1028. FH681, FH779, FH954 crashed in US before delivery. FH908 ground instruction aircraft as A559.

RCAF ex-RAF serials: FT542–931 to '14381–14670', FT542 ex-42-70957, FT931 ex-42-71246, FV100–464 to '15001–15365' c/n T4-4670–T4-6034, FV100 ex-42-65585, FV449–464 ex-42-65734–42-65749, FW881–930 to '16601–16650' ex-42-71247–42-71296, FW910 c/n FA516, FZ197 ex-43-36247 c/n FC251 to RCAF '10750', FZ213–242 to '10766–10795', FZ248–354 to '10801–10907', FZ261 ex-43-36311, FZ295 c/n FA430, FZ305 ex-43-36355, FZ334 c/n FA568, FZ354 ex-43-36404.

On Thursday 21 October 1943 Fleet Aircraft Limited, Fort Erie, Ontario, Canada celebrated the completion of its 1,000th aircraft of the Fairchild Cornell type. This was '10835' for the RCAF ex-FZ282 under a Lend-Lease contract. Taken on charge on 2 November 1943. It was flight-tested by Tom Williams, chief test pilot. It was christened *Spirit of Fleet*.

Massive orders for the Fairchild PT-26 Cornell trainer in 1941 not only doubled the company's production facilities, but exceeded the capacity at Hagerstown, Maryland. This resulted in a large number of Lend-Lease Cornells being manufactured by Fleet at Fort Erie, Canada these being designated PT-26A and PT-26B. Depicted is a Fairchild-built PT-26 Cornell FJ695. (Via Kent A Mitchell).

CORONADO Consolidated

Mark No.	US Desig.	Company	Requisition	Contract	RAF Serials	US Serials
GR1	PB2Y-3B	Consolidated	152	LL85402	JX470–501(32)	

Ten only delivered, JX470/471/472/486/490/494/495/496/498/501.

Based briefly at Beaumaris and intended for Coastal Command. Switched to Transport Command early in 1944 as transatlantic transports with 231 Squadron.

LEND-LEASE AIRCRAFT IN WORLD WAR II

CORSAIR Vought-Sikorsky Model V-166B

Mark No.	US Desig.	Company	Requisition	Contract	RAF Serials	US Serials
I	F4U-1	United	N-2	NOa(S)198	JT100–194(95)	18122–18191(70)
II	F4U-1D	United	N-2	NOa(S)198	JT195–704(510)	
III	F3A-1	Brewster	N-1113	NOa(S)172	JS469–888(420)	04689–04774(86)
					JT963–972(10)	08550–08797(248)
						11067–11162(96)
IV	FG-1D	Goodyear	N-1450	NOa(S)1871	KD161–560(400)	14592–14991(400)
					KD561–867(307)	76139–76445(307)
					KD868–999(132)	87949–87998(50)
					KE100–117(18)	88134–88158(25)
					KE310–429(120)	88269–88293(25)
						88404–88428(25)
						92171–92195(25)

To speed up production contracts were placed with Brewster Aeronautical Corporation, Long Island City, New York; Goodyear Aircraft Corporation, Akron, Ohio and Chance-Vought Division, United Aircraft Corporation (later Chance-Vought Aircraft Inc.), Dallas, Texas and Vought-Sikorsky Division, United Aircraft Corporation, Stratford, Connecticut. Main deliveries to Blackburn Aircraft Ltd, Roosevelt Field, New York for modification.

Excellent photo showing six Corsair II aircraft, including JT187 '3BD' and JT235 '3BB' seen in starboard echelon formation. The unit is No.738 Squadron which was formed at Quonset Point, Rhode Island, USA on 1 February 1943 with a variety of aircraft supplied under Lend-Lease including Corsairs. It provided advanced carrier training for RN pilots who had trained at various US Navy air stations. They were taught British flying methods, and instruction on map reading, flight formation, simulated forced and dummy deck landings, navigation and night flying. The 'JT' batch of Corsairs included 605 Mk.I/II (F4U-1/1D) JT100–704 delivered to Blackburn Aircraft in the USA for modification to Royal Navy standard. (Via Peter M Bowers).

The Cessna T-50 originally produced in 1939 as a commercial five-seat light transport, was adopted in 1940 for use as a conversion trainer for the huge Commonwealth Joint Air Training Plan in Canada where the type was known as the Crane. Power plant change to 245 hp Jacobs R-775-9s in 1941 changed the designation to AT-17. Equipment changes produced the designations AT-17A, B and C. A total of 550 AT-17A aircraft went to Canada under Lend-Lease initially with RAF serials FJ100–649. Depicted is JF-186 which in Canada became RCAF '8837'. (Via Philip Jarrett).

CRANE Cessna Model T-50

Mark No.	US Desig.	Company	Requisition	Contract	RAF Serials	US Serials
IA	AT-17A	Cessna	6226	DA-785	FJ100–649(550)	42-13617–14166(550)

Transferred to the RCAF but retaining RAF serials. One source quotes identities as follows: FJ100–239 ex-42-13617–13756, FJ248–289 ex-42-13765–13806. Used in the huge Empire Air Training Scheme (EATS).

RCAF Mk IA   FJ100–199(100) c/n 2301–2400 given RCAF serial .8751–8850.

FJ200–239   c/n 2401–2440

FJ248–289   c/n 2449–2490.

FJ200 ex-42-13717, FJ207 ex-42-13724, FJ235 ex-42-13752.

CUB Piper J3C-65

Mark No.	US Desig.	Company	Requisition	Contract	RAF Serials	US Serials
I	L-4B	Piper	40247	AC-30126	FR886–889(4) HK936–939(4) VM286(1)	43-743, 750, 751, 787 Serials as above 43-630(1)

Ex-USAAF L-4B for evaluation. VM286 ex-L-4B-PI 43-630 also used by RAF.

One of the three US commercial lightplanes selected by the US Army in 1941 for evaluation was the Piper J3C-65 Cub which was eventually produced in large numbers. Depicted is L-4B Cub 43-1404 one of four known to have been evaluated by the RAF in May 1943, but it still carries US markings. The type was used for artillery spotting, gun-laying and general front line liaison duties. (Via Bruce Robertson).

DAKOTA Douglas Commercial Three (DC-3)

Mark No.	US Desig.	Company	Requisition	Contract	RAF Serials	US Serials
I	C-47	Douglas	2849	DA-167	FD768(1)	
			2849	AC-20669	FD769–788(20)	
			7204	DA-1043	FD789–818(30)	
					HK993(1)	
II	C-53		1050	AC-18393/20667		41-20084,-20085, -20099,-20105,-20115, -20117, 42-6479, -6481, -6502(9)
					FG857(1)	
					FJ709 FJ712(2)	
					HK867(1)	
					HK893(1) Built from spares.	
					TJ168–170(3)	
III	C-47A		2849, 7204	AC-20669-1	FD819–967(149)	
					FL503–543(41)	
			7204	AC-28405	FL544–652(109)	
					FZ548–698(151)	
					KG310–729(420)	
			7204	AC-40652	KG730–769(40)	
					KG770–809(40)	
IV	C-47B		7204	AC-40652	KJ801–999(199)	
					KK100–220(121)	
					KN200–201(2)	
IV	C-47B		43194	AC-40652	KN202–284(83)	
			43194	AC-2032	KN285–701(417)	
					KP208–279(72)	
III	C-47A				TS422–427(6)	
					TS431–436(6)	
					TP187(1)	
IV	C-47B				TP181(1)	

RAF Serials	USAF Serials	RAF Serials	USAF Serials	RAF Serials	USAF Serials	RAF Serials	USAF Serials
FD768	41-38564	FD879-898	42-23669-88	FL570-571	42-92201-02	FZ554-581	42-92303-28
FD769-773	42-5635-39	FD899-908	42-23759-68	FL572-580	42-92204-12	FZ582-622	42-92347-83
FD774-788	42-5650-64	FD909-928	42-23814-33	FL581-589	42-92213-21	FZ623-631	42-92384-92
FD789-798	42-32817-26	FD929-935	42-23900-06	FL590-598	42-92222-30	FZ632-649	42-92402-10
HK993	41-38625	FD936	42-23908	FL599-607	42-92231-39	FZ650-658	42-92411-19
FJ709	42-6479	FD937-938	42-23973-74	FL608-616	42-92240-48	FZ659-663	42-92420-24
FJ710	42-6481	FD939-958	42-23998-17	FL617	42-92249	FZ664	42-108836
FJ711	42-6485	FD959-967	42-24083-91	FL618-623	42-92258-63	FZ665	42-108839
FJ712	42-47371	FL503	42-24092	FL624	42-92266	FZ666	42-92445
HK867	42-6457	FL504-513	42-24160-69	FL625-626	42-92267-68	FZ667	42-92446
TJ167	42-6478	FL514-533	42-24235-54	FL627-630	42-92270-73	FZ668-672	42-92451-55
FD819-828	42-23319-28	FL534-543	42-24347-56	FL631	42-92275	FZ673	42-108841
FD829-838	42-23373-82	FL544-548	42-92136-40	FL632-640	42-92276-84	FZ674-675	42-92463-64
FD839-858	42-23445-64	FL549-557	42-92141-49	FL641-649	42-92285-93	FZ676-678	42-92467-69
FD859-868	42-23543-52	FL558-566	42-92150-58	FL650-652	42-92294-96	FZ679-685	42-92472-77
FD869-878	42-23625-34	FL567-569	42-92161-63	FZ548-553	42-92297-02	FZ686	42-92479
						FZ687	42-92481

RAF Serials	USAF Serials	RAF Serials	USAF Serials	RAF Serials	USAF Serials	RAF Serials	USAF Serials
FZ688-692	42-92485-89	KG424-432	42-92636-44	KG546-554	42-93149-57	KG662-670	42-93554-62
FZ693-698	42-92492-97	KG433	42-108862	KG555	42-108919	KG671	42-108964
KG310-315	42-92498-02	KG434-442	42-92645-53	KG556	42-93158	KG672-680	42-93608-16
KG317-332	42-92506-19	KG443	42-108863	KG557-565	42-93257-65	KG681	42-108970
KG333-334	42-92522-23	KG444-452	42-92654-62	KG566	42-108931	KG682-690	42-93617-25
KG337-340	42-92533-36	KG453	42-108864	KG567-575	42-93266-74	KG691	42-108971
KG341	42-108850	KG454-462	42-92663-71	KG576	42-108932	KG692-700	42-93626-34
KG342-350	42-92537-45	KG463	42-108865	KG577-584	42-93393-00	KG701	42-108972
KG351	42-108851	KG464-466	42-92672-74	KG585	42-108946	KG702-710	42-93635-43
KG352	42-92546	KG467-475	42-92744-52	KG586-594	42-93401-09	KG711	42-108973
KG353-358	42-92549-54	KG476	42-108874	KG595-596	42-93417-18	KG712-720	42-93644-52
KG359	42-108852	KG477-485	42-92753-61	KG597	42-108948	KG721	42-108974
KG360-368	42-92555-63	KG486	42-108875	KG598-606	42-93419-27	KG722-723	42-93653-54
KG369	42-108853	KG487	42-92950	KG607-608	42-93453-54	KG724-726	42-93776-78
KG370-378	42-92564-72	KG488-496	42-92951-59	KG609	42-108952	KG727	42-108988
KG379	42-108854	KG497-505	42-92960-68	KG610-618	42-93455-63	KG728	42-93779
KG380	42-92573	KG506	42-92969	KG619	42-108953	KG729	42-93783
KG381-387	42-92593-99	KG507-513	42-93043-49	KG620-627	42-93465-72	KG730-769	43-48013-52
KG388	42-108857	KG514	42-108907	KG628	42-108954	KG770-809	43-48186-25
KG389-396	42-92600-07	KG515-523	42-93050-58	KG629-636	42-93473-80	KJ801-839	43-48324-62
KG397-402	42-92612-17	KG524	42-108908	KG637-645	42-93527-35	KJ840	43-48364
KG403	42-108859	KG525-526	42-93059-60	KG646	42-108961	KJ841-842	43-48444-45
KG404-412	42-92618-26	KG527-534	42-93132-39	KG647-650	42-93536-39	KJ843-879	43-48521-57
KG413	42-108860	KG535	42-108917	KG651	42-108962	KJ880-882	43-48564-66
KG414-422	42-92627-35	KG536-544	42-93140-48	KG652-660	42-93545-53	KJ883-893	43-48652-62
KG423	42-108861	KG545	42-108918	KG661	42-108963	KJ894-912	43-48664-82

Lend-Lease Dakota deliveries included a number of Dakota II ex C-53 Skytrooper with the single fuselage door and small cargo door aft. They were used for VIP duties and depicted is TJ170 built at Long Beach and seen in the Western Desert during World War 2. The two VIPs walking from the Dakota are Air Marshals Sir Arthur Tedder and Sir Arthur Coningham. (IWM CNA 1792).

RAF Serials	USAF Serials	RAF Serials	USAF Serials	RAF Serials	USAF Serials	RAF Serials	USAF Serials
KJ913-915	43-48819-21	KN244-249	43-49853-58	KN361-362	44-76396-97	KN519	44-76728
KJ916-919	43-48823-26	KN250-251	43-49860-61	KN363-365	44-76399-01	KN520	44-76730
KJ920-923	43-48828-31	KN252-253	43-49917-18	KN366-368	44-76403-05	KN521-522	44-76732-33
KJ924-927	43-48833-36	KN254	43-49920	KN369-371	44-76407-09	KN523-524	44-76736-37
KJ928-931	43-48838-41	KN255-257	43-49922-24	KN372-374	44-76411-13	KN525-526	44-76740-41
KJ932-935	43-48843-46	KN258-261	43-49926-29	KN375-377	44-76415-17	KN527	44-76743
KJ936-939	43-48848-51	KN262-265	43-49931-34	KN378-380	44-76419-21	KN528-529	44-76746-47
KJ940-942	43-48853-55	KN266-267	43-49937-38	KN381-387	44-76423-29	KN530-531	44-76750-51
KJ943-965	43-48974-96	KN268-270	43-49940-42	KN388	44-76431	KN532-533	44-76754-55
KJ966-969	43-48998-01	KN271-273	43-49944-46	KN389	44-76477	KN534	44-76757
KJ970-972	43-49003-05	KN274-277	43-49948-50	KN390-395	44-76479-84	KN535	44-76760
KJ973-976	43-49148-51	KN278-280	43-49953-55	KN396-402	44-76487-93	KN536	44-76775
KJ977-980	43-49153-56	KN281	43-49957	KN403-409	44-76495-01	KN537-538	44-76805-06
KJ981-985	43-49158-62	KN282-283	43-49959-60	KN410-416	44-76503-09	KN539-540	44-76808-09
KJ986-999	43-49164-77	KN284	43-49962	KN417-420	44-76511-14	KN541	44-76811
KK100-102	43-49178-80	KN285-287	44-76200-02	KN421-422	44-76516-17	KN542-543	44-76814-15
KK103-107	43-49292-96	KN288-289	44-76204-05	KN423-427	44-76519-23	KN544-545	44-76817-18
KK108-111	43-49298-01	KN290-292	44-76207-09	KN428-436	44-76525-33	KN546-547	44-76820-21
KK112-115	43-49303-06	KN293-295	44-76211-13	KN437-443	44-76535-41	KN548-549	44-76824-25
KK116-119	43-49308-11	KN296-299	44-76215-18	KN444-445	44-76580-81	KN550	44-76827
KK120-123	43-49313-16	KN300-302	44-76220-22	KN446-449	44-76584-87	KN551	44-76829
KK124-127	43-49318-21	KN303-305	44-76224-26	KN450-453	44-76589-92	KN552-554	44-76831-33
KK128-131	43-49323-26	KN306-307	44-76228-29	KN454-457	44-76594-97	KN555-556	44-76835-36
KK132	43-49328	KN308	44-76255	KN458-464	44-76599-05	KN557-558	44-76839-40
KK133-136	43-49453-56	KN309	44-76260	KN465-469	44-76607-11	KN559-561	44-76842-44
KK137-141	43-49458-62	KN310	44-76262	KN470-471	44-76613-14	KN562-563	44-76846-47
KK142-149	43-49464-71	KN311-312	44-76280-81	KN472-473	44-76616-17	KN564-565	44-76850-51
KK150-162	43-49473-85	KN313-315	44-76283-85	KN474-479	44-76619-24	KN566	44-76853
KK163-181	43-49593-11	KN316-318	44-76287-89	KN480-485	44-76626-31	KN567-571	44-76855-59
KK182-185	43-49618-21	KN319	44-76291	KN486-488	44-76633-35	KN572	44-76862
KK186-192	43-49623-29	KN320	44-76293	KN489-490	44-76673-74	KN573-574	44-76864-65
KK193-196	43-49708-11	KN321-323	44-76295-97	KN491-492	44-76677-78	KN575-576	44-76867-88
KK197-200	43-49713-16	KN324-326	44-76299-01	KN493-494	44-76681-82	KN577-578	44-76871-72
KK201-204	43-49718-21	KN327-329	44-76303-05	KN495	44-76684	KN579	44-76875
KK205-208	43-49723-26	KN330-332	44-76307-09	KN496-498	44-76687-89	KN580	44-76878
KK209-212	43-49728-31	KN333-335	44-76311-13	KN499-500	44-76692-93	KN581	44-76879
KK213-216	43-49733-36	KN336	44-76317	KN501	44-76695	KN582	44-76881
KK217-220	43-49738-41	KN337-339	44-76319-21	KN502-503	44-76698-99	KN583	44-76883
KN200-201	43-49743-44	KN340-342	44-76323-25	KN504-505	44-76702-03	KN584	44-76885
KN202-204	43-49805-07	KN343-345	44-76327-29	KN506-507	44-76706-07	KN585-587	44-76887-89
KN205-209	43-49809-13	KN346-348	44-76331-33	KN508-509	44-76709-10	KN588-591	44-76891-94
KN210-220	43-49815-25	KN349-351	44-76379-81	KN510-511	44-76713-14	KN592	44-76896
KN221-225	43-49827-31	KN352-354	44-76383-85	KN512-513	44-76717-18	KN593	44-76898
KN226-237	43-49833-44	KN355-357	44-76387-89	KN514-515	44-76720-21	KN594	44-76901
KN238-243	43-49846-51	KN358-360	44-76391-93	KN516-518	44-76724-26	KN595-596	44-76903-04

RAF Serials	USAF Serials	RAF Serials	USAF Serials	RAF Serials	USAF Serials	RAF Serials	USAF Serials
KN597-598	44-76906-07	KN644-646	44-77002-04	KN682-684	44-77060-62	KP232-236	44-77185-89
KN599-607	44-76910-18	KN647	44-77006	KN685-686	44-77064-65	KP237-279	44-77207-49
KN608-609	44-76920-21	KN648-649	44-77008-09	KN687-689	44-77067-69	TS422	42-100882
KN610	44-76923	KN650-651	44-77011-12	KN690-691	44-77071-72	TS423	42-100884
KN611	44-76925	KN652	44-77014	KN692-694	44-77074-76	TS424	42-100887
KN612-616	44-76927-31	KN653-654	44-77016-17	KN695-697	44-77078-80	TS425	42-100890
KN617-618	44-76933-34	KN655-656	44-77020-21	KN698-700	44-77082-84	TS426	43-15103
KN619-620	44-76937-38	KN657	44-77023	KN701	44-77086	TS427	43-15085
KN621-622	44-76940-41	KN658-659	44-77025-26	KP208	44-77087	TS431	43-15147
KN623-626	44-76944-47	KN660	44-77028	KP209-211	44-77089-91	TS432	42-100898
KN627-628	44-76949-50	KN661-664	44-77030-33	KP212-213	44-77093-94	TS433	43-15113
KN629-631	44-76953-55	KN665-666	44-77036-37	KP214-217	44-77096-99	TS434	43-15108
KN632	44-76957	KN667-669	44-77039-41	KP218-219	44-77101-02	TS435	43-15100
KN633	44-76985	KN670-671	44-77043-44	KP220-222	44-77104-06	TS436	42-100886
KN634-636	44-76987-89	KN672-673	44-77046-47	KP223-224	44-77108-09	TP187	42-92271
KN637	44-76991	KN674-675	44-77049-50	KP225-227	44-77111-13		
KN638-641	44-76993-96	KN676-678	44-77052-54	KP228-230	44-77115-17		
KN642-643	44-76999-00	KN679-681	44-77056-58	KP231	44-77119		

DAKOTA

RCAF Mk III FL598, 615, 616, 618, 621, 636, 650, FZ557, 558, 571, 575, 581, 583, 584, 586, 596, 634, 635, 669, 671, 678, 692, 694, 695, KG312, 317, 320, 330, 337, 345, 350, 354, 368, 382, 389, 394, 395, 400, 403, 414, 416, 423, 430, 441, 455, 479, 485, 486, 526, 545, 557, 559, 562, 563, 568, 577, 580, 587, 600, 602, 623, 632, 634, 635, 641, 665, 668, 692, 693, 713, 769, 808, 827, 828 **MkIV** KJ956, KK101, 102, 143, 160, KN200, 201, 256, 258, 261, 269, 270, 277, 278, 281, 291, 392, 427, 436, 443, 448, 451, 485, 511, 665, 666, 676, KP221, 224, 227.

Ground instruction aircraft KN451 as A655: KG600 as A601.

Notes: FD906–908, 956–958 diverted direct to South African Air Force.

FD819, 841, 879, 930 diverted to Royal Indian Air Force.

HK867 impressed in Middle East. TJ170 VIP aircraft for Lord Tedder.

FL503–652 main deliveries to RAF in India. Eighteen to SAAF, sixteen to BOAC, two to RCAF, one to RAAF.
FZ548–698 Nineteen to RCAF, twelve to BOAC, two to RCAF, one to RAAF.

KG310–809 Fifty to BOAC, RAAF, RCAF, SAAF and Russia. KG507, 542, 723, 765 to VIP standard. KG507 used by Lord Wavell in India. KG508 crashed on delivery off Brazilian coast. Three Dakotas crashed prior to delivery and could be KG316, 335, and 336.

KN200–701 KN267, 327, 483, 669–671 to SAAF. KN628, 647 VIP aircraft. KN437, 465–467, 501–505, 523–527, 537, 539–544, 548–555, 557, 559, 585–587 fitted with glider pick-up hook and winch.

On 21 September 1944 during Arnhem re-supply mission 48 Squadron lost FZ620, KG346, KG350, 404, 417, 579.

The following Dakotas were equipped with glider pick-up hook and winch. KN437, 523–527, 548–555, 557, 559, 466, 467, 501–505, 537, 539–544, 585, 586, 587, 465.

Lend-Lease Douglas Dakota FD947 ex 42-24006 C-47A-40-DL c/n 9868 arrived in the United Kingdom on 11 August 1943 for the RAF. Eight days later it arrived in India and was transferred to the USAAF on 26 October 1944 and struck off charge, presumably after battle damage, on 31 December 1945. It is depicted somewhere in South East Asia Command with visible damage and carrying the unique markings of the USAAF 2nd Air Commando Group. Between 12 November 1944 and 4 October 1945 the group was based at Kalaikunda, India. (Via Peter M Bowers).

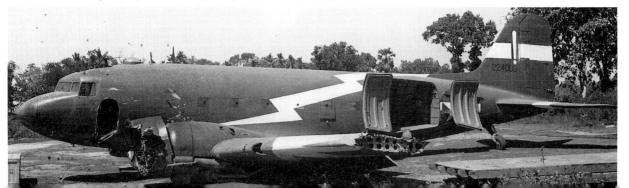

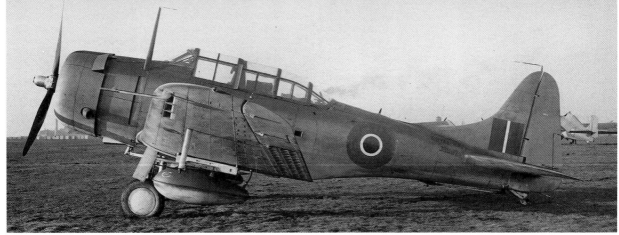

Official photo dated December 1943 depicting JS997 the first Douglas SBD-5 Dauntless DB.I one of nine for evaluation by the RAF and the Royal Navy. It was rejected for use with the Fleet Air Arm. The SBD-5 was the main production version of this successful US dive-bomber with a total of 2,964 of this model being built. Power was a 1,200 hp Wright R-1820-60 Cyclone engine. (Via Philip Jarrett).

DAUNTLESS Douglas

Mark No.	US Desig.	Company	Requisition	Contract	RAF Serials	US Serials
DB I	SBD-5	Douglas	N-1004	NOa(S)269	JS997–999(3)	36022/36023/36456
					JT923–928(6)	54191–54196(6)

Nine ex-US Navy SBD-5s supplied for evaluation by the RAF and Royal Navy.

Royal Navy – JS997/999, JT923/927/928; Royal Air Force – JS998, JT923/925/926.

DC-2 Douglas Commercial Two

Mark No.	US Desig.	Company	Requisition	Contract	RAF Serials	US Serials
DC-2K	C-33	Douglas			AX755(1)	
					AX767, 768, 769(3)	
					DG468–479(12)	
					HK820, 821(2)	
					HK837(1)	
					HK847(1)	
					HK867(1)	
					HK993(1)	

AX755 ex-NC14268, AX767 ex-VT-ARA, AX768 ex-NC14966, AX769 ex-NC14277, DG468 ex-VT-AOU, DG469 ex-VT-AOQ, DG470 ex-VT-AOR, DG471 ex-VT-AOS, DG472 ex-VT-AOT, DG473 ex-VT-AOV, DG474 ex-VT-AOW, DG475 ex-VT-AOX, DG476 ex-VT-AOY, DG477 ex-VT-AOZ, DG478 ex-VT-APA, DG479 ex-VT-APB, HK820 ex-NC14290, HK821 ex-NC14271, HK837 ex-NC14950, HK847 ex-NC14280, HK867 ex-NC14278, HK993 ex-VT-CLE.

NC14279 sold to US Treasury in May 1941 for the British Purchasing Commission but crashed at Bathurst, The Gambia on 2 August 1941 while en route to the Egyptian Canal Zone and the RAF.

Seen parked at Willingdon, New Delhi on 31 July 1945 is Douglas DC-2 VT-ARA of Indian National Airways still carrying the RAF serial AX767. This transport was bought by the British Purchasing Commission on 5 July 1941 and became AX767 at RAF Khartoum on 14 October that year. It was operated by RAF transport squadrons and in September 1945 was still a DC-2K as the type was known in the RAF. Broken up for spares. (Peter M Bowers).

Through the British Purchasing Commission the RAF operated a handful of hybrid DC-3 airliners including MA925 depicted. It was a right-hand door DC-3-277D NC33653 c/n 4116 operated by American Airlines but bought by the US Government on 9 July 1941. It went to Pan American in Africa during October and to the RAF on 1 May 1942. It served with two RAF transport squadrons then on 19 September 1942 went to AHQ India Comm Flight based at New Delhi. It was bought by Indian National Airlines in 1943 and registered VT-ATB. (R J S Dudman via J D R Rawlings).

DC-3 Douglas Commercial Three

Mark No.	US Desig.	Company	Requisition	Contract	RAF Serials	US Serials
DC-3	C-48	Douglas			LR230(1)	42-14297
	C-49G				LR231(1)	42-38252
	C-49H				LR232(1)	42-38253
	C-49D				LR233(1)	42-38256
	C-53				LR234(1)	41-20081
	C-49G				LR235(1)	42-38255
	C-49H				MA925(1)	42-38250
					MA928(1)	
					MA929(1)	
	C-49H				MA943(1)	42-38251

LR230 ex-NC30004, LR231 ex-NC16094, LR232 ex-NC33675, LR233 ex-NC17313, LR234 ex-NC25623, LR235 ex-NC16082, MA925 ex-NC33653, MA943 ex-NC33655.

ELECTRA Lockheed Model 10 & 12

Mark No.	US Desig.	Company	Requisition	Contract	RAF Serials	US Serials
	12A	Lockheed			R8987(1)	
	12A				V4732(1)	
	12A				X9316(1)	
	10A				AX699–701(3)	
	12A				AX803(1)	

Two from the batch of five RAF Lockheed 12A Electra twin-engined low-wing monoplane light airliners, including LA619 depicted, operated with No.24 Squadron during World War 2. RAF Electra AX700 was assigned in 1945 as the personal transport of the Governor of Bengal. The batch LA619–623 has been quoted as ex USAAF UC-40D, this designation being allocated to ten commercial Model 12A's impressed into military service during 1942. (MAP).

LEND-LEASE AIRCRAFT IN WORLD WAR II

Mark No.	US Desig.	Company	Requisition	Contract	RAF Serials	US Serials
	12A				HM573(1)	
	12A				HX798(1)	
	UC-40D				LA619–623(5)	
	12A				LV700(1)	
	12A				LV760–762(3)	
	12A				NF753(1)	

R8987 ex-G-AEMZ impressed November 1939 for RAE. V4732 ex-VT-AJN impressed in India. X9316 ex-G-AEOI impressed. AX699–701 taken on charge in Middle East ex-YU-SAV, YU-SDA, YU-SBB. AX803 VT-AJS impressed in India. HM573 ex-G-AGDT impressed. HX798 ex-VT-AMB ex-G-AFXP loaned by the Maharajah of Jaipur. LA619–623 ex-UC-40D. LV760–762 ex-Dutch L2-32, L2-30, L2-01. NF753 purchased in US for use by Prince Bernhard.

EXPEDITER Beechcraft Model C-18S

Mark No.	US Desig.	Company	Requisition	Contract	RAF Serials	US Serials
	C-45	Beech	43458		None	40-182
I	C-45B		41044	AC-40082	FR940–948(9)	
I			41044	AC-40082	HB100–206(107)	
I(RN)			41570	AC-40082	FT975–979(5)	
II	C-45F		41044	AC-40082	HB207–299(93) KJ468–560(93)	
II			43193	AC-40082	KN100–109(10)	
II			43193	AC-3213	KN110–149(40)	
II(RN)			41570	AC-40082	FT980–996(17) HD752–776(25)	
II(RN)			43302	AC-40082	KP100–102(3)	
II(RN)			43302	AC-3213	KP103–124(22) HB759(1)	

FR940–948 (9) All to 32 Operational Training Unit (OTU) in Canada. HB100–206 (107) Some delivered to RCAF. HB207–299 (93) Some delivered to RCAF. KN100–149 (50) delivered to India 1945. KN150–199 (50) cancelled. HB759 no delivery record.

RCAF Mk 3T FR940 c/n 5954, 941 c/n 5964 43-35540, 942 c/n 5966 43-35541, 943 c/n 6142, 944 c/n 6154 43-35635, 945 c/n 6162, 946 c/n 6174 43-35645, 947 c/n 6186 43-35651, 948 c/n 6190 43-35653, HB100 c/n 5768, 101 c/n 5776, 102 c/n 5780 43-35466, 103 c/n 5784 43-35467, 104 c/n 5786 43-35468, 105 c/n 5792, 106 c/n 5816 43-35475, 107 c/n 5820 43-35476, 108 c/n 5824 43-35477, 109 c/n 5828 43-35478, 110 c/n 5832 43-35479, 111 c/n 5836 43-35480, 112 c/n 5840 43-35481, 113 c/n 5844 43-35482, 114 c/n 5848 43-35483, 115 c/n 5852 43-35484, 116 c/n 5854 43-35485, 117 c/n 5856 43-35486, 118 c/n 5858 43-35487, 119 c/n 5860 43-35488, 120 c/n 5864 43-35490, 121 c/n 5866 43-35491, 122 c/n 5868 43-35492, 123 c/n 5870 43-35493, 124 c/n 5872 43-35494, 125 c/n 5874 43-35495, 126 c/n 5876, 127 c/n 5712 43-35449, 129 c/n 5756 43-35460,

A number of Beechcraft Expeditor II (C-45F) were supplied to the Royal Navy for use mainly as a six-eight seat communications aircraft. Depicted is KP110 from the batch of 22 KP103–124. Despite being wartime Lend-Lease aircraft the type served in the RN well into the 1950s. KP103 served at Donibristle as 807/DO with 782 Squadron: KP107 at Lee-on-Solent as 851/LP with 781 Sq.: KP111 in Australia with 724 Sq as 'VJ-AAN' and KP115 in Malta, at Hal Far as 811/HF with 728 Squadron. (AP Photo Library).

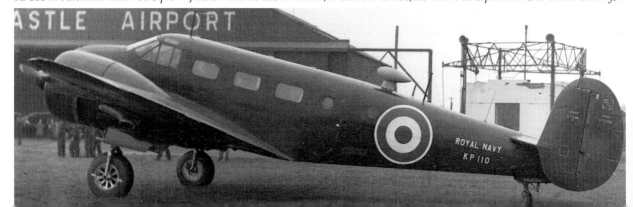

130 c/n 5996, 131 c/n 5998, 134 c/n 5978 43-35547, 135 c/n 5980 43-35548, 136 c/n 5982 43-35549, 137 c/n 5984 43-35550, 138 c/n 5986 43-35551, 139 c/n 5988 43-35552, 140 c/n 5990 43-35553, 141 c/n 6002 43-35555, 142 c/n 5716 43-35450, 143 c/n 5736 43-35455, 144 c/n 5744, 145 c/n 5748 43-35458, 146 c/n 5752, 148 c/n 5796, 151 c/n 5812 43-35474, 185 c/n 6112 43-35614, 186 c/n 5958 43-35537, 207 c/n 6220 43-35668, 210 c/n 6226 43-35671, 212 c/n 6264 43-35690, 266, 267, 268 43-35881, 269.

Ground instruction aircraft: HB106 as A511, HB120 as A676, HB121 as A512, HB102 as A640, HB146 as A393, HD317 as A547, FR947 as A627.

FORTRESS Boeing Model 299

Mark No.	US Desig.	Company	Requisition	Contract	RAF Serials	US Serials
I	B-17C	Boeing			AN518–537(20)	40-2043/4/51/2/3/5 40-2056/7/60/1/4/5 40-2066/8/9/71/3/5 40-2076/9(20)
II	B-17F				FA684(1)	
II	B-17F		149	DA-16	FA695–700(6)	41-24594–24599(6)
			149	AC-20292	FA701–713(13)	FA711 ex-42-5238
IIA	B-17E		149	AC-15677	FK184–213(30) FL449–460(12) FL462–464(3)	
III	B-17G		149	AC20292	HB761–782(22) HB783–788(6) HB789–790(2)	42-97098–97119(22) 42-102434–102439(6) 42-102940–102941(2)
III	B-17G	Lockheed-Vega	149	AC-35321	HB791–793(3) HB795–796(2) HB799–803(5) HB805(1)	42-98021–98023(3) 42-98025–98026(2) 42-98029–98033(5) 42-98035
III	B-17G	Lockheed-Vega	149	AC-40031	HB815–820(6) KH998–999(2) KJ100–102(3) KJ103–110(8) KJ111–115(5) KJ116–125(10)	44-8082–8087(6) 44-8240–8241(2) 44-8242–8244(3) 44-8336–8343(8) 44-8534–8538(5) 44-8619–8628(10)
III	B-17G	Lockheed-Vega	43300	AC-40031	KJ126–127(2) KL830–832(3) KL833–837(5)	44-8861–8862(2) 44-8863–8865(3) 44-8966–8970(5)
IIIA	B-17G	Boeing			SR376–389(14)	

FA684 photo discovered in USAAF Technical Manual – used for spares. *AN518–537* initially marked 'AM' in error. One B-17C-BO taken over by USAAF in India. FK192 to RCAF. FL461 not received or contracted. HB778/G HB796/G carried special equipment. HB761, 764, 766, 770, 771, 781, 783, 784, 794, 797, 798, 804, 806–814 diverted back or retained by USAAF. KH998, 999, KJ100–127 delivered as from October 1944. Twelve retained in Canada. SR376–389 supplied for use by 214 Squadron.

GANNET Grumman Model G-50. Original name allocated to Hellcat

GOOSE Grumman G-21

Mark No.	US Desig.	Company	Requisition	Contract	RAF Serials	US Serials
IA	JRF-6B	Grumman			BW778–827(50)	66325–66374(50)
I	JRF-5	Grumman	N-1147	NOa(S)463	FP470–473(4)	37780, 37793, 37796, 37806(4)
IA	JRF-6B	Grumman	666	LL86447	FP475–524(50)	

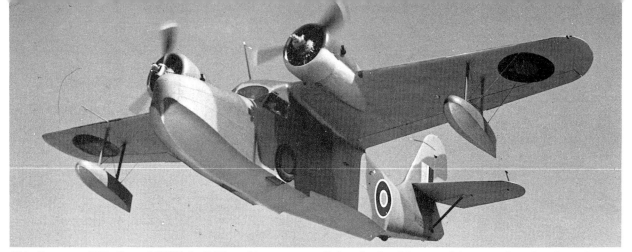

This Grumman JRF- Goose MV993 in RAF markings was supplied under Lend-Lease and is unusual in that the underwing roundels are Type B being red/blue. The type served both with the RAF and the Fleet Air Arm. Many in the RN served at the air station located at Piarco, Trinidad from 1942 and were used along with other types for training air observers with No.749 Squadron, the inventory including Goose I FP503 'W2W'. (Via Peter Mr Bowers).

Mark No.	US Desig.	Company	Requisition	Contract	RAF Serials	US Serials
I	JRF-5	Grumman			FP474(1)	
I	JRF-5	Grumman			FP738–747(10)	
		Grumman			HK822(1)	
					MV993(1)	

FP475–524 replaced BW778–827. FP471/3 used by British Air Commission in Canada and US 24 April 1944 to 5 March 1945. Main deliveries to Royal Navy at Piarco, West Indies. Most returned to US Navy after World War Two. HK822 c/n 1049 G-21A ex-G-AFKJ transferred to RAAF. Used by 24 Squadron RAF at Hendon. FP738/739/741/743/747 retained by US Navy. FP471 c/n 37793, FP473 c/n 37806.

GOSLING Grumman G-44

Mark No.	US Desig.	Company	Requisition	Contract	RAF Serials	US Serials
I	J4F-2	Grumman	N-1117	NO(a)S455	FP455–469(15)	From FP456 as follows 32986/37714/37722/ 37723/37727/37728/ 37732/37733/37737/ 37738/37741/37742/ 37745/37746(14)

Ex-US Navy and used by the Royal Navy in the West Indies. See Widgeon.

HADRIAN Waco Model CG-4

Mark No.	US Desig.	Company	Requisition	Contract	RAF Serials	US Serials
I	CG-4A	Waco		40236	FR557–580(24)	
II	CG-4A	Ford		40236	FR581–600(20)	
II	CG-4A	Waco		40236	FR601–724(124)	
					FR726–778(53)	
					KH871–992(122)	
					KK569–787(219)	
					KK792–923(132)	
					NP664(1)	

Other sources quote serial blocks as follows: FR556–778 (223), KH871–992 (122), KK569–968 (4) which included CG-13A KK790, 791. FR580 to Canada. KH871–992 Main deliveries to India. KH944–947 to Canada. Hadrian first supplied to the RAF in 1943, and 129 were towed by Dakotas into action in the Allied invasion of Sicily in July 1943. Apart from Sicily, Hadrians were not used operationally by the RAF, though they equipped a number of units in South-East Asia Command (SEAC) in late 1944 and early 1945 ready for a possible invasion of Japan. Units equipped were 668, 669, 670 Squadrons of 343 (Fatchjang) Wing and 671, 672, 673 Squadrons of 344 (Bikram) Wing.

KH944 ex-42-56424, KH945 ex-42-74524, KH946 ex-42-79361, KH947 ex-42-42236. Retained by RCAF.

VJ 120–413(200) ex-USAAF. VJ120–165, 198–222, 239–284, 313–349, 368–413. VJ426–VK874 ex-USAAF VJ735–781, 821–847, VK573–609, VK623–655. Others allocated but not taken up. VJ426–459, 481–520, 538–559, 583–628, 650–687, 712–731, 850–876, 890–908, 912–951, 986–999, VK127–159, 183–222, 261–303, 321–369, 392–431, 467–487, 491–527, 555–571, 661–693, 712–747, 777–783, 786–829, 841–874.

Identified Hadrians include:

FR557, 558 ex-42-61318, 42-61327.

FR564–575 42-45659–45670.

FR659, 660 43-41868, 43-41879.

FR661, 662 42-56596, 42-56598.

FR663, 664 42-56601, 42-56603.

FR665, 666 42-56605, 42-56606.

FR667–670 43-36738–36741.

FR671   43-40274.

FR673   43-40037

FR679   43-40957.

FR778   43-42140.

Three CG-4As were obtained as instructional airframes and included 42-61897 (5561M), 43-39744 (5241M) and 43-40593 (5071M).

Other CG-4A Hadrian gliders known to have been delivered to the RAF include the following:

CG-4A-BB (Babcock Aircraft, Deland, Florida) 42-47411.

CG-4A-CE (Cessna Aircraft, Wichita, Kansas) 42-62193.

CG-4A-CM (Commonwealth Aircraft, Kansas City, Kansas) 42-53233, 53236, 74346, 74482, 74521, 74523, 74553, 74573, 74608, 74612.

CG-4A-FO (Ford Motor Co., Willow Run, Michigan) 42-77065, 77067, 77131, 77341, 77363, 77516, 77898, 77965, 43-39662, 39697, 39919, 45-6129, 6168.

CG-4A-GA (G&A Aircraft, Willow Grove, Pennsylvania) 42-57563, 79439, 79446, 79447, 79529, 79537, 79542.

CG-4A-GE (General Aircraft, Astoria, Long Island, New York) 43-19721, 19764, 19769, 19779, 19829, 43-40849, 41053, 41061, 41220.

CG-4A-GN (Gibson Refrigerator, Greenville, Michigan) 42-52858, 73883, 73890, 73912, 73931, 73934, 73976, 73997, 74027, 43-41384, 41387.

CG-4A-LK (Laister-Kauffman Aircraft Co., St Louis, Missouri) 42-43665, 43666.

CG-4A-PR (Tratt, Read & Co., Deep River, Connecticut) 42-56129, 56168, 56214, 56240, 56331, 56361, 56532, 56561, 56596, 43-42001.

CG-4A-RO (Robertson Aircraft, St Louis, Missouri) 42-78797, 78811, 78812, 78813, 78115, 78818, 78819, 78820, 78824, 78825, 78827, 78828, 78830, 78831, 78833, 78834.

CG-4A-TI (Timm Aircraft, Van Nuys, California) 42-62745.

CG-4A-WO (Waco Aircraft Co., Troy, Ohio) 42-79027, 79217, 79306, 79315, 79345, 79349, 79409.

HARVARD North American Model NA-49. NA-16-1E, NA-66, NA-76, NA-81, NA-88.

Mark No.	US Desig.	Company	Requisition	Contract	RAF Serials	US Serials
I		North			N7000–7199(200)	
I		American			P5783–5982(200)	

The Harvard was one of the first US aircraft ordered by the British Purchasing Commission for the RAF in June 1938. The Harvard I was the RAF version of the USAAC BC-1 of 1937, and the initial contract for 200 (N7000–7199) was completed in June 1939. Depicted is the first of many to see Allied service, hundreds being delivered later under Lend-Lease to the huge Commonwealth Air Training Scheme based at flying schools in Canada, Rhodesia and the United Kingdom. N7000 was evaluated by the A&AEE Martlesham Heath, Suffolk during December 1938. On 16 February 1939 the aircraft's tendency to spin claimed N7000 as the first Harvard victim when it crashed at Eyke, near Woodbridge, Suffolk, killing both occupants. (Via Philip Jarrett).

Mark No.	US Desig.	Company	Requisition	Contract	RAF Serials	US Serials
II					AH185–204(20)	
II					AJ538–987(450)	
II					BD130–137(8)	ex RCAF 2521–2528(8)
II					BJ410–411(2)	2529–2530(2)
II					BJ412–415(4)	2534–2537(4)
II					BS808(1)	2538(1)
II					BW184–207(24)	
II					DG430–431(2)	
II					DG432–439(8)	ex RCAF 2539–2546
IIA	AT-6C		147	DA-8	EX100–846(747)	41-33073–33819(747)
III	AT-6D		147	DA-8	EX847–999(153) EZ100–249(150)	41-33820-34122(303)
III	AT-6D		147	AC-29317	EZ250–458(209)	
III					EZ459–799	Cancelled
IIB	AT-16	Noorduyn	2553	DA-215	FE267–999(733) FH100–166(67)	42-464–963(500) 42-12254–12553(300)
IIB	AT-16	Noorduyn	2553	AC-31737	FS661–999(339) FT100–460(361)	43-12502–13201(700)
III		North America			FT955–974(20)	42-44538–44557(20)
IIB	AT-16	Noorduyn	65/40/4092	AC-238	FX198–497(300)	43-34615–34771(156)FX198-354(156)
					KF100–999(900) KG100–309(210)	Cancelled
III	SNJ-4	North America	BAC/N-1990		KE305–309(5)	26800, 26812, 26816, 26817, 26818(5)

RCAF AJ538–987 AJ538–585, 586–597, 643–662, 683–737, 753–767, 788–802, 823–836, 847–854, 893–910, 912–984. *BW184–207* inclusive. *FE267–999* FE268–352, 383–412, 433–527, 533–592, 618–662, 688–695, 721, 765, 790–877, 902–961, 976–999. *FH100–166* FH100–106, 117–166. *AH185–204* inclusive. FS661–681, 857–878, 957–978, FT265–301.

N7000–7199 British Purchasing Commission contract. 124 to Southern Rhodesia under Empire Air Training Scheme. N7020 retained in the USA, later to Canada.

P5783–5982 P5783–5915 shipped to the UK of which eighty-nine later went to Southern Rhodesia direct from P5916. 5921 to South African Air Force.

AJ538–987 AJ602–642, 663–682, 703–722, 738–752 shipped direct to Southern Rhodesia. AJ855–892 became NZ968–1005 with RNZAF. Offsets to RCAF, SAAF, only fifty reached RAF.

BD130–137 130 to UK, 131–134 to Rhodesia, 135–137 to USAAF.

BJ400–419 400–408 to Rhodesia. Record only of 410, 412–415 being delivered.

The Harvard Mk I, charge number NA49, was similar to the BC-1, powered by a 600 hp R-1340-S3HI and had a fabric-covered rear fuselage. The Harvard Mk II (NA76) was based on the BC-1A. Lend-Lease models were the Mk IIA (AT-6C), Mk IIB (AT-16), and Mk III (AT-6D/SNJ-4). The Harvard MK 4 was a post-war Canadian Car & Foundry built model for the RCAF. The model designation NA-16-IE was also applied to the Harvard Mk I. RCAF versions of the Mk I and Mk II had North American charge number NA61 and NA75 respectively.

Mk I 400 aircraft. N7000–7199, P5783–5982, with c/n 49-748–947 and 49-1053–1252.

Mk II 519 aircraft. AH185–204, AJ538–987, BD130–137, BJ410–415, BS808, BW184–207, DG430–439. BD135, 136, 137 diverted to the USAAF.

Mk IIA NA81.

RCAF Notes: AH185–204 c/n 66-2747–66-2766, FE527 c/n 14-261, FE553–592 c/n 14-287 14-326, FE553–563 ex-42-750–42-760, FE618–649 c/n 14-352 14-383, FE800–877 c/n 14-534 14-611, FE902–961, c/n 14-636 14-695, FE976–999 c/n 14-710 14-733, FH143 ex-42-12530, FT267 c/n 14A-1307 ex-43-13008, FE755, 798, 799 to USAAF. FE800, 802, 859, 867, 906, 907, 908, 909, 910 Sold USAAF Fort Dix. FT268–271, FT281–288, 290, 291, 293, 294, 295, 297, 298, 299, 300, 301, USAAF Fort Dix.

Lost at sea in transit to India and Ceylon: FE364, 375, 376, 417, 418, 419, 421, 486, 493, 497; FE529, 530, 531, 532, 536, 537, 541.

HAVOC Douglas DB-7B. Conversions from Boston

Mark No.	US Desig.	Company	Requisition	Contract	RAF Serials	US Serials
I	A-20	Douglas			AW392–414(23)	
					AX848–851(4)	
					AX910–918(9)	
					AX920–975(56)	
					BB890–912(23)	
					BD110–127(18)	
					BJ458–501(43)	
					BK882–883(2)	
					BL227–228(2)	
					BT460–465(6)	
					BV203(1)	
					DG554–555(2)	
II	A-20	Douglas			AH430–529(100)	

As the Douglas DB-7s taken over by the United Kingdom lacked the necessary range for bombing operations from UK bases, the decision was taken to modify the R-1830-S3C4-G-powered aircraft, including earlier models which were re-engined, for night-intruder and night-fighter duties. *AW392–414* 393, 395, 400, 401, 405, 407, 411, 412 fitted out as Turbinlites. *AX848–851* ex-French. *AX910–918* ex-French AX913 Turbinlite and fitted with Long Aerial Mine, later to USAAF. *AX920–975* 922, trainer to USAAF, 924, 930 Turbinlites, *BB890–912* BB897, 899, 907–909 Turbinlites. 891, 896 to USAAF. 902 trainer, 906 to Royal Navy. *BD100–127* 110, 111, 120 Turbinlites. 115, 116 trainers, 121, 122 to Royal Navy. *BJ458–501* ex-French. BJ458–477, 485–501, 474 converted to Mk II. Several converted to trainers of which BJ464 was prototype. 460, 461, 466, 469, 470 Turbinlites. 490, 493, Long Aerial Mine. 461, 466, 473, 488, 489 to USAAF. *BK882–883* 882 Turbinlite. 883 intruder version with Long Aerial Mine. *BL227–228* 227 to Royal Navy. 228 trainer. *BT460–465* 465 fitted with Long Aerial Mine, 464 to USAAF. *DG554–555* 554 fitted with Long Aerial Mine. *AH430–529.* 430 crashed during company test flight. 431, 432, 434–436, 446–450, 452, 453, 456–458, 460, 466, 468, 470, 472, 473, 476–485, 489–491, 493, 497, 503 Turbinlites. Ten to USAAF.

Havoc III designation initially given to Havoc I (Pandora) fitted with Long Aerial Mine.

Havoc IV designation initially given to Havoc I (Intruder) fitted with Turbinlite.

Seen in yellow colour scheme, early 1946 postwar roundels, and code 9X-E from 1689 Ferry Training Flight is KF998 the pen-ultimate RAF Harvard. It later served with 25 Reserve Flying School (RFS) at Wolverhampton, with 11 RFS at Perth, and finally with 1 Flying Training School at Moreton-in-the-Marsh before being struck off charge in May 1957. (Via Bruce Robertson).

LEND-LEASE AIRCRAFT IN WORLD WAR II

HELLCAT Grumman Model G-50. Originally named Gannet

Mark No.	US Desig.	Company	Requisition	Contract	RAF Serials	US Serials
I	F6F-3	Grumman	7207	LL90071	FN320–329(10)	04850–04859(10)
					FN330–339(10)	04945–04954(10)
					FN340–349(10)	08894–08903(10)
					FN350–359(10)	08954–08963(10)
					FN360–369(10)	09029–09038(10)
					FN370–379(10)	25778–25787(10)
					FN380–389(10)	25868–25877(10)
					FN390–399(10)	25958–25967(10)
					FN400–409(10)	26053–26062(10)
					FN410–419(10)	26148–26157(10)
					FN420–429(10)	65962–65971(10)
					FN430–439(10)	66082–66091(10)
					FN440–449(10)	66222–66231(10)
I	F6F-3	Grumman	N-3	NOa(S)846	JV100–221(122)	
II	F6F-5	Grumman	N-3	NOa(S)846	JV222–234(13)	58220–58232(13)
					JV235–297(63)	58733–58795(63)
					JV298–301(4)	58996–58999(4)
					JV302–324(23)	69992–70014(23)
					JW700–722(23)	70015–70037(23)
					JW723–772(50)	70238–70287(50)
					JW773–784(12)	70463–70474(12)
					JW857–894(38)	70475–70512(38)
					JW895–899(5)	70688–70692(5)
					JX670–739(70)	70693–70762(70)
					JX740–814(75)	71163–71237(75)
					JX815–889(75)	71638–71712(75)
					JX890–964(75)	72113–72187(75)
NFII	F6F-5N	Grumman	N-3	NOa(S)846	JX965–967(3)	72989–72991(3)
NFII	F6F-5N	Grumman	N-3	NOa(S)2676	JX968–999(32)	
					JZ775–827(53)	
					JZ890–999(110)	
					KD108–160(53)	
					KE118–254(148)	

A number were converted to MkFRII with a camera installation in the rear fuselage. These were modified by Blackburn Aircraft who fitted British rocket projectile launchers to a number of F6F-3s.

HELLDIVER Curtiss Model 84

Mark No.	US Desig.	Company	Requisition	Contract	RAF Serials	US Serials
I	SBW-1B	Canadian Car & Foundry	N-5	NXs-LL-139	JW100–125(26)	60010/21201 21203(3) 60013–60035(24)

450 SBW-1s were intended for the Royal Navy but only twenty-six delivered as SBW-1Bs in 1944.

Delivered to 1820 Squadron but never used operationally. JW119 to the RAF.

Grumman Hellcat II JV270 coded 2-C from No.1840 Squadron based on HMS Indefatigable *in 1944. It is from the batch of 225 JV100–324 Mk.I/II (F6F-3/5). The aircraft is named* Ivy *and is fitted with rocket rails. First Hellcats were delivered to the Royal Navy under Lend-Lease, some 1,182 being allocated by the end of hostilities. (Peter M Bowers).*

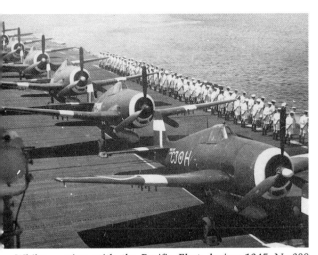

Whilst serving with the Pacific Fleet during 1945 No.800 Squadron with its Hellcats served on board HMS Emperor *as seen in this photo. These were Hellcat II supplied under Lend-Lease and included JZ999 'C3-H' when the squadron was with the 29th Naval Fighter Wing. Earlier it was with the 3rd Naval Fighter Wing and included Hellcat II JV304 'K3-G'. It also used Hellcat I JV134 'EZ'. In May 1945 the unit assisted in the capture of Rangoon followed by attacks on shore targets and shipping off the Tenasserim coast during which eight Hellcats operated from HMS* Shah. *A Hellcat II seen damaged at Trincomalee, Ceylon in October 1945 was JZ931 'C3-M'. (Via Michael J F Bowyer).*

A total of 26 Curtiss Helldiver I (SBW-1B) dive-bombers, JW100–125, were delivered to the Royal Navy under Lend-Lease in 1944. No.1820 Squadron was formed at Brunswick, USA on 1 April with nine aircraft including JW-104 '4L' and JW-121. After work-up these embarked in HMS Arbiter *in July 1944 for passage to the UK, but the type was found unsatisfactory, the squadron losing several aircraft and crews through accidents, including three aircraft which failed to pull out of vertical dives. These 26 Helldivers were built by the Canadian Car & Foundry Factory. Depicted as JW-117 which was flight tested in the UK. (Via Peter M Bowers).*

HOVERFLY I Sikorsky Model R-4

Mark No.	US Desig.	Company	Requisition	Contract	RAF Serials	US Serials
I (RN)	YR-4	Sikorsky	40145	AC-29005	FT833–834(2)	42-107238, 107240(2)
I (RN)	YR-4B		40189	AC-29005	FT835–839(5)	42-107246; 43-28228, 28232, 28233, 42-28226(5)
I (RN)	R-4B		40189	AC-41023	KK969–971(3) KK973–975(3) KK977–978(2)	43-46508–46510(3); 43-46513–46515(3) 43-46518, 46519(2)
I (RN)	R-4B		41203	AC-41023	KK979–984(6) KK986–993(8) KK996–999(4) KL100–102(3) KL106–109(4) KL111–113(3)	
I (RAF)	R-4B		41623	AC-41023	KK972, 976, 985 994, 995(5) KL103–105(3) KL110(1)	43-46511, 46516, 46540 46562, 46558(5) 43-56581, 56580, 56587(3) 56596(1)

KL110 to RCAF.

By the time the Sikorsky R-6A Hoverfly II was delivered under Lend-Lease, World War 2 was virtually over, and during the 'austerity' period which followed in 1946/7 a severe US dollar shortage in the UK created difficulties in obtaining spare parts. This resulted in only a few of the type being flown. The Maintenance Unit which handled the helicopter was No.29 at High Ercall, Shropshire. Depicted is KN856 evaluated at the A&AEE Boscombe Down in October 1945. (Via Philip Jarrett).

HOVERFLY II Vought-Sikorsky Model 316A

Mark No.	US Desig.	Company	Requisition	Contract	RAF Serials	US Serials
IIA	R-6A	Nash-Kelvinator	43393	AC-40217	KN837–986(150)	

First forty delivered mainly to RAF. KN855/879 to Royal Navy. KN864 to Canada. 107, KN880–986, cancelled.

HUDSON Lockheed Model 14-F62, 214, 314, 414

Mark No.	US Desig.	Company	Requisition	Contract	RAF Serials	US Serials
	Model 14	Lockheed			AX681–682(2) AX688(1) HK982(1) HK984(1)	Impressed.
I	Model 214				N7205–7404(200) P5116–5165(50) R4059(1) T9266–9365(100)	
II	Model 314				T9366–9385(20)	
III	Model 414				T9386–9465(80) V8975–8999(25) V9020–9065(46) V9066–9069(4) V9090–9129(40) V9150–9199(50) V9220–9254(35) AE485–657(173) AM930–953(24)	
IIIA	A-29	Lockheed	62,2467	DA-5	BW361–777(417)	41-23223–23639(417)
IIIA	A-29		62,2467	DA-151	FH167–260(94)	41-36968–37061(94)
IIIA	A-29		3371	DA-151	FH261–366(106)	41-37062–37167(106)
IIIA	A-29		2817	DA-151	FH367–466(100)	41-37168–37267(100)
IIIA	A-29A		7201	DA-908	FK731–813(83)	42-47287–47369(83)
IVA	A-28		63	DA-5	A16–101/152(52)	41-23171–23222 RAAF(52)
IV	A-29				AE609–638(30)	
V	A-29				AM520–702(181)	

The Lockheed Hudson proved itself as a workhorse with the RAF, being involved in a multitude of tasks. Depicted is a long-range Hudson III V9150 from a batch of 200 V8975–9254 delivered before Lend-Lease. Carries the markings of an Air-Sea Rescue squadron of RAF Coastal Command. It is fitted with a Mk. 3 airborne lifeboat the first to be dropped in combat. (Via Philip Jarrett).

Mark No.	US Desig.	Company	Requisition	Contract	RAF Serials	US Serials
V	A-29	Lockheed			AM703–909(207)	
VI	A-28A		2817	DA-471	EW873–972(100)	42-6582–6681(100)
VI	A-28A		7201	DA-908	FK381–730(350)	42-46937–47286(350)

Mk I Military version of the Lockheed 14-F62 airliner, with transparent nose cone, two 0.303 inch nose guns and a dorsal turret. Two 1,100 hp R-1820-G102As. A total of 351 were built for the RAF as Model 214: N7205–7404, P5116–5165, R4059, T9266–9365.

Mk II Model 314. As Mk I but with spinnerless constant speed airscrews, reinforced airframe. Twenty were delivered: T9366–9385.

Mk III Model 414. Two 1,200 hp R-1820-G205As. Retractable ventral gun position. Four hundred and twenty-eight (428) were built: T9386–9465, V8975–8999, V9020–9065, V9220–9254 as Hudson III(SR); V9066–9069, V9090–9129, V9150–9199, AE485–608, AM930–953 as Hudson III(LR). Two ex-BOAC aircraft, G-AGDC c/n 2585 ex-V9061 and G-AGDK c/n 3757, became Hudson CIII VJ416 and JV421 respectively. Hudson III(LR) AE520–528, 542, 543, 567, 570–572, 584–608 and AM930 transferred to USAAF.

Mk IIIA First Lend-Lease model, ex-A-29 and A-29A-LO. 800 were built. Many were transferred to the air forces of Australia, Canada, China and New Zealand. BW361–380 went to the US Navy as PBO-1 Bu.No.03842–03861, whilst BW461–613 were repossessed by the USAAF.

Mk IV Model 414. Based on the Mk II but powered by two 1,050 hp R-1830-SC3-Gs and ventral gun deleted. Thirty were delivered AE609–638.

MK IVA For some reason fifty-two A-28-LOs delivered under RAF Lend-Lease order DA-5 to RAAF. Powered by two 1,050 hp R-1830-45s and a 0.05 inch gun on a dorsal mounting.

MkV Mk III version with two 1,200 hp R-1830-S3C4-G engines. Four hundred and nine (409) were delivered: AE639–657, AM520–702 as Hudson V(SR) and AM703–909 as Hudson V(LR). Many were transferred to the RCAF and RNZAF. AM633, 667, 668 were returned to the USAAF.

Mk VI Ex-A-28A-LO. 450 were delivered. Some were converted to CVI, others went to the RCAF and RNZAF. At least three, FK487, 496, 618, were transferred to the USAAF.

RCAF: Mk III T9385, V9069, 9171, 9223, BW381–384, 399–408, 410, 412, 423, 430–434, 436–439, 441–444, 447–454, 456–458, 460, 614, 616–635, 638–660, 682, 683, 685–698, 700–713, 715–720, 722–724, 728, 768, 770–772, 775–777, FH340, 395, 416, 466.

Mk V AM576, 720, 721, 723, 726, 729, 733, 736, 737, 745, 747–749, 751, 752, 755, 759, 761, 763–767, 769, 770, 772, 773, 886–896, 899, 901–903, 905.

Mk VI EW873, 956. FK393, 399, 408, 409, 443, 460, 464, 465, 467, 468, 470, 495, 506, 511, 512, 514, 518, 534, 539, 541, 546–548, 550, 553, 560–564.FK524 fuselage only used as ground instruction, as A334. Ground instruction aircraft FK393 salvaged RAF Hudson. BW708 as A181, AM905 as A190, BW423 as A247, AM736 as A248, BW689 as A291, N7371 as A420.

Lend-Lease were programmed to deliver a total of 140 Douglas Invader I (A-26) to the RAF as KL690–829, but only KL690 and 691 apparently delivered. The remainder apparently went to the US Navy with effect from June 1945. Very rare photo depicts KL692 in RAF markings identified from the USAAF tail number '322604' as a Tulsa-built Douglas A-26C-25-DT Invader 43-22604 c/n 18751 from a consecutive batch of 187. (Via Peter M Bowers).

INVADER Douglas

Mark No.	US Desig.	Company	Requisition	Contract	RAF Serials	US Serials
I	A-26	Douglas			KL690–829(140)	

Only two delivered: KL690/1 ex Bu.No. 80621/2, KL702 ex-Bu.No. 77154. Other Bu.Nos. were 77139 and 77224. Remainder went to the US Navy with effect from June 1945.

The Boeing-Stearman Model 75-Kaydet trainer series, US Army PT-13, 17, 18 and 27, US Navy N2S- had been in production by Stearman for the USAAC since 1936, but the majority of production was turned out during World War 2 after Stearman became a division of Boeing. Depicted are Stearman variants including 41-25453 PT-17; BuNo.05235 N2S-3 and FD972 Kaydet the latter supplied under Lend-Lease, one of 300 all of which were retained in Canada. (Via Philip Jarrett).

KAYDET Boeing-Stearman Model X70

Mark No.	US Desig.	Company	Requisition	Contract	RAF Serials	US Serials
I	PT-27	Boeing-Stearman	6562	DA-1338	FD968–999(32) FJ741–999(259) FK100–108(9)	42-15570–15601(32) 42-15602–15860(259) 42-15861–15869(9)

All retained in Canada and the US under the Commonwealth Air Training scheme. FD968–999 c/n 733759–753790, FJ741–999 c/n 753791–754049, FK100–108 c/n 75050–754058.

KINGCOBRA Bell Model 33

Mark No.	US Desig.	Company	Requisition	Contract	RAF Serials	US Serials
I	P-63A	Bell	20794	AC-29318	FR408(1)	42-68937(30)
I	P-63A	Bell	20794	AC-29318	FZ440(1)	42-69423(70)

Both to Royal Aircraft Establishment, Farnborough for evaluation.

FR408 arrived Speke, Liverpool on 17 May 1944 and took part in an aerodynamic research programme at the RAE relating to boundary-layer wings. In August 1944 it made a wheels-up landing and was subsequently scrapped. It was replaced by FZ440 and used for similar testing between April 1945 and September 1948 before being dismantled, its wings used for wind tunnel trials.

Depicted is Bell P-63A Kingcobra FR-408, one of two evaluated at RAE Farnborough during 1944/5. This one arrived at Speke, Liverpool by sea on 17 May 1944 and took part in an aerodynamic research programme relating to boundary-layer wings. During August 1944 it made a wheels-up landing and was subsequently scrapped. It was replaced by P-63A FZ440 and both Kingcobras were supplied under Lend-Lease. (Via Philip Jarrett).

One of the many Lend-Lease types evaluated at the A&AEE Boscombe Down was the Kingfisher I landplane. Depicted on 6 May 1942 is FN656 from a batch of 100 supplied, FN650–749 ex US Navy OS2U-3. Deliveries were mainly to the Middle East, West Africa and Jamaica, serving with two Fleet Air Arm second-line squadrons here in the United Kingdom. (Via Philip Jarrett).

KINGFISHER Vought-Sikorsky VS-310

Mark No.	US Desig.	Company	Requisition	Contract	RAF Serials	US Serials
I	OS2U-3	Vought	7951	LL 76493	FN650–679(30)	Bu.No. 5811–5840(30)
I	OS2U-3	Vought	7951	LL 76493	FN680–749(70)	09513–09582(70)

Deliveries mainly to the Middle East, West Africa and Jamaica. FN678 based with 765 Squadron at Sandbanks near Poole, Dorset. Used by 764 Squadron at Lawrenny Ferry, Pembrokeshire.

Curtiss Kittyhawk IIA (P-40F) FL220 ex US Army Air Force 41-13698 seen shortly after delivery to the United Kingdom. From this batch of 230 FL219–448 a number were returned to the USAAF, whilst seven were lost at sea during transit from the USA, and a further seven went to the Free French Air Force. (Via Bruce Robertson).

KITTYHAWK Curtiss Model Hawk 81

Mark No.	US Desig.	Company	Requisition	Contract	RAF Serials	US Serials
I/IA	P-40D/E	Curtiss	322	DA-3	ET100–999(900)	41-24776–25195(42)
I/IA	P-40D/E		322	DA-3	EV100–699(600)	41-35874–36953(10)
IIA	P-40F		322	AC-15802	FL219–368(150)	
IIA	P-40F		Not known		FL369–448(119)	
III	P-40K-1		322	DA-913	FL710–713(4)	
III	P-40K		322	AC-22714	FL875–905(31)	
III	P-40K-1		322	DA-913	FR111–115(5)	
III	P-40K		322	AC-22714	FR116–140(25)	
III	P-40K-1		322	DA-913	FR210–361(152)	
III	P-40K		322	AC-22714	FR385–392(8)	
III	P-40K		322	AC-22714	FR412–521(110)	
III	P-40M		322	AC-30491	FR779–872(94)	
IV	P-40N		Not known		FR884–885(2)	
III	P-40M		322	AC-30491	FS100–269(170)	All to USSR
IV	P-40N-1		322	AC-34423	FS270–399(130)	All to USSR
II	P-40L		322	AC-22714	FS400–499(100)	
IV	P-40N		322	AC-34423	FT849–954(106)	
IV	P-40N		322	AC-34423	FX498–847(350)	

ET100–EV699 Many diversions by ship direct to Australia and New Zealand, others by rail to Canada. Later diversions to SAAF. At least thirty-four were lost at sea in transit.

FL219–448 Offset from USAAF 41-13697–14599 (902).

FL710–730 Offset from USAAF 43-5403–6002 (599). Deliveries direct to Middle East, autumn 1942.

FL875–905 Delivered to Middle East late 1942. *FR111–140* Delivered to Middle East.

FR210–361 Main deliveries to Middle East. *FR385–392* Delivered to Middle East.

FR412–521 FR460–471 diverted from RAF deliveries. *FR779–872* Mainly direct to Middle East.

FR884–885 Delivered October 1943. *FS100–499* FS100–269 diverted to USSR.

FT849–954 FT898–904 lost at sea during transit.

FX498–847 Late deliveries, many diversions.

RCAF Mk IA The following twelve aircraft received the RCAF serials '720–731' inclusive: ET845 c/n 1306, 847 c/n 1308, 849 c/n 1310, 850 c/n 1311, 852 c/n 1313, 854 c/n 1315, ET856 c/n 1317, 858 c/n 1319, 860 c/n 1321, 862 c/n 1323, 863 c/n 1324, 866 c/n 1327.

Ground instruction aircraft: AK893 as A388, AL110 as A390, AL113 as A391, AL124 as A392.

Costs of P-40s varied considerably between models as detailed in the following descriptions, but the cost breakdowns of three representative production models are presented here:

Item	P-40	P-40E	P-40N
Airframe	$24,889	$28,482	$27,189
Engine	17,126	16,855	10,702
Propeller	3,425	2,481	3,110
Electronics	1,360	3,160	7,154
Ordnance	1,922	5,940	2,646
Other	2,816	2,700	2,068
Grand Total	$51,538	$59,618	$52,869

LIBERATOR Consolidated Model 32

Mark No.	US Desig.	Company	Requisition	Contract	RAF Serials	US Serials
II	B-24C	Consolidated			AL503–667(165)	
LB-30A					AM258–263(6)	
I	B-24				AM910–929(20)	
V	B-24D		141		BZ711–959(249)	
VI	B-24J		141	AC-26992–35312	BZ960–999(40) EV812–899(188) EW100–249(150)	
VII	C-87		41635	AC-811	EW611–618(8)	44-39219–39226(8)

This Consolidated 32 Liberator (B-24A) AM910 was used for various airborne experiments and it is seen heavily modified with ASV radar aerials as used by RAF Coastal Command, whilst a bulge under the forward fuselage houses a cannon. Ground testing of this caved in the bomb doors whilst it was being fired. Photo was taken during July 1941. (Via Philip Jarrett).

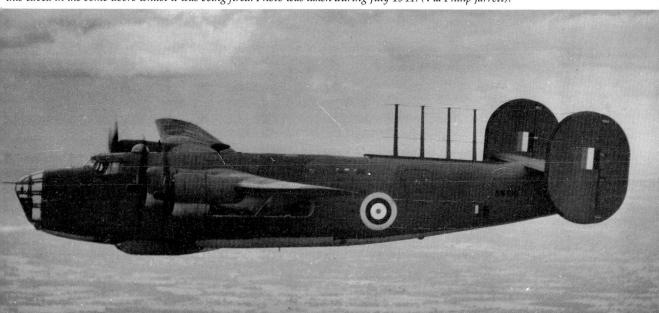

Mark No.	US Desig.	Company	Requisition	Contract	RAF Serials	US Serials
					EW619–620(2)	44-39236–39237(2)
					EW621–634(14)	44-39248–39261(14)
VI/VIII	B-24J	Consolidated	141	AC-40715	EW250–322(73)	44-10253–10325(73)
					KG821–978(158)	44-10326–10483(158)
					KG979–999(21)	44-10644–10664(21)
					KH100–187(88)	44-10665–10752(88)
III	B-24D		141		LV336–346(11)	41-1107, 41-1087, 41-1127, 41-1096, 41-1122, 41,1097, 41-1114, 41-1111,
					FL906–995(90)	41-1093, 41,1124, 41-1108(11)
VI/VIII	B-24J		141–43200	AC-40033	FK214-245(32) KH188–258(71)	44-44049–44119(71)
					KH259–420(162)	44-44130–44291(162)
					KK221–278(58)	44-44292–44349(58)
					KK279–378(100)	44-44360–44459(100)
					KL348–388(41)	44-44460–44500(41)
VI/VIII	B-24J	Ford	43200	AC-21216	KL392–470(79)	
VI/VIII	B-24L		43200	AC-21216	KL390–391(2)	
					KL471–689(219)	
					KN702–788(87)	
					KN789–836(68)	
					KP125–196(72)	
IX	RY-3	Consolidated	N-1422	NOa(S)3236	JT973–999(27)	90021–90047(27)
					JV936–999(64)	90048–90111(64)
					KE266–285(20)	90112–90131(20)
II	B-24C				FP685(1)	
VI	B-24J				TS519–539(21)	
VI	B-24J				TT336,340,343(3)	44-10597, 42-94797, 42-51350(3)
VI	B-24J				TW758–769(12)	
VI	B-24J				VB852(1)	42-50744(1)
					VB904(1)	42-52766(1)
					VD245(1)	42-52681(1)
					VD249(1)	44-10533(1)

Mk I Six Model LB30As, AM258–263, and twenty LB30Bs, AM910–929, of which AM927 crashed before delivery, was later repaired and used by the USAAF as a C-87 with its RAF serial retained. Five temporarily used by BOAC: AM259 (G-AGCD), AM262 (G-AGHG), AM263 (G-AGHG), AM918 (G-AGDS), AM920 (G-AGHYB). A few with 120 Squadron fitted with a ventral tray housing four 20mm cannon.

Mk II One hundred and sixty-five aircraft, AL503–667, of which AL504 was later fitted with a single fin and rudder as Winston Churchill's personal aircraft. Number converted to CII and used by BOAC: AL507 (G-AHYC), AL512 (G-AGEL), AL514 (G-AGJP), AL516 (G-AHZP), AL522 (G-AHYD), AL524 (G-AGTJ), AL528 (G-AGEM), AL529 (G-AHYE), AL541 (G-AGTI), AL547 (G-AGKU), AL552 (G-AHZR), AL557 (G-AGZI), AL571 (G-AGZH), AL592 (G-AHYF), AL603 (G-AHYG), AL619 (G-AGKT).

The following were transferred to the USAAF and operated as LB30s retaining the RAF serial: AL532–541, 543–589, 604–609, 611–613, 615, 617, 618, 621–623, 626, 628, 631–634, 637, 639–641. MkII FP685 was on temporary loan from the USAAF.

Mk III One hundred and fifty-six aircraft. Some became MkIIIA with ASV radar in place of the ventral turret. FL992 became a CIII.

Mk IV Not officially taken up and would have been equivalent to the USAAF B-24E. Some MkVIs were converted to MkIVs. BZ970 delivered as a CIV as were TS521–523, 527, 529, 530, 533, 534, 536, 538, 539, VB904 and VD249, the latter two being ex-B-24H-FO 42-52766 and B-24J-CF 44-10533. TS519, 520, 524–526, 528, 531, 532, 535, 537 were BMk IV. TT336 and TT340 converted to BMk IV and TT343 and VB852 to CMk IV.

Mk V Aircraft delivered to Coastal Command as GR V included BZ711–832, 861–889, 910–921, 930, 931, 937–945, FL927, 937, 938, 941, 942, 944, 946–991, a total of 236 aircraft, of which BZ723, 743, 744, 760–762, 769, 773, 781, 783, 786, 792, 793, 804, 806, 862, 869, 871, 931, 941, FL941, 970, 979 were converted to CV.

Mk VI The following were probably not delivered: EW127–137, KG932, 935, KH137–142, 144, 145, 152–154, 185–188, 190–197, 201, 202, 219, 220, 285–289, 295, 297, 299–301, 303, 307, 321, 324, 343, 345, 409, KL389, 395–470, 506, 518, 519, 535, 539, 555, 602–606, KN708–718. Many conversions. BZ971, 972, 981, 986 delivered as C VIs. A number were transferred to the military air arms of India and Czechoslovakia.

Mk VII Total of twenty-four C-87-CFs delivered.

Mk VIII Fifty, KP147–196, not delivered.

Mk IX Of the batch JV936–999 (64) only JV936 ex-Bu.No.90048 delivered. JT973 ex-Bu.No.90021 to RCAF as *Rockcliffe Ice Wagon*.

Transfer to RCAF: BZ725 as '589' ex-42-40447, BZ727 as '591' ex-42-40451, BZ728 as '590' ex-42-40452, BZ729 as '587' ex-42-40453, BZ732 as '586' ex-42-40456, BZ733 as '588' ex-42-40460, BZ734 as '599' ex-42-40461, BZ735 as '595' ex-42-40557, BZ736 as '593' ex-42-40470, BZ737 as '592' ex-42-40471, BZ738 as '597' ex-42-40231, BZ739 as '594' ex-42-40480, BZ747 as '596' ex-42-40466, BZ755 as '600' ex-42-40557, BZ756 as '598' ex-42-40560.

RCAF aircraft: Mk VI EW127 ex-42-99793, 128 ex-42-99794, 129 ex-42-99827, 130 ex-42-99809, 131 ex-42-99812, 132 ex-42-99815, 133 ex-42-99817, 134 ex-44-99820, 135 ex-42-99821, 136 ex-42-99822, 137 ex-42-99823, 208 ex-42-99894, 209 ex-42-99895, 210 ex-42-99896, 211 ex-42-99897, 212 ex-42-99898, 213 ex-42-99899, 214 ex-42-99900, 216 ex-42-99902, 217 ex-42-99903, 218 ex-42-99904, 270 ex-41-10273, 281 ex-44-10284, 282 ex-44-10285, KG880 ex-44-10385, 886 ex-44-10391, 888 ex-44-10392, 891 ex-44-10396, 892 ex-44-10397, 894 ex-44-10399, 920 ex-44-10425 c/n 30–334, 922 ex-44-10427 c/n 30–336, 923 ex-44-10428, c/n 30–337 B-24J-50, 924 ex-44-10429 c/n 30–338, 929 ex-44-10434, 930 ex-44-10435, 931 ex-44-10436, 978 ex-44-10483, KH105 ex-44-10670, 106 ex-44-10671, 107 ex-44-10672, 108 ex-44-10673, 109 ex-44-10674, 110 ex-44-10675 B-24J-75, 171 ex-44-10736, 172 ex-44-10737, 173 ex-44-10738, 174 ex-44-10739, 175 ex-44-10740, 176 ex-10741, 285 ex-44-44156, 286 ex-44-44157, 287 ex-44-44158, 288 ex-44-44159, 237 ex-44-44308, 238 ex-44-44309, 239 ex-44-44310, 240 ex-44-44311, 241 ex-44-44312, 242 ex-44-44313, 267 ex-44-44338 c/n 29–277 B-24J-95.

EW130 ground instruction aircraft as A427.

LIGHTNING Lockheed Model 222

Mark No.	US Desig.	Company	Requisition	Contract	RAF Serials	US Serials
I	P-38	Lockheed			AE978–999(22)	
I	P-38	Lockheed			AF100–220(121)	
II	P-38	Lockheed			AF221–744(524)	

Only a few Mk Is delivered, rest reverted to USAAF.

First production aircraft, AE978, delivered during December 1941.

AF105 and 106 flight-tested at Boscombe Down. Mk II batch cancelled.

Depicted whilst on an evaluation flight from Boscombe Down is Lightning I AF106, later returned to the USAAC, and seen with standard RAF camouflage and including gas detector paint 'diamonds' at the rear of the booms. This early model was powered by the original specified Allison V-1710-C15 engines. Only one RAF Lightning II AF221 was completed by Lockheed and as a P-38F-13-LO was used by the company for testing smoke-laying canisters and aerial torpedoes from racks. (Via Bruce Robertson).

LEND-LEASE AIRCRAFT IN WORLD WAR II

LODESTAR Lockheed Model 18-07/08

Mark No.	US Desig.	Company	Requisition	Contract	RAF Serials	US Serials
I	18-08	Lockheed			AX685–687(3)	ex-SAAF 231–233(3)
I	18-08				AX717–723(7)	
I	18-08				AX756–759(4)	
I	18-08				AX763–765(3)	
I	18-07				HK855(1)	
I	18-07				HK973(1)	
I	18-08				HK974–975(2)	
I	18-07				HK980(1)	
I	18-08				HK981(1)	
I	18				HK990(1)	
I	18				HX793(1)	
IA	C-59		1049	DA-53	EW976–982(7)	41-29626–29632(7)
II	C-60		1049	DA-53	EW983–997(15)	41-29633–29647(15)
II	C-60		40221	DA-1039/ AC-26618	FreeFrench FreeFrench	42-32192, -32193, -55913, -55917, -55943(5)

AX717–723 717 (G-AGCV), 718 (G-AGCR), 719 (G-AGCW), 720 (G-AGCU), 721 (G-AGCP), 722 (G-AGCT), 723 (G-AGCS). *AX756–759* 756 (NC25630/G-AGCN), 757 to Free French Air Force, 758, 759 to BOAC, HK855 (G-AGIL impressed), HK973 (G-AGBO impressed). *HK974–975* 974 (G-AGCT ex AX722), 975 (G-AGCW ex-AX719) impressed. HK980 G-AGBP impressed. 981 G-AGCX impressed, 990 impressed. HX793 (VT-AAM) impressed in India.

Three extra aircraft were EW973–975, retained in the US. EW976 became G-AGIN, EW977 G-AGIM, EW980 G-AGIG, EW982 G-AGJH.

MARAUDER Martin Model 179

Mark No.	US Desig.	Company	Requisition	Contract	RAF Serials	US Serials
I/IA	B-26A	Martin	150	AC-13243	FK109–160(52) FK362–380(19)	
II	B-26C		150	AC-19342/38728	FB418–517(100)	
III	B-26F		150	AC-31733	HD402–601(200)	42-96329–96528(200)
III	B-26G		41698	AC-31733	HD602–676(75)	43-34465–34539(75)
III	B-26G		41698	AC-1871	HD677–751(75)	44-67990–68064(75)

Note: Several other sources quote Mk II batch as FB400–522 (123).

Captain Don McVicar flew the first Martin B-26A Marauder I FK138 for the RAF from Gander to Prestwick on 2 September 1942. It is depicted after arrival in the UK and was from the first batch of Lend-Lease Marauders FK109–160 totally 52. (Via Philip Jarrett).

FK109–160 FK109, 111 to UK, rest direct to Middle East. FK113, 114, 125, 129, 140, 146, 158 lost in transit. *FK362–380* FK368, 369, 372, 379, 380 crashed before delivery. *FB418–517* Main deliveries to Middle East, some transferred to SAAF. *HD402–751* Main deliveries to Middle East. HD432, 512, 605, 632, 654, 664, 666 crashed during delivery flight.

Known identities as follows: FB486 41-35538, FB493–511(19) 42-107497–107515(19), FB449–450(2) 41-35385–35386(2), FB462 41-35500, FB476–477(2) 41-35513–35514(2), FB486 41-35538.

The twin-engined Martin PBM- patrol-bomber flying-boat for the US Navy made its maiden flight in 1939. A total of 33 Martin PBM-3B/C Mariner GR.I flying-boats were allocated to the RAF under Lend-Lease JX100–132 but apparently only 28 were delivered. Depicted is JX-117 seen moored at Beaumaris in Anglesey where Saro handled the type after delivery to the United Kingdom. (AP Publications).

MARINER Martin Model 162

Mark No.	US Desig.	Company	Requisition	Contract	RAF Serials	US Serials
GR Mk I	PBM-3B/C	Martin	N-7	N-76927	JX100–132(33)	

Only twenty-eight delivered. JX101/120/126/128/130 not delivered. JX103/G trials aircraft. JX100/105/106/110/122/131 used by 524 Squadron at Oban 20 October to 7 December 1943.

Photo dated 6 April 1941 depicting a Grumman F4F-3 Martlet I AL257 one from the first batch for the Royal Navy AL231–262 procured by the British Purchasing Commission and which were ex French Navy. The first five from the batch went to Canada, the remainder going to the RN air station at Donisbristle, Fifeshire for the Fleet Air Arm. The type was named Wildcat when delivered under Lend-Lease. (Via Philip Jarrett).

LEND-LEASE AIRCRAFT IN WORLD WAR II

MARTLET Grumman Model G-36A. Renamed Wildcat for Lend-Lease aircraft

Mark No.	US Desig.	Company	Requisition	Contract	RAF Serials	US Serials
I	F4F-	Grumman	ex-French Navy		AL231–262(32)	
			ex-French Navy		AX725–747(23)	
			ex-French Navy		BJ554–570(17)	
			ex-French Navy		BT447–456(10)	
III	F4F-3A		ex-Greece		AX753–754(2)	Bu.No.3875–6(2)
			ex-Greece		AX761(1)	3877(1)
			ex-Greece		AX824–829(6)	3878–3883(6)
			ex-Greece		BJ507–527(21)	3884–3904(21)
II	F4F-4				AJ100–153(54)	
					AM954–999(46)	
III	F4F-3				AM954–963(10)	

AL231–262(32) AL231–235 to Canada, remainder mainly diverted to Donibristle for Royal Navy. AX725–747(23) Delivered to Middle East. BT447–456(10) all lost at sea on delivery. AX753–754(2) believed lost at sea in transit. AX824–829 assembled at Prestwick by Scottish Aviation. AJ100–153(54) Main deliveries direct to India. AJ107, 109, 110, 111 lost at sea in transit. AM954–999(46) AM954–963(10) delivered with non-folding wings later replaced by standard wings except for AM954 lost in transit. Deliveries commenced on 27 July 1940 and were completed three months later. The first fixed-wing Model G36B, AM954, was flown at Bethpage in October 1940. First G-36B with folding wings, AM964, first flew on 8 July 1941. Deliveries were made between March 1941 and April 1942, but five were lost at sea.

AL231–262(32) British Purchasing Commission Contract F292. AL257 to BPC 28 August 1940, shipped, arrived Scottish Aviation, Prestwick 1 December 1940. Unpacked and assembled, test-flown 10 December, ferried for storage at RNAS Donibristle 17 December. BJ447–456 lost at sea on delivery.

BJ515 and 562 from 804 Squadron, first US fighter in service with British forces to shoot down a German aircraft, 25 December 1940.

MARYLAND Martin Model 167

Mark No.	US Desig.	Company	Requisition	Contract	RAF Serials	US Serials
I	A-22	Martin			AH205–279(75)	
					AR702–751(50)	
					BJ421–428(8)	
					BS760–777(18)	
II					AH280–429(150)	
					HK836(1)	
					HK845(1)	Martin 167F ex-Vichy

Designed to meet requirements for a USAAC attack-bomber specification the Martin 167W first flew in February 1939. As the A-22 it was unsuccessful in the US so the type was offered for export. The French government purchased it as the Model 167F, but few had been delivered by the surrender of France in 1940, so the remainder were diverted to the RAF. First examples reached Burtonwood in June 1940. Depicted is Maryland I AR711 in this photo dated October 1941. (Via Philip Jarrett).

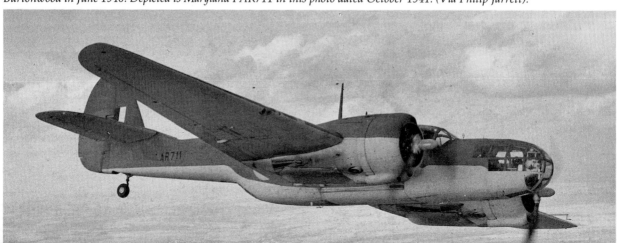

AH205–279 Mk I delivered direct to South African Air Force.

AH280–429 c/n 1827–1976 Mk II mainly delivered direct to Takoradi.

AH301–311, AH313–331, AH371–380, AH386–395, AH406–429 renumbered 1600–1699 SAAF.

AR702–751 First thirty-five had no provision for British equipment.

AR720/736/740 to Royal Navy. AR716 to Free French Air Force.

AR708/742/745/746/747 lost at sea en route from US.

BJ421–428 Ex-French contract to Middle East via UK and Takoradi. BJ422/4/6 lost en route.

BS760–777 Ex-French order. BS777 to Free French Air Force.

BS770 converted to target-tug. BS773 to South African Air Force.

MITCHELL North American NA-40

Mark No.	US Desig.	Company	Requisition	Contract	RAF Serials	US Serials
I	B-25B	N. American	4617	AC-13258	FK161–181(23)	
II	B-25C	N. American	4617	AC-16070	FL164–218(55) FL671–709(39) FR362-384(23)	
				AC-27390	FR393–397(5) FV900–939(40)	
II	B-25D	N. American	4617	AC-19341	FV940–999(60) FW100–280(181) HD302–345(44)	
II	B-25D	N. American	4617	AC-19341	KL133–161(29)	
II	B-25C	N. American			FR141–207(67)	
	B-25G	N. American	40540	AC-27390	FR208–209(2)	42-64822–64823(2)
III	B-25J	N. American	4617	AC-19341	KJ772–787(16) KJ788–800(13) KP308–311(4) KP312–328(17)	44-31145–31160(16) 44-31260–31276(17) 44-31422–31438(17)

FR141–207 allocated to Dutch units under RAF. FR148 lost in transit and FR153/4/5 not delivered. Many transferred to Royal Netherlands AF in 1947. FR362–368 Inglewood built. FR369 lost in transit. Deliveries mainly to 111 OTU Nassau. FR393–397 Inglewood built. FR395 not delivered. FK161–183 FK161, 162, 165 only to UK. FK168 retained in Canada. FK178 crashed before delivery; rest to 111 OTU Nassau.

Known identities: HD310 43-3764, HD312–315(4) 43-3780–3783(4), HD317–320(4) 43-3785–3788, HD322 43-3790, HD323–326(4) 43-3794–3797(4), HD331–335(5) 43-3844–3848, HD337–345(9) 43-3850–3858(9), KL133 41-30548, KL134 41-30596, KL135 41-30637, KL136 41-30757, KL137–139(3) 41-30758–30760(3), KL140 41-30814, KL141 42-87146, KL142 42-87288, KL143 42-87290, KL144 42-87352, KL145 42-87379

Excellent air-to-air portrait of a North American Mitchell II FL212 coded EV-W for Whisky from No.180 Squadron RAF showing nine bomb silhouettes each recording a raid over enemy territory with No.2 (Bomber) Group. The squadron received its first B-25 Mitchell at the end of September 1942 and by the beginning of November it had 22 of the type on strength. Another Mk.II was FL198 EV-P for Peter and a Mk.III was KJ705 EV-T for Tommy. (Via Bruce Robertson).

KL146 43-3629, KL147 42-87501, KL148 43-3634, KL149 43-3647, KL150–154(5) 43-3300–3304(5), KL155–156(2) 43-3307–8(2), KL157–159(3) 43-3310–3312(3), KL160 43-3316, KL161 43-3318.

RCAF Mk I FK164, 166, 171, 176–178, 180. *Mk II* FW220, 237, 246, 251, 259, 260, 272–274, 278–280, HD310–315, 317–320, 322–326, 331–335, 337–345, KL133–161.

Mk III KJ641, 764.

FW220 ex-43-3540, 237 43-3557, 246 43-3566, 251 43-3686, 259 43-3694, 260 43-3695, FW272 43-3710, 273 43-3712, 274, 43-3718, 278 43-3751, 279 43-3752, 280 43-3753. HD310 43-3764, 311 43-3779, 312 43-3780, 313 43-3781, 314 43-3782, 315 43-3783, HD317 43-3785, 318 43-3786, 319 43-3787, 320 43-3788, 322 43-3790, 323 43-3794, HD324 43-3795, 325 43-3796, 326 43-3797, 331 43-3844, 332 43-3845, 333 43-3846, HD334 43-3847, 335 43-3848, 337 43-3850, 338 43-3851, 339 43-3852, 340 43-3853, HD341 43-3854, 342 43-3855, 343 43-3856, 344 43-3857, 345 43-3858. KL133 41-30548, 134 41-30596, 135 41-30637, 136 41-30757, 137 41-30758, 138 41-30759, KL139 41-30760, 140 41-30814, 141 42-87146, 142 42-87288, 143 42-87290, 144 42-87352, KL145 42-87379, 146 43-3269, 147 42-87501, 148 43-3634, 149 43-3647, 150 43-3300, KL151 43-3301, 152 43-3302, 153 43-3303, 154 43-3304, 155 43-3307, 156 43-3308, KL157 43-3310, 158 43-3311, 159 43-3312, 160 43-3316, 161 43-3318.

FW273 ground instruction aircraft A402.

MOHAWK Curtiss Model 75

Mark No.	US Desig.	Company	Requisition	Contract	RAF Serials	US Serials
III/IV	P-36	Curtiss			AR630–694(65)	
IV					AX799(1)	
I/II					AX800–898(19)	
IV					BB918–979(62)	
IV					BJ434–453(20)	
IV					BJ531–550(20)	
III					BK574–588(15)	
I/II					BK876–879(4)	
I/II					BL220–223(4)	
IV					BS730–747(18)	
IV					BS784–798(15)	
IV					BT470–472(3)	
IV					LA147–165(9)	

The US government permitted Curtiss to sell models to France and later Norway and the Netherlands. Nearly 200 served as an effective fighter until the fall of France in 1940. Other Hawk 75s en route were diverted to loyalist French ports and to French Africa. The UK took over the French 75s still in the factory plus some escapees from France and named them Mohawks. While the RAF made little combat use of its Mohawks, many were reassigned to other nations and did well in less active theatres of operations. The type fought on both sides. The Germans captured some still in shipping crates in France and Norway and sold them to Finland, whose pilots used them against the Russians. Other Hawk 75s in Vichy-controlled French North Africa fought briefly against US forces during the Allied landings.

One hundred H75-A1s (RAF Mohawk I) powered with 1,050 hp P & W R-1830-SC3G engine, delivered to France commencing December 1938. After fall of France, some H75-A1s escaped to the UK and as Mohawk I/IIs were given RAF serials. A further one hundred H75-A2s for France (RAF Mohawk II) delivered from May 1939. Two additional wing guns and the R-1830-S1C3G engine making them more like the USAAF P-36D. Some reached UK. One hundred and thirty-five H75-A3s (RAF Mohawk III) for France with 1,200 hp engine. Deliveries commenced in February 1940. Approximately sixty reached France, others diverted to French Morocco with more than twenty taken over by the RAF. Refitted with British equipment, these were transferred to Portugal, South Africa and India. Two hundred and eighty-four H75-A4s (RAF Mohawk IV) were built out of 795 ordered by France. Powered by 1,200 hp Wright R-1820-G205A Cyclone. Only six H75-A4s reached France before the surrender. Four were lost at sea in transit, twenty-three were diverted to Martinique remaining there, and the remainder came to the UK.

The exact total of RAF Mohawk IVs cannot be determined from RAF serial numbers since some blocks apply to both IIIs and IVs. The numbers appearing as IVs total 278, only six less than the total of H75-A4s built. However some Mohawks other than -A4s became IVs, including the ten A9s for Persia and at least six of the former Chinese A5s assembled in India. The Cyclone-powered H75-A5 was intended to be assembled in China, but the operation was never completed, but at least six A5s are known to have been assembled by Hindustan Aircraft in Bangalore, India. These were absorbed into the RAF as Mohawk IVs. Ten H75-A9s for Persia were powered by Wright R-1820-G205A engine. Taken over by the RAF and transferred for use in India.

Of over 200 Curtiss Model 75 (P-36) Mohawks supplied to the RAF, over 100 were shipped to the UK between July and September 1940. After assembly and modification they were distributed for storage at the Maintenance Units located at Little Rissington, Wroughton, Colerne and Lossiemouth. They were never used operationally in Europe but at the end of 1941 were sent to India. For a period eight comprised the sole fighter defence of NE India. They remained operational in Burma until December 1943. Depicted is a Mohawk IV BS734. (Via Philip Jarrett).

Mohawks arriving in the UK after assembly and modification were distributed to RAF MUs located at Little Rissington, Wroughton, Lossiemouth and Colerne and held in reserve. Apparently batch BK574–588 was never delivered to the RAF.

MUSTANG North American (USAAF version initially named Apache) Model NA-73, NA83, NA-91, NA-97, NA-99, NA-104, NA-111

Mark No.	US Desig.	Company	Requisition	Contract	RAF Serials	US Serials
	A-36	North American	40273	AC-27390	EW998(1)	42-83685
I	P-51				AG345–664(320) AL958–999(42) AM100–257(158) AP164–263(100)	
IA	P-51		282	DA-140	FD418–567(150)	41-37320–37469(150)
II	P-51A		282	AC-30479	FR890–939(50)	43-6023–6032(10), 43-6093–6107(15), 43-6208–6232(25)
III	P-51B		282	AC-33923/30479	FX848–999(152) FZ100–147(48) FZ149–197(49) FB100–124(25) FR411(1)	

Excellent air-to-air photo of Mustang I AG351 from the first production batch carrying prototype markings whilst under test and evaluation at the A&AEE Boscombe Down on 9 February 1942. The fighter proved far superior to any contemporary US fighter largely because of the use by North American of a laminar-flow wing and the provision of a smooth nose by locating the radiator well back. (Via Philip Jarrett).

In June 1943 this Mustang I AG357 was experimentally fitted with rocket projectiles as shown in this photo. The /G added to the RAF serial indicated that the aircraft had to be under strict guard 24-hours a day. Early RAF Mustangs were used by Army Co-operation Command being fitted with an oblique camera fitted behind the pilot on the port side. (Via Philip Jarrett).

Mark No.	US Desig.	Company	Requisition	Contract	RAF Serials	US Serials
		North American	282	AC-33940	FB125–399(275) HB821–961(141) KH421–430(10)	42-103019–103194(176) See L2B3-1 for balance of Serials.
			282	AC-40063	KH431–640(210)	
IV	P-51D		282	AC-40063	KH641–670(30)	44-11168–11187(20) 44-11253–11262(10)
			43196	AC-40063	KM493–532(40) KM533–572(40) KM573–623(51) KM624–663(40) KM664–695(32)	44-12903–12942(40) 44-12960–12999(40) 44-13050–13100(51) 44-13141–13180(40) 44-13221–13252(32)
			43196	AC-2400	KM696–743(48)	44-84391–84397(7) 44-84468(1) 44-84681–84720(40)
V	P-51F		40505		FR409(1)	43-43334
IV	P-51G		40505		FR410(1)	43-43336
	P-51H		43465		KN987(1)	44-64181
IV	P-51K		282	AC-40063	KH671–870(200)	44-11374–11413(40) 44-11478–11517(40) 44-11579–11618(40) 44-11699–11738(40) 44-11819–11858(40)
					KM100–139(40)	44-11953–11992(40)
			43196	AC-40063	KM140–310(171) KM311–361(51) KM362–441(80) KM442–492(51)	44-12263–12433(171) 44-12552–12602(51) 44-12628–12707(80) 44-12759–12809(51)
III	P-51B/C				SR406–440(35)	
IV	P-51K				TK586 & 589(2)	Trials aircraft

The type owed its origin to a RAF requirement for a fighter for European service, as no existing US fighter during 1940 could meet the requirement. In January of that year, North American Aviation undertook to design a new fighter in which the early lessons from aerial combat over Europe could be taken account of. The company accepted a 120-day limit for the construction of a prototype. An in-line engine was specified and the British armament of eight machine-guns was also required. The design engineers not only kept inside the 120-day limit, but also succeeded brilliantly in meeting all requirements with their NA-73 design. The prototype, NX19998, flew for the first time on 25 October

1940. Production began almost immediately to meet contracts placed by the British Purchasing Commission, and the first production example flew before the end of 1941. The introduction of Lend-Lease led to an order for the RAF of 150 fighters. Supplied to the RAF as Mustang IAs some were requisitioned for defence of the United States after Pearl Harbor, these flying in British camouflage and RAF serial numbers but with US star insignia. To further improve the high-altitude performance of the new fighter, it was proposed in the UK that the Rolls-Royce Merlin should be installed. Four RAF Mustang Is were converted at the engine factory at Derby. Flight tests commencing on 30 November 1942 showed an increase of 50 mph in max. speed at optimum altitude to a new high of 441 mph. These four Mustang Is were AL963, AL975, AM203 and AM208 fitted with Merlin 61 or 65 engines driving four-blade airscrews and having radiator fittings. They were designated Mk X fighters.

Mk I AG345–664 (320) Twenty-one lost at sea during delivery. Ten re-shipped to Russia. AG357 experimentally fitted with rocket projectiles. AL958–AM257(200) AL975/G was Mk III prototype. AM106/G used on various armament tests. AP164–263(100) for RAF Army Co-operation Command. EW998(1) Used for evaluation as fighter-bomber.

Mk III FB100–399(300) FB205 crashed before delivery. FB235, 237, 238 not delivered. Some to SAAF squadrons in Italy.

Mk IA FD418–567(150) FD510–527 retained in the US. FD473 used for Malcolm hood trials.

Mk II FR890–939(50) FR901 had special long-range tanks fitted by Air Service Training.

Mk III FX848–FZ197(250) FX992 crashed before delivery. FX848–851, 856, 857, 861, 863, 867–870, 875, 877, 879, 883, 886, 891, 894, 902, 905–907, 909–911, 913–916, 918, 927, 928, 932, 948 were handed back to the USAAF on arrival in the UK.

Mk V/IV/III FR409–411(3) FR409 Mk V, FR410 Mk IV, FR411 Mk III.

Mk III HB821–961(141) Delivered after April 1944 except HB920 which crashed before delivery. HB838 to USAAF.

Mk II/IV/IVA KH421–870(450). KH421–640 Mk III. KH641–670 Mk IV. KH671–870 Mk IVA. KH470, 687 crashed before delivery.

Mk IV/IVA KM100–799(700). KM100–492 Mk IVA. KM493–743 Mk IV. KM744–799 not delivered.

Mk III SR406–440(35) Ex-USAAF P-51B/C. SR439 not delivered.

Mk IV TK586, 589(2) Trials aircraft. TK589 ex-44-13332.

FR410 ex-XP-51G-NA 43-43336. Mk V FR409 ex-XP-51F-NA 43-43334. KN987 Mk IV (P-51H) for evaluation.

Mk III	SR406 ex-43-12162	SR415 ex-43-7039	SR423 ex-42-106683	SR432 ex-43-7152
	SR407 ex-43-12407	SR416 ex-43-6831	SR424 ex-42-106630	SR433 ex-43-7135
	SR408 ex-43-12412	SR417 ex-43-12155	SR425 ex-42-106687	SR434 ex-42-103209
	SR409 ex-43-12473	SR418 ex-43-12188	SR426 ex-43-7071	SR435 ex-42-106478
	SR410 ex-43-12484	SR419 ex-43-12456	SR427 ex-43-7144	SR436 ex-42-106431
	SR411 ex-43-12427	SR420 ex-43-12480	SR428 ex-43-5595	SR437 ex-43-7007
	SR412 ex-43-7014	SR421 ex-43-12399	SR429 ex-43-7171	SR438 ex-43-12420
	SR413 ex-43-12189	SR422 ex-42-106663	SR430 ex-43-6829	SR439 Cancelled
	SR414 ex-43-12177		SR431 ex-43-12420	SR440 ex-43-7159

NAVIGATOR Beechcraft Model B-18S

Mark No.	US Desig.	Company	Requisition	Contract	RAF Serials	US Serials
	AT-7B	Beechcraft	40269	AC-24998	FR879–883(5)	42-2508/9 42-43475–43477

FR880 became 'PB2' for Prince Bernhard of the Netherlands. FR881/2 to India.
FE882/3 were given incorrectly to FR882/3 Expediters.

NOMAD Northrop 8A-5

Mark No.	US Desig.	Company	Requisition	Contract	RAF Serials	US Serials
I	A-17A	Northrop			AS440–462(23) AS958–976(19) AW420–438(19)	

LEND-LEASE AIRCRAFT IN WORLD WAR II

Only AS958/967/971/AW421 to RAF. Rest to South African Air Force. Eight of first batch and six of second batch lost at sea. Surplus USAAF A-17A. French Purchasing Commission obtained ninety-three which were returned to Douglas to be refurbished and re-engined. With the fall of France sixty-one taken over by British Purchasing Commission and thirty-two went to RCAF.

NORSEMAN Noorduyn

Mark No.	US Desig.	Company	Requisition	Contract	RAF Serials	US Serials
IV	UC-64A	Noorduyn	40496	AC-28393	FR405–406(2) FZ441–442(2)	43-5137–5138(2) 43-5386–5387(2)

Ex-RCAF aircraft on temporary loan and possibly retained in Canada.

FZ441 c/n 377 ex-RCAF '2495', FZ442 c/n 378 ex RCAF '2496' operated by 413 Squadron RCAF.

RELIANT Stinson Model SR-8. V-77

Mark No.	US Desig.	Company	Requisition	Contract	RAF Serials	US Serials
	SR-9D	Stinson			W5791(1)	
	SR7-10				W7978–7984(7)	
	SR-5				X8518–8522(5)	
	SR-8				X9596(1)	
I	AT-19		3328	DA-1072	FK814–999(186) FL100–163(64)	42-46640–46889 43-43964–44213(500)
I	AT-19		40407	DA-1072-10	FB523–772(250)	

W5791 ex-G-AFBI, W7978 ex-G-AFRS, W7979 ex-G-AEFY, W7980 ex-G-AEVX, W7981 ex-G-AFHB, W7982 ex-G-AEXW, W7983 ex-G-AFTM, W7984 ex-G-AEVY, X8518 ex-G-ACSV, X8519 ex-G-ADDG, X8520 ex-G-AEJI, X8521 ex-G-AEYZ, X8522 ex-G-AFUW, X9596 ex-G-AELU impressed May 1940.

FK814–FL163 mainly for Royal Navy. FB523–722 mainly for Royal Navy.

Aircraft built to British contracts but which were diverted to the US Navy included Bu.No. 30481–30452, plus Bu.No. 37637/8 and 99085–99088 which were cancelled.

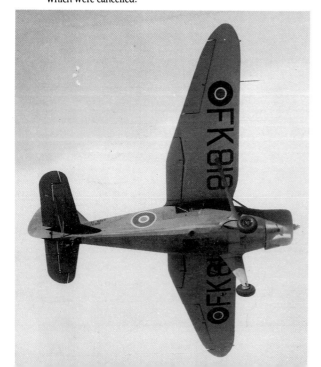

The US-built civil version of the Stinson Reliant first appeared in 1933. Some 500 military versions were transferred to the Royal Navy under Lend-Lease and employed for navigation training and communications with some 24 second-line squadrons. Depicted in this A&AEE Boscombe Down photo dated 14 June 1943 is Reliant I FK818. (Via Philip Jarrett).

The Curtiss Seamew was a two-seat reconnaissance aircraft suitable for catapult launch and equipped with either land or seaplane undercarriage. It was the Lend-Lease version of the US Navy SO3C-2C but saw no operational service with the Royal Navy and from 1943 was relegated to training. Depicted is Seamew I FN473 from a batch of 200 FN450–649 there being on record that only 13 were delivered. (Via Philip Jarrett).

The Vultee-Stinson L-5 Sentinel was widely used by the Allies in South-East Asia Command (SEAC) during World War 2 for communications, air ambulance and spotting duties. A total of 100 were delivered for use by the RAF. Power was from a 185 hp Lycoming engine. The ambulance version was the Sentinel IB (L-5B) the RAF operating 60 of this version. Depicted is an un-identified Sentinel with RAF serial LG552 which belongs to an Airspeed Horsa glider. (APN).

SEAMEW Curtiss Model 82

Mark No.	US Desig.	Company	Requisition	Contract	RAF Serials	US Serials
I	SOC3-2C	Curtiss			FN450–649(200) JW550–669(120)	22007–22207(200) 22208–22256

For Royal Navy, but FN453/463–467/472/483/489/573/608/622/631/ only delivered. JW550–669 for Royal Navy but full delivery not made.

Total of 250 destined for the Royal Navy, to have been SO3C-1Bs were designated SO3C-2C. Seventy went to Canada. See Seamew Drone.

Canada: Eighty-two. FN480–486, 489–496, 498, 499, 600–608, 610–613, 615, 616, 618–620, 622, 623, 625, 627, 629–642. Sold to Royal Navy at Worthy Down. JW576–578, 580–583, 614–618, 621, 622, 634, 638, 640, 642. Sold to Royal Navy. JW618 damaged in transit, written off.

SEAMEW DRONE Curtiss Model 84

Mark No.	US Desig.	Company	Requisition	Contract	RAF Serials	US Serials
I	SO3C-1K	Curtiss	BAC/N-1857		JX663–669(7) JZ771–774(4) KE286–304(19)	

Known in the Royal Navy as Queen Seamew MK 1. Batch KE286–304 cancelled.

SENTINEL Stinson

Mark No.	US Desig.	Company	Requisition	Contract	RAF Serials	US Serials
I	L-5	Stinson	41831	AC-34453	KJ368–407(40)	42-99487–99506(20) 42-99549–99558(10) 42-99539–99548(10)
IB	L-5B	Stinson	41831	AC-34453	KJ408–467(60)	42-99591–99610(20) 42-99673–99689(17) 42-99700–99702(3) 44-16969–16988(20)

For use in Air Command South-East Asia.

LEND-LEASE AIRCRAFT IN WORLD WAR II

SKYMASTER Douglas DC-4

Mark No.	US Desig.	Company	Requisition	Contract	RAF Serials	US Serials
I	C-54B	Douglas	41719	AC-20284	EW999	43-17126(1)
I	C-54D	Douglas	43195	AC-27311	KL977–986(10)	42-72442/72484/ 42-72530/72532/ 42-72584/72585/ 42-72644/72645/ 42-76678/72679(10)
I	C-54D	Douglas			KL988–999(12)	

Used by the RAF with 232 and 246 Squadrons and were returned to the US Navy and US Marine Corps after World War Two. Bu.No. 91994 (KL977), 91995 (KL979), 91996 (KL980), 91997 (KL982), 91998 (KL984), 91999 (KL985), 92000 (KL986), 92002 (KL981), 92003 (KL978).

TARPON Grumman Model G-40 (See Avenger). Renamed Avenger on 13 January 1944

THUNDERBOLT Republic P-44

Mark No.	US Desig.	Company	Requisition	Contract	RAF Serials	US Serials
I	P-47D	Republic	41278	AC-29279	FL731–850(120) HB962–999(38) HD100–181(82)	
II	P-47D	Republic	41278	AC-29279	HD182–301(120) KJ128–367(240) KL168–347(180) KL838–841(4)	
II	P-47D	Republic	43197	AC-24579	KL842–887(46) KL888–976(89)	44-90076-120(45) 90335(1)

Notes: KL888–976(89) cancelled. Deliveries mainly direct to India. FL738 crashed in US. HD182 delivered to UK.

The Thunderbolt II was the most widely used version with the RAF which equated to the USAAF P-47D-25 and had a 'tear-drop' moulded canopy as shown on KJ299. This improved all-round vision. In all 830 Thunderbolts were supplied under Lend-Lease of which 240 were Mk.Is and 590 Mk.IIs. (Via Peter M Bowers).

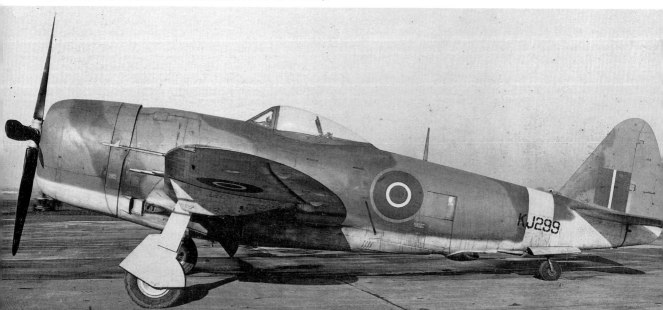

Two Grumman F7F-2N Tigercat aircraft were supplied from the US Navy to the Royal Navy for evaluation at the end of 1945 and allocated the serials TT346 and TT349 but retained US markings. One went to the A&AEE at Boscombe Down to test its suitability for carrier operations. The second went to RAE Farnborough to test single-engine recovery capability, and the use of the power boosted rudder. The Tigercat I was considered to be a most attractive aircraft possessing good and bad deck operating characteristics. Depicted is a ground shot of TT346. (Via Philip Jarrett/Bruce Robertson).

TIGERCAT Grumman Design 51

Mark No.	US Desig.	Company	Requisition	Contract	RAF Serials	US Serials
I	F7F-2N	Grumman			TT346, 349(2)	

Ex-US Navy and transferred to Royal Navy for evaluation.

TIGER MOTH De Havilland (Canada) DH-82C

Mark No.	US Desig.	Company	Requisition	Contract	RAF Serials	US Serials
	PT-24	de Havilland	2670	DA-230	FE100–266(167) FH618–650(33)	42-964–1163(200)

Allocated the RCAF serials 1100–1299 c/n 1303–1502 before being funded under Lend-Lease with USAAF serials and delivered with RAF serials and retained in Canada.

FE100–266 (167) c/n 1303–1469 transferred to RCAF with serials '1100–1266'.

A total of 2,949 de Havilland Tiger Moths were built in Australia and New Zealand for use by pilots training under the huge Commonwealth Air Training Plan. A further 200 were funded under Lend-Lease by the United States as the PT-24 with initially USAAF serials and then RAF serials FE100–266 (167) FH618–650 (33). They remained in Canada and the first 167 were allocated RCAF serials. Depicted somewhere in Canada are Lend-Lease Tiger Moths which were fitted with a canopy, an item very necessary in winter. (AP Photo Library).

Depicted is an early Curtiss Tomahawk I AH762 equivalent to the USAAC P-40B and from the RAF batch AH741–880 – 140 aircraft. A number from this allocation were shipped to Russia and RAF deliveries commenced in April 1940 but the RAF quickly decided that this model was unsuitable for combat duties and relegated them to training roles. (Via Philip Jarrett).

TOMAHAWK Curtiss Model Hawk 81

Mark No.	US Desig.	Company	Requisition	Contract	RAF Serials	US Serials
I	P-40C	Curtiss	1016	AC-15802	None	41-13389, 13390(2)
						41-13396–13401(6)
						41-13406, 13407(2)
I	P-40B	Curtiss			AH741–880(140)	
IIA	P-40B				AH881–990(110)	
IIB	P-40C				AH991–999(9)	
IIB	P-40C				AK100–570(471)	
IIB	P-40C				AM370–519(150)	
IIB	P-40C				AN218–517(300)	

AH774, 793, 840 to Canada. AH936, 952, 965–971, 974–985, 987, 989–990 to USSR. Nine, AH991–999, to USSR. AK210–224, 226–241 lost in transit at sea. One to Turkish Air Force. Nine, including AK254, 434, 440, 448, 470, 561, to Royal Egyptian Air Force. Thirty-six to the American Volunteer Group in China. AM370–519, over sixty, to AVG in China. AN469–517 to USSR. Eight to Egypt and twenty-four to Turkey.

RCAF Mk I Ground instruction aircraft: AH774 c/n 14479, AH793 c/n 14498, AH840 c/n 14545.

Mk IIA AH938 c/n 14188.

TRAVELLER Beechcraft Model 17

Mark No.	US Desig.	Company	Requisition	Contract	RAF Serials	US Serials
	YC-43	Beech			DR628(1)	39–139(1)
	C-17R				DS180(1)	
					EB279–280(2)	
I	C-43		5911	DA-1042	FL653–670(18)	43-38674–38691(18)
I	GB-2		41097	AC-31386	FT461–535(75)	32867–32915(49)
I	C-43		40787	AC-31386	FZ428–435(8)	43-10870–10877(8)
			40787	AC-31386	FZ436–439(4)	43-10884–10887(4)
					FZ442–443(2)	43-10874–10875(2)

Amongst the 105 Beechcraft Model 17 aircraft supplied under Lend-Lease some 25 were ex US Navy GB-2s FT461–535 for use by the Royal Navy and named Traveller. Depicted is Traveller II FT461 still carrying GB-2 and BuNo.23657 on the tail. After World War 2, 49 of this batch were returned to the USA and allocated new US Navy BuNo's – FT461 c/n 6669 became BuNo.32867. The type was used by both the RAF and the Royal Navy. (Via Philip Jarrett).

Beech D-17S YC-43 c/n 295 39–139 to DR628 allotted for personal use of Prince Bernhard. FL653–670 mainly to Middle East but FL659–670 were lost at sea en route. FT461–535 for RN ex-US Navy and USAAF. FZ429 crashed in US before delivery. FZ432 Middle East 1944. FZ438 '310886' c/n 4934 shipped to Middle East 1 February 1944. DS180 c/n 118 G-AESJ impressed C-17R in May 1941. EB279–280 impressed in the US for British Air Commission, Washington DC.

The British (RN & RAF) received a total of 105 Beechcraft Model D17s under Lend-Lease, which were designated Traveller Mk I. The RN aircraft were flown from the Beech Aircraft factory at Wichita to Fort Dix, McGuire AFB, where they were dismantled and crated for transport by rail to Newark, New Jersey. Here they were loaded aboard ship for the Atlantic crossing to the UK. The thirty Travellers delivered to the RAF were shipped in batches from New York to Suez in the Middle East in March 1943 aboard SS *Tabian*, in April aboard the SS *Agumonte*, and in October aboard the SS *Philip Schugler*. Twelve of these aircraft were lost at sea when the SS *Agumonte* was torpedoed by a U-boat on 29 May 1943 at position 34° 52'S, 19° 33'E off Quoin Point, Cape Province, South Africa. At least six, including FZ432, served with the Communication Flight based at RAF Khormaksir, Aden; operated on daily reconnaissance flights along the coastline looking for any indications of landings by enemy submarine crews on the beaches.

VANGUARD Vultee Model 48C

Mark No.	US Desig.	Company	Requisition	Contract	RAF Serials	US Serials
I	P-66	Vultee			BW208–307(100)	

Batch of one hundred initially ordered by Sweden, offered to the UK as advanced trainers but eventually shipped to the Chinese Air Force. Two aircraft, BW208 and 209, flew for a short period in RAF livery.

Vultee completed a prototype of its Model 48C Vanguard fighter (P-66) in September 1939 and obtained an export order from Sweden for 144. Deliveries to Sweden were barred, so the order became assigned to the RAF, the RCAF and eventually China under Lend-Lease arrangements. A total of 100 BW208–307 were offered to the RAF as advanced trainers but only BW208 and BW209 flew in RAF livery as depicted in the photos. Eventually the batch was shipped to China. (Via Bruce Robertson).

The first contract for the Vultee V-72 Vengeance was signed on 3 July 1940 by officials from the British Purchasing Commission and Vultee Aircraft, covering 200 dive-bombers. Contract price was $14,202.200 per 200 aircraft and $2,840,400 for spares. An additional $800 per aircraft boxed for export was also to be paid. Depicted in flight on 22 August 1942 is Vengeance I AN889 from the RAF batch AN838–999. (Via Philip Jarrett).

VENGEANCE Vultee Model 72

Mark No.	US Desig.	Company	Requisition	Contract	RAF Serials	US Serials
I	A-31	Vultee			AN838–999(162) AP100–137(38)	
I/IA	A-31	Northrop	2648	DA-120	EZ800–999(100)	41-30848–31047(200)
II	A-31	Vultee			AN538–837(300)	
II	A-31	Northrop		A-557	AF745–944(200)	
III	A-31C	Vultee	2647	DA-119	FB918–999(82) FD100–117(18)	41-31048–31147(100)
IV-1	A-35B	Vultee	145	DA-119	FD118–221(104)	41-31258, 31260, 31291, 31261 41-31311–31410(100)
IV-2	A-35B	Vultee	145	AC-24664	FD222–417(196) HB300–550(251) KG810–820(11) FP686(1)	

Origin of the type conceived as a result of negotiations with French government whose purchasing visits to US in 1938/39/40 by French Air Force officers sought new designs to supplement their ailing military aircraft programme with emphasis on a dive-bomber. British Purchasing Commission saw the Vultee design during its search for dive-bombers. First contract signed 3 July 1940 for 200 dive-bombers. Two prototypes, AF745, 746.

AN838, 993 retained in the US and AN670 crashed before delivery as did AN679 which was replaced by FP686. AN869–871, 873, 877, 879, 971, 973, 974 sunk en route to India. AN853–857, 872, 874–876, 878, 892, 894, 896–898 shipped from Los Angeles to Sydney for RAAF. *EZ800–999* EZ800–818 Mk I, EZ819–999 Mk IA. EZ880–888, 906–974 not delivered and eighty-four offset to RAAF. Main deliveries to RAF in India to 301 MU Drigh Road for assembly and flight testing. *AF745–944* AF758, 778, 797, 800, 814, 820, 828, 840, 849, 859, 860, 862, 869, 874, 878, 888, 912, 918, 931 shipped direct to Australia for RAAF. Remainder diverted to USAAF. *FB918–FD417* FD122–124, 126, 128–130, 134, 137, 159, 167, 180, 184, 187, 188, 190, 193–196, 200, 201, 204, 207–209, 212, 213, 215, 217, 220 retained by USAAF. FD288, 307, 339, 381, 415 crashed in US before delivery. Mk III mainly delivered to India, Mk IV to UK where many were converted to target-tugs. FD221, 224, 246, 287, 290, 303, 320, 325, 327, 334, 341, 351, 353, 355, 358, 359, 361, 372, 377, 383, 392, 339, 405 to Royal Navy. *KG810–820* for RAF except KG812, 818 which went to Royal Navy.

AF759 used by USAAF as flying test-bed for Wright 2,200 hp R-3350-13 Double Cyclone engine. FD186 used at USAAF proving ground. AN581–608 to Brazil. HB335 MK IV to RN as target tug. The NACA establishment located at Lewis, Cleveland on Lake Erie had two Vengeance aircraft for testing, quoted as YA-31C models EZ887 and AF782, between July 1944 and July 1945. The first one for R-3350 mixture distribution problems, the other for ground tests and instrumentation development connected with the R-3350 engine.

VENTURA Lockheed Model 37

Mark No.	US Desig.	Company	Requisition	Contract	RAF Serials	US Serials
I	B-34	Lockheed			AE658–845(188)	
II	B-34				AE846–957(112)	
II	B-34				AJ163–537(375)	
IIA	B-34		41018	DA-152	FD568–767(200)	41-38020–38219(200)
GRV	PV-1		N-517	NOa(S)198	FN956–967(12) FN969–999(31) FP537–548(12)	
GRV	PV-1		N-517	NOa(S)284	FP549–684(136) JS889–984(96) JT800–898(99)	

AE658–957(300) Sixteen crashed en route before delivery. Forty-two held in Canada for the RCAF, eighty-two diverted to the SAAF. AE850, 857–861, 863–870, 890, transferred to the USAAF. AJ163–537 of which only forty-one served with the RAF due to offsets to RCAF, SAAF and losses during ferrying. AJ165, 168–170, 172–180, 185, 187, 189–192, 195, 197–205, 207–215, 217–223, 227–278, 280–358, 360–372, 374, 376–382, 384–387, 400–401, 403, 405–406, 408, 410–428, 432–442, 530 transferred to the USAAF. AJ511 became USN Bu.No.33925 and AJ537 33951. FD568–767(200) Twenty-three diverted to RNZAF and others including FD568 to the USAAF. FN956–999(43) FN965, 967, 968, 972–974, 977–979, 987, 991, 992, 995, 996 retained in Canada. Some retained by US Navy. FP537–684(148) Ninety only delivered, FP645, 647 crashed before delivery. FP642-644, 648, 649 were retained by the US Navy. JS889-984(96) delivered to Middle East. JS900, 971 crashed in Brazil during delivery flight. JS903, 904, 921–925, 938, 939, 941, 942, 976–979 direct to SAAF. JS896, 909, 930, 953, 956, 975 transferred to SAAF in 1945. RCAF operated 129 Ventura I/IIs ex-RAF, twenty GRVs also ex-RAF.

RCAF Mk I AE658, 659, 661, 663–674, 676–678, 696, 703, 728.

Mk II AE849, 851, 860, 866–869, 871, 872, 874, 878, 879, 882, 886, 887, 889, 893, AE905, 907, 911, 912, 922, 923, 925, 926, 928–932, 934, 936, 942–944, 946, AE950, 952–954. AJ164, 173, 186, 194, 211, 230, 247, 270, 302, 335, 358, AJ373, 375, 383, 388, 389, 402, 404, 407, 409, 429, 430, 448. FD572, 574, 621, 637, 643, 645, 646, 649, 654, 660, 662, 668, 675, 677, 685, FD688, 689, 692, 693, 697, 699, 700–702, 705, 707, 710–714, 721, 728–733, FD738–740, 742, 752, 754, 755.

GR Mk V FN967, 971–983, FP542–547.

Ground instruction aircraft: AE664 as A287, AE671 as A324, AE953 as A578, AE934 as A577, AE912 as A447.

Once the idea of using light aircraft for field liaison and communication duties had been established by their use in large-scale manoeuvres early in World War 2, contracts were negotiated, mainly in the USA, for a number of different types. Eight Stinson L-1 Vigilant were assigned to the RAF under Lend-Lease followed by 96 L-1A many of the latter being retained by the USAAF and operated in a combination of both British and USAAF markings. Both HL429 and HL430 were evaluated at the A&AEE Boscombe Down during November and December 1941. Both carried (P) markings for some unknown reason. (Via Philip Jarrett).

LEND-LEASE AIRCRAFT IN WORLD WAR II

VIGILANT Stinson Model 74

Mark No.	US Desig.	Company	Requisition	Contract	RAF Serials	US Serials
IA	O-49/L-1A	Stinson	2292	AC-17910	BZ100–154(55)	
IA	O-49A/L-1A	Stinson	2292	AC-17910	BZ155–195(41)	
I	O-49/L-1	Stinson	2292	AC-13098	FR401–404(4)	
I	O-49/L-1	Stinson			HL429–432(4)	

BZ101, 102, 110 used as spares. RAF serials of 40-262/3/4/5 not known. BZ109, 111–154 not delivered. BZ155–195 cancelled. Origin of HL429–432 not known.

WIDGEON Grumman G-44

Mark No.	US Desig.	Company	Requisition	Contract	RAF Serials	US Serials
I	J4F-2	Grumman	N-262	N-5229	JS996(1)	32956(1)
(Used at Miami, Florida. See Gosling.)						
I	J4F-2	Grumman	N-1117	NOa(S)455	FP455–469(15)	

For use by the Royal Navy in the West Indies. Originally named Gosling.

A total of 16 Grumman J4F-2 Widgeon amphibians were delivered to the Royal Navy under Lend-Lease and were utilised on communications duties mainly in the West Indies between 1943/45. In British service the type was originally known as the Gosling. Depicted is Widgeon I FP460 from the batch of 15 FP455–469. JS996 was a single delivery ex US Navy BuNo.32956. (Via Peter M Bowers).

The US Navy designation F4F-4B identified the Wildcat IV delivered to the Royal Navy under Lend-Lease. Fleet Air Arm aircraft were assigned serials FN100–319 of which 220 of these fighters were produced between February/November 1942. Six – FN109/110/111/205/206/207 – were lost at sea in transit. Main deliveries were to the UK but FN172–188 went direct to Mombasa. Depicted is FN202 heavily armed with underwing rocket-projectiles and seen after modification at the Brough Factory of Blackburn Aircraft (AP Publications)

WILDCAT Grumman Model G-36A. Lend-Lease version. See Martlet.

Mark No.	US Desig.	Company	Requisition	Contract	RAF Serials	US Serials
III	F4F-3	Grumman	1465	N-75736	AX753–754,761, 824–829 BJ507–527(30)	38 75–3904(3) Grumman c/n
IV	F4F-4B		154, 7207	LL 83734	FN100–319(220)	
V	FM-1	Gen. Motors	N-4	LL 99036	JV325–636(312)	
VI	FM-2	Gen. Motors	N-4	NOa(S)227	JV637–924(288) JW785–836(52) JZ860–889(30)	

FN109–111, 205–207 lost at sea in transit. FN172–188 delivered direct to Mombasa. FM-1 and FM-2 built by Eastern Aircraft Division of the General Motors Corporation. JZ860–889(30) delivered to Far East and Australia. Contract N-75736 initially destined for Greece. AX753–754 believed lost at sea.

Known ex-US Navy Bu.Nos.

	Bu.No.	
JV687–711(25)	47043–47067(25)	
JV712–736(25)	47368–47392(25)	
JV737–756(20)	55305–55324(20)	
JV757–776(20)	56759–56778(20)	
JV777–781(5)	57079–57083(5)	

WACO CG-13A

Mark No.	US Desig.	Company	Requisition	Contract	RAF Serials	US Serials
	CG-13A	Ford	41926	AC-28380	KL162–167(6)	43-43875–43877(3) 43-43879–43881(3)
					KK790–791(2)	

Gliders for evaluation. KL162/3 to the UK. KL164/5/6/7 to India.

During the early days of World War 2 the Autogiro Company of America and the Pitcairn-Larsen organisation completed the design of the PA-39 tandem two-seater autogiro under a British government contract. It was intended to operate from the small deck area of a convoy vessel using a vertical jump take-off, and scout for German U-boats which were raising havoc with Allied convoys. A total of seven PA-39s were produced for the RAF these being remanufactured PA-18 autogiros purchased back from their owners. Depicted is PA-39 BW833 seen at the A&AEE Boscombe Down on 11 December 1941. It was written-off in a flying accident on 19 November 1942. (Via Philip Jarrett).

PITCAIRN AUTOGYRO PA-39

Mark No.	US Desig.	Company	Requisition	Contract	RAF Serials	US Serials
	PA-39	Pitcairn			BW828–834(7)	

BS828, 829, 830 lost at sea in transit.

MONOCOUPE Universal 90-AF

Mark No.	US Desig.	Company	Requisition	Contract	RAF Serials	US Serials
	L-7A	Universal	40166FF	AC-23802	None	42-88638–88654(17) 42-88656/7(2) 42-88655 cancelled

The Monocoupe Model 90 was introduced by the Monocoupe Corporation in 1930, and this two-seat cabin high-wing monoplane was progressively improved until 1942 when production was suspended. Nineteen Model 90-AF Monocoupes powered by 90 hp Franklin 0-200-1 engine were sent to France.

LEND-LEASE SERIALS NTU

With the end of World War Two large aircraft contracts placed in the United States for both the USAAF, US Navy and the Lend-Lease programme were cancelled, mounting to thousands of aircraft of many types.

Here in the United Kingdom this resulted in RAF serial numbers allocated for Lend-Lease aircraft not being taken up. The block KP329 to KV300, involving nearly 5,000 aircraft, was reserved but not taken up and so never used.

A further batch involved RZ435 to RZ999, some 815 aircraft, reserved for Lend-Lease aircraft and dated 14 January 1944. This was the first part of the fifth and final batch of serials allotted to the British Aeronautical Commission in Washington DC for allocation to Lend-Lease aircraft constructed in the US and Canada. The fifth batch total comprised some 9,100 serials extending to SL534. It is known that SA100 to SA549 were allocated but not used; there is no evidence that the numbers RZ435 to RZ999 were ever allocated.

RZ410 to RZ581 were reserved for Hamilcar Mk I gliders of which RZ410 to 431 were built and allocations to RZ581 cancelled. The serials SL541 to SM698 were allocated to Spitfires.

Appendix B

This includes RAF serial block allocation, the corresponding USAAF and US Navy numbers, plus the company construction numbers for the well-known North American Harvard training aircraft.

Detailed listing of Consolidated B-24 Liberators allocated to the RAF under Lend-Lease, some with no RAF serials and used in the European and Mediterranean theatres of operations. Full listing of B-24 USAAF serials, this corresponding to the RAF serial blocks. In odd cases extra USAAF serials were allocated as replacements for aircraft which were damaged before delivery to the United Kingdom.

Detailed production blocks from the Douglas Aircraft Company involving Lend-Lease contracts which include RAF Dakota transports.

Serial Numbers

BRITISH MILITARY SERIAL NUMBERS ALLOCATED TO HARVARDS

RAF serial	Mk.	USAAF serials	Qty	
N7000–7199	I	-	200	
P5783–5982	I	-	200	
AH185–204	II	-	20	
AJ538–987	II	-	450	Originally Ordered by French Air Force
BD130–137	II	-	8	ex RCAF 2521–2528
BJ410,411	II	-	2	ex RCAF 2529, 2530
BJ412–415	II	-	4	ex RCAF 2534–2537
BS808	II	-	1	ex RCAF 2538
BW184–207	II	-	24	
DG430,431	II	-	2	
DG432–439	II	-	8	ex RCAF 2539–2546
EX100–846	IIa	41-33073/33819	747	
EX847–999	III	41-33820/33972	153	
EZ100–249	III	41-33973/34122	150	
EZ250–258	III	42-84163/84171	9	
EZ259–278	III	42-84182/84201	20	
EZ279–298	III	42-84282/84301	20	
EZ299–308	III	42-84362/84371	10	
EZ309–328	III	42-84453/84472	20	
EZ329–348	III	42-84543/84562	20	
EZ349–358	III	42-84633/84642	10	
EZ359–378	III	42-84723/84742	20	
EZ379–398	III	42-84803/84822	20	
EZ399–408	III	42-84923/84932	10	
EZ409–428	III	42-85013/85032	20	
EZ429–448	III	42-85103/85122	20	
EZ449–458	III	42-85223/85232	10	
EZ459–799	III	-		Cancelled
FE267–766	IIb	42-464/963	500	
FE767–999	IIb	42-12254/12486	233	
FH100–166	IIb	42-12487/12553	67	
FS661–999	IIb	43-12502/12840	339	
FT100–460	IIb	43-12841/13201	361	
FT955–974	III	42-44538/44557	20	
FX198–497	IIb	43-34615/34914	300	Not in strict order
KE305	III		1	ex USN 26800
KE306	III		1	ex USN 26812
KE307–309	III		3	ex USN 26816–26818
KF100–757	IIb	-	658	Not in strict order
KF758–900	IIb	-		Cancelled
KF901–999	IIb	-	99	
KG100–309	IIb	-		Cancelled

Totals:		
	Mk.I	400
	Mk.II	519
	Mk.IIa	747
	Mk.IIb	2557
	Mk.III	537
		4760

Construction numbers

In the following list, the North American Aviation construction numbers for Harvards Mk IIa and Mk III are incomplete and those shown should be treated as provisional. The Noorduyn construction numbers for Mk IIb aircraft in the FX and KF serial batches were not necessarily in strict order of serial number.

RAF serial	Const. nos.	RAF serial	Const. nos.
N7000–7199	49.748–947	EX789–796	88.13903–13910
P5783–5982	49.1053–1252	EX811–828	88.14161–14178
AH185–204	66.2747–2766	EX835–847	88.14371–14383
AJ538–987	76.3508–3957	EX857–868	88.14483–14494
BD130–137	66.2254–2261	EX873–884	88.14544–14555
BJ410,411	66.2262,2263	EX890–909	88.14657–14676
BJ412–415	66.2267–2270	EX925–946	88.14870–14890
BS808	66.2271	EX972–989	88.15052–15069
BW184–207	81.4109–4132	EX997–999	88.15122–15124
DG430,431	66.	EZ100–105	88.15125–15130
DG432–439	66.2272–2279	EZ144–177	88.15334–15367
EX100–224	88.9179–9303	EZ184–194	88.15688–15698
EX225–244	88.9611–9630	EZ229–258	88.15856–15885
EX245–254	88.9641–9650	EZ259–278	88.15896–15915
EX255–264	88.9661–9670	EZ279–296	88.15996–16013
EX265–284	88.9681–9700	EZ297,298	88.16081,16082
EX285–294	88.9721–9730	EZ299–308	88.16143–16152
EX295–304	88.9748–9757	EZ309–328	88.16234–16253
EX305–314	88.9778–9787	EZ329–348	88.16324–16343
EX315–324	88.9808–9817	EZ349–358	88.16414–16423
EX325–334	88.9838–9847	EZ359–378	88.16504–16523
EX335–344	88.9868–9877	EZ379–398	88.16584–16603
EX345–354	88.9913–9822	EZ399–408	88.16704–16713
EX355–364	88.9958–9967	EZ409–428	88.16794–16813
EX365–372	88.10008–10015	EZ429–448	88.16884–16903
EX392–396	88.10108–10112	EZ449–458	88.17004–17013
EX398–401	88.10154–10157	FE267–999	14.001–733
EX421–432	88.10251–10262	FH100–166	14.734–800
EX433–584	88.10528–10677	FS661–999	14A.801–1139
EX585–619	88.12029–12063	FT100–460	14A.1140–1500
EX633–646	88.12127–12140	FX198–497	14A.1501–1800
EX660–688	88.12326–12354	KE305,306	88.11444,11445
EX692–705	88.12758–12771	KE307–309	88.11460–11462
EX741–749	88.13187–13194	KF100–757	14A.1801–2458
EX779–786	88.13598–13605	KF901–999	18.002–100

USAAF serial numbers of B-24 Liberators allocated to the Royal Air Force under Lend-Lease.

Theatre transfers

European Theatre of Operations		Mediterranean Theatre of Operations	
41-28868	42-52771	41-11906	42-78110
41-29568	42-94771	41-28722 +	42-78113 +
42-50744	42-94797	41-29278 +	42-78129
42-51226	42-94813	42-52205 +	42-78143 +
42-51350	42-94847	42-64341 +	42-78144 +
42-51529	42-94856	42-78080 +	42-78153 +
42-52483	42-94981	42-78096 +	
42-52572	44-10421*		
42-52573	44-10533	+ Returned to ASAAF after VE Day	
42-52591	44-10574		
42-52620	44-10594		
42-52681	44-10597		
42-52712	44-10611		
42-52731	44-40380		
42-52766	44-40457		

* Returned to USAAF April 1945.

USAAF serial numbers of B-24 Liberators allocated to the Royal Air Force under Lend-Lease.

40-2350	41-11610	41-11672	41-11722	42-40157
41-1087	41-11611	41-11679	41-11723	42-40158
41-1093	41-11612	41-11681	41-11724	42-40159
41-1096	41-11621	41-11682	41-11725	42-40160
41-1097	41-11626	41-11683	41-11726	42-40161
41-1107	41-11627	41-11684	41-11727	42-40162
41-1108	41-11628	41-11685	41-11734	42-40163
41-1109	41-11633	41-11687	41-11735	42-40284
41-1110	41-11634	41-11690	41-11736	42-40285
41-1111	41-11635	41-11692	41-11737	42-40286
41-1112	41-11643	41-11694	41-11738	42-40287
41-1114	41-11644	41-11696	41-11740	42-40288
41-1115	41-11645	41-11697	41-11741	42-40289
41-1119	41-11647	41-11699	41-11748	42-40291
41-1120	41-11648	41-11700	41-11749	42-40292
41-1121	41-11649	41-11701	41-11750	42-40293
41-1122	41-11651	41-11702	41-11751	42-40294
41-1124	41-11654	41-11703	41-11752	42-40300
41-1126	41-11658	41-11705	41-11753	42-40301
41-1127	41-11659	41-11710	41-11754	42-40302
41-1129	41-11660	41-11711	41-11755	42-40303
41-11589	41-11661	41-11712	41-11756	42-40304
41-11590	41-11662	41-11713	42-40098	42-40305
41-11594	41-11664	41-11714	42-40099	42-40306
41-11599	41-11665	41-11715	42-40124	42-40307
41-11604	41-11666	41-11716	42-40136	42-40308
41-11605	41-11667	41-11718	42-40138	42-40309
41-11606	41-11668	41-11720	42-40148	42-40310
41-11607	41-11670	41-11721	42-40150	42-40444

42-40445	42-64161	42-100395	44-49214	44-49800
42-40448	42-64187	42-100397	44-49215	44-49802
42-40449	42-64204 to 42-64233	42-100399	44-49217	44-49803
42-40454	42-64244	44-10253	44-49218	44-49804
42-40455	42-64252	44-10256 to 44-10436	44-49220	44-49805
42-40457	42-64259	44-10438	44-49221	44-49806
42-40458	42-64261	44-10439	44-49223	44-49812
42-40459	42-64263 to 42-64322	44-10441 to 44-10483	44-49426	44-49813
42-40462	42-64324 to 42-64330	44-10644 to 44-10752	44-49439	44-49815
42-40463	42-64332	44-44049 to 44-44119	44-49440	44-49817
42-40464	42-64333	44-44130 to 44-44349	44-49441	44-49819
42-40465	42-64334	44-44360 to 44-44500	44-49443	44-49820
42-40467	42-64335	44-48798	44-49444	44-49821
42-40546	42-64336	44-48859	44-49447	44-49823
42-40547	42-64338	44-48885	44-49449	44-49824
42-40548	42-64345	44-49026	44-49452	44-49825
42-40556	42-64352	44-49049	44-49453	44-49828
42-40558	42-64355	44-49052	44-49455	44-49830
42-40559	42-64357	44-49056	44-49457	44-49831
42-40569	42-64360	44-49058	44-49459	44-49832
42-40582	42-64366	44-49061	44-49462	44-49833
42-40583	42-64375	44-49064	44-49465	44-49834
42-40585	42-64376	44-49066	44-49470	44-49835
42-40586	42-64377	44-49069	44-49473	44-49836
42-40587	42-64378	44-49072	44-49475	44-49842
42-40589	42-64379	44-49076	44-49477	44-49843
42-40590	42-64381	44-49078	44-49671	44-49846
42-40591	42-64382	44-49081	44-49682	44-49856
42-40592	42-64383	44-49083	44-49686	44-49861
42-40593	42-64384	44-49090	44-49689	44-49862
42-40599	42-64386	44-49092 to 44-49111	44-49692	44-49871
42-40625	42-64387	44-49113 to 44-49122	44-49697	44-49874
42-40633	42-64432	44-49126	44-49701	44-49883
42-40641	42-99736 to 42-99745	44-49133	44-49706	44-49888
42-40643	42-99747	44-49137	44-49709	44-49891
42-40652	42-99750	44-49139	44-49713	44-49893
42-40672	42-99751	44-49140	44-49717	44-49898
42-40674	42-99753	44-49142	44-49722	44-49901
42-40678	42-99756	44-49144	44-49729	44-49903
42-40693	42-99757	44-49145	44-49755	44-49906
42-40696	42-99765	44-49147	44-49756	44-49909
42-40698	42-99767	44-49148	44-49757	44-49917
42-40700	42-99769	44-49150	44-49758	44-49922
42-40703	42-99774 to 42-99794	44-49151	44-49760	44-49931
42-63807 to 42-63865	42-99796	44-49153	44-49761	44-49934
42-63867 to 42-63892	42-99797	44-49154	44-49762	44-49951
42-63898	42-99800	44-49155	44-49765	44-49956
42-63901	42-99804	44-49156	44-49766	44-49959
42-63902	42-99806	44-49158	44-49768	44-49962
42-63911 to 42-63952	42-99809	44-49159	44-49769	44-49968
42-63992 to 42-63999	42-99810	44-49160	44-49770	44-49969
42-64000 to 42-64036	42-99811	44-49162 to 44-49171	44-49774	44-49978
42-64057	42-99812	44-49173	44-49775	44-49979
42-64058	42-99814	44-49176	44-49777	44-49982
42-64059	42-99815	44-49178	44-49778	44-49985
42-64060	42-99817 to 42-99848	44-49195	44-49780	44-49987
42-64062	42-99850	44-49196	44-49781	44-49992
42-64063	42-99852	44-49199	44-49782	44-49993
42-64065 to 42-64100	42-99857	44-49200	44-49785	44-49994
42-64121	42-99859	44-49203	44-49787	44-49996
42-64122	42-99861	44-49205	44-49790	44-49997
42-64123	42-99863 to 42-99935	44-49206	44-49792	44-49998
42-64124	42-100349	44-49207	44-49793	44-50001
42-64125	42-100383	44-49209	44-49794	44-50003
42-64126	42-100384	44-49210	44-49798	44-50008
42-64128 to 42-64152	42-100386 to 42-100392	44-49212	44-49799	44-50010

44-50013	44-50053	44-50130	44-50178	44-50246
44-50014	44-50055	44-50131	44-50179	
44-50016	44-50056	44-50134	44-50181	C-87s
44-50017	44-50057	44-50135	44-50183	
44-50019	44-50059	44-50137	44-50184	44-39219
44-50020	44-50060	44-50138	44-50185	44-39220
44-50021	44-50061	44-50139	44-50187	44-39221
44-50023	44-50063 to 44-50079	44-50140	44-50191	44-39222
44-50025	44-50081	44-50147	44-50192	44-39223
44-50026	44-50082	44-50148	44-50193	44-39224
44-50027	44-50086	44-50151	44-50195	44-39225
44-50029	44-50087	44-50153	44-50196	44-39226
44-50032	44-50088	44-50154	44-50197	44-39236
44-50033	44-50099	44-50155	44-50198	44-39237
44-50034	44-50100	44-50157	44-50199	44-39248
44-50035	44-50101	44-50158	44-50202	44-39249
44-50036	44-50102	44-50159	44-50206	44-39250
44-50037	44-50104	44-50160	44-50208	44-39251
44-50038	44-50107	44-50161	44-50210	44-39252
44-50039	44-50112	44-50163	44-50212	44-39253
44-50041	44-50114	44-50164	44-50213	44-39254
44-50042	44-50116	44-50165	44-50215	44-39255
44-50043	44-50118	44-50167	44-50217	44-39256
44-50044	44-50120	44-50168	44-50226	44-39257
44-50045	44-50121	44-50171	44-50227	44-39258
44-50046	44-50123	44-50172	44-50228	44-39259
44-50047	44-50124	44-50174	44-50230	44-39260
44-50049	44-50125	44-50175	44-50232	44-39261
44-50051	44-50127	44-50176	44-50234	
44-50052	44-50128	44-50177	44-50242	

Douglas Dakota

Many Douglas C-47s were delivered off the production lines direct to Allied forces under the Lend-Lease agreement. These came from USAAF contracts and all the initial paperwork involved was completed by the USAAF, after which the aircraft were handed over to the appropriate air arm whose government normally had a team of representatives based at the Douglas factories. After an acceptance air test the transports were ferried to the point of embarkation. For the RAF this was 45 Group at Montreal. By far the largest number went to the RAF, who named the transport Dakota.

Douglas C-53-DO (Santa Monica)

AC-18393	C-53	41-20045–20136

Douglas C-47-DL (Long Beach)

DA-AC-1043	C-47-DL	42-32786–32923
	C-47A-DL	42-32924–32935
AC-20669	C-47-DL	42-5635–5704
	C-47A-5-DL	42-23347–23355
	C-47A-10-DL	42-23356–23379
	C-47A-15-DL	42-23380–23412
	C-47A-30-DL	42-23581–23787
	C-47A-35-DL	42-23788–23961
	C-47A-40-DL	42-23962–24088
AC-20669-2	C-47A-45-DL	42-24089–24138
AC-20669	C-47A-50-DL	42-24139–24321
	C-47A-60-DL	42-24338–24407
	C-47A-DL	43-30640–30761

Douglas C-47-DK (Oklahoma City)

AC-28405	C-47A-DK	42-92024–92091
	C-47A-1-DK	42-92092–92415
	C-47A-5-DK	42-92416–92572
		42-108837–108854
	C-47A-10-DK	42-92573–92743
		42-108855–108873
	C-47A-20-DK	42-92924–93283
		42-108894–108933
	C-47A-25-DK	42-93284–93823
		42-108934–108993
AC-40652	C-47A-30-DK	43-47963–48255
	C-47B-1-DK	43-48263–48562
	C-47B-5-DK	43-48563–48912
	C-47B-10-DK	43-48913–49262
	C-47B-15-DK	43-49263–49612
	C-47B-20-DK	43-49613–49962
AC-2032	C-47B-25-DK	44-76195–76538
	C-47B-30-DK	44-76539–76854
	C-47B-35-DK	44-76855–77184
	C-47B-40-DK	44-77185–77294

Appendix C

Table of American aircraft types, symbols and RAF names, taken from *The Aircraft and Spotters Note Book* issued during World War Two and used by the author. It emphasises the initial designation and name problem which was solved with the introduction of Lend-Lease aircraft listing.

AMERICAN TYPES, SYMBOLS & R.A.F. NAMES

British Name	Maker's Name	American Name	U.S Army No.	U.S Navy No.	Maker's No.
Airacobra I	Bell	Airacobra	P–39D	–	P–400
Argus I	Fairchild	Forwarder	UC–61/68	–	Fairchild 24W–41
Avenger	Grumman	Avenger	–	TBF–1	–
Baltimore I	Martin	–	A–30	–	Glenn Martin 187B1
Bermuda I	Brewster	Buccaneer	–	SB2A–2	Brewster 340
Black Widow	Northrop	Black Widow	P–61	–	–
Boston III	Douglas	–	A–20C	BD–2	DB–7B
Buffalo II	Brewster	Buffalo	–	F2A–3	Brewster 339
Caravan	Curtiss	–	C–76	–	Caravan
Catalina I	Consolidated	Catalina	–	PBY–5	Model 28–5
Catalina III	,, Amphibian	Catalina	–	PBY–5A	Consolidated 28–5A
Chesapeake	Vought-Sikorsky	Vindicator	–	SB2U–3	V–156
Commando	Curtiss	–	C–46	R5C–1	CW20
Constellation	Lockheed	–	C–69	–	–
Coronado I	Consolidated	Coronado	–	PB2Y–3	Model 29–3
Corsair	Vought-Sikorsky	Corsair	–	F4U–1	–
Crane	Cessna	Bobcat	C–78 AT–17	–	T–50T
Dakota I	Douglas	Skytrain	C–47	R4D–1	DC–3
Dakota II	Douglas	Skytrooper	C–53	R4D–3	DC–3A
Digby	Douglas	Bolo	B–18A	–	DB–280
Fortress II	Boeing	–	B–17F	–	B–299P
Goose I	Grumman	–	OA–9	JRF–2	G–21B
Gosling I	Grumman	Widgeon	–	J4F–3	G–44
Harvard II	North American	Texan	AT–6	SNJ–3	NA–16–3
Havoc II	Douglas	Nighthawk	P–70	–	DB–7A
Hellcat	Grumman	Hellcat	–	F–6F	–
Helldiver	Curtiss	–	–	SB2C–1	Curtiss
Hudson III	Lockheed	–	A–29	PBO	414–56–01
Kingcobra	Bell	Kingcobra	P–63	–	–
Kingfisher I	Vought-Sikorsky	Kingfisher	–	OS2U–3	VS–310
Invader	Douglas	Invader	A–26	–	–
Kittyhawk II	Curtiss	Warhawk	P–40F	–	Hawk 87A4
Liberator Express	Consolidated	–	C–87	–	Model 32
Liberator III	Consolidated	–	B–24D	PB4Y	Model 32–4
Lightning I	Lockheed	Atalanta	P–38D	–	322–61
Lodestar	Lockheed	Lodestar	C–56	R50–4	L18
Marauder I	Martin	Marauder	B26B	–	Glenn Martin 179
Mariner I	Martin	Mariner	–	PBM–3	Glenn Martin 162

British Name	Maker's Name	American Name	U.S Army No.	U.S Navy No.	Maker's No.
Mars	Martin	–	–	PB2M	–
Maryland I	Martin	–	A–22	–	Glenn Martin 167A
Mitchell I	North American	Mitchell	B–25B	PBJ–1	NA–62B
Mohawk IV	Curtiss	–	P–36E	–	Hawk 75A4
Mustang I	North American	Apache	P–51	–	NA–73
Norseman	Noorduyn	–	UC–64A	–	–
Nomad I	Northrop	–	A–17A	BT–1	8A–3P
Seamew	Curtiss	Seagull	–	SO3C	–
Skymaster	Douglas	Skymaster	C–54	R5D–1	DCHA
Superfortress	Boeing	–	B–29	–	–
Thunderbolt I	Republic	Thunderbolt	P–47B	–	Thunderbolt
Tomahawk II	Curtiss	–	P–40C	–	Hawk 81A3
Vengeance I	Vultee	Georgia	A–31/35	TBV–1	Vultee 72
Ventura I	Lockheed-Vega	Lexington	B–34	PV–1	Lockheed-Vega 37
Vigilant I	Vultee–Stinson	–	L–49B	–	O–74
Wildcat	Grumman	Wildcat	–	F4F–3	G–36A
Yale I	North American	–	BT–24	–	NA–64

Appendix D

By the end of World War Two, RAF Ferry Command and No.45 Atlantic Transport Group had been involved in the ferrying of well over 9,000 aircraft across the North Atlantic, South Atlantic and Pacific oceans. This is an interesting listing of Lend-Lease aircraft involved.

Lend-Lease aircraft deliveries – west to east

Aircraft	Number	Destination
Consolidated B-24 Liberator	847	United Kingdom
	902	Middle East
Douglas C-47 Dakota	1,174	United Kingdom
	543	Middle East
Martin A-30 Baltimore	1,000	Middle East
Lockheed A-28 A-29 Hudson	661	United Kingdom
North American B-25 Mitchell	659	Middle East
Lockheed B-34 PV-1 Ventura	306	Middle East
	222	United Kingdom
Martin B-26 Marauder	368	Middle East
	70	United Kingdom
Consolidated PBY Catalina	435	United Kingdom
	37	Pacific
Douglas A-20 Boston	324	United Kingdom
	110	Middle East
Consolidated PB2Y Coronado	169	United Kingdom
	51	South-East Asia
Boeing B-17 Fortress	153	United Kingdom
Martin PBM Mariner	137	United Kingdom
Douglas C-54 Skymaster	15	United Kingdom
Lockheed C-60 Lodestar	15	United Kingdom
Douglas A-26 Invader	15	United Kingdom
Waco CG-4A Hadrian	1	United Kingdom

Appendix E

Aircraft held with 107 Maintenance Unit, Kasfareet, Canal Zone, Egypt recorded on Sunday 3 August and Wednesday 13 August 1947. Adjacent aircraft dumps are included.

Baltimore
AH156, FA132, 152, 184, 199, 209, 210, 235, 237, 257, 262, 263, 275, 279, 302, 336, 342, 369, 408, 482, 599, 610, 629, 636. FW368, 429, 442, 444, 475, 500, 526, 604, 635, 725, 737, 783, 788 (Greek), 840, 877.
FW429 Greek.
FW844 A-30A-30-MA ex-43-9001 Greek.

Boston
AL729

Dakota
FD784, 785, 792, 804, 805, 807, 808, 816, 817. KN646. FD807 'ODSH', possibly ex-BOAC.

Expediter
KJ493

Hellcat
JX818

Kittyhawk
FR862

Lockheed 18
EW992, 993. HK975, 981, VR955.

Marauder
FB410, 420, 422, 423, 432, 442, 450, 462, 466, 468, 469, 474, 476, 485, 493, 494, 495, 497, 498, 499, 500, 510, 514, 519, 520, 521, 522.
USAAF identities still on aircraft.
FB462 135500, 450 135386, 493 2107497, 497 2107501, 449 135385.
FB468 B-26C-33-MO
FB477 B-26C-33-MO 41-35514
FB483 B-26C-33-MO: *Livia*
FB486 B-26C-33-MO 41-35538
FB511 B-26C-26-MO 42-107515

FB513 B-26C-26-MO
HD408, 410, 415, 422, 424, 426, 430, 431, 438, 453, 473, 478, 481, 489, 493, 495, 502, 503, 506, 508, 514, 530, 542, 545, 546, 553, 554, 566, 568, 571, 598, 602, 604, 612, 630, 633, 635, 655, 660, 661, 680, 683, 684, 687, 689, 690, 703, 705, 709, 741.
USAAF identities still on aircraft
HD415 B-26F-2-MA 42-96342
HD424 B-26F-2-MA
HD430 B-26F-2-MA 42-96357
HD564 B-26G-21-MA 44-68017
HD646 B-26G-11-MA
HD696 B-26G-21-MA 44-68009

Maryland
AR738

Mustang
FB343 P-51C-1-NT, KM372 P-51K-15-NT 44-12738
KH797 AK-A unit unknown.

Thunderbolt
FL330, 757, 830. HD144. KJ139, 154, 164, 353.
KL186, 288.
FL757 P-47D-22-RE
FL830 P-47D-22-RE
HD144 P-47D-22-RE

Ventura
FB631. FN957, 960, 993, 994, 997. FP547, 556, 565, 578, 582, 595, 602, 609, 669, 676. JS892, 907, 910, 912, 926, 929, 936, 943, 948, 950, 961, 962, 963, 966, 967, 972, 974, 978, 957, 983, 967. JT803, 804, 809, 815, 817, 818, 823, 832, 835, 887.

Appendix F

Record Transatlantic Flights

The following list indicates some of the fastest flights on main stages of the North Atlantic bomber delivery and the return ferry services. In all cases the Liberators were carrying the maximum load of 56,000 lb and the twin-engined aircraft – Ventura, Hudson, Boston and Catalina flying boats – were also fully laden with passengers and war freight. A dead-heat between two captains, both flying Venturas on the Newfoundland–Iceland passage, will be noted.

All times given are from take-off to landing, and in the case of stops at North American coastal bases, the brief stop-over periods are excluded from the time shown:-

East to West

	Statute Miles	Aircraft	Pilot	Flying Time
UK–Iceland	850	Ventura	Capt E. G. Carlisle OBE	4h. 3m.
UK–Labrador	2,400	Liberator	Air Commodore G. J. Powell	14h. 27m.
UK–Newfoundland	2,200	Liberator	Capt Richard Allen	10h. 18m.
UK–New Brunswick	2,750	Liberator	Capt T. G. Thomlinson	12h. 18m.
UK–Nova Scotia	2,700	Liberator	Capt Richard Allen	13h. 52m.
UK–Maine, USA	2,840	Liberator	Capt W. L. Steward	13h. 54m.
Iceland–Newfoundland	1,620	Liberator	Capt T. G. Thomlinson	9h.–
Iceland–Labrador	1,550	Liberator	Capt A. Andrew	10h. 31m.

West to East

Newfoundland–UK	2,200	Liberator	Capt W. S. May	7h. 47m.
Labrador–UK	2,400	Liberator	Capt S. W. A. Scott	9h. 43m.
Iceland–UK	850	Boston	F/Lt N. Bicknell	3h. 4m.
Bermuda–UK	3,400	Catalina	Capt R. E. Perlick	19h. 50m.
Newfoundland–Iceland	1,620	Ventura	Capt A. Harris	7h. 36m.
		Ventura	Capt S. Klusek	7h. 36m.
Labrador–Iceland	1,500	Ventura	Capt D. B. Jacques	7h. 15m.

Britain–Canada Flights

UK–Montreal (non-stop)	3,100	Liberator	Capt E. R. B. White	13h. 30m.
Montreal–UK (non-stop)	3,100	Liberator	Capt S. T. B. Cripps DFC	12h. 51m.

East to West Exclusive of Brief Stop

UK–Montreal (stop at Newfoundland)	3,150	Liberator	Capt Richard Allen	15h. 7m.
UK–Montreal (stop at New Brunswick)	3,200	Liberator	Capt W. J. Vanderkloot OBE	14h. 20m.
UK–Montreal (stop at Maine USA)	3,130	Liberator	Capt W. L. Stewart	15h. 50m.
UK–Montreal (stop at Iceland)	3,200	Liberator	Capt W. S. May	15h. 56m

West to East Exclusive of Brief Stop

Montreal–UK (stop at Newfoundland)	3,150	Liberator	Capt S. W. A. Scott	12h. 21m.
Montreal–UK (stop at Nova Scotia)	3,200	Liberator	Capt S. W. A. Scott	11h. 50m

Appendix G

Significant dates affecting Lend-Lease ferry operations across the Atlantic

July 1940 The Atlantic Ferry Organisation, or ATFERO, was formed to ferry by air US military aircraft purchased by Britain.

9 September 1940 An Overseas Air Movement Control Unit (OAMCU) was established to control the non-operational flights operating outside of UK airspace, including the then small number of aircraft from North America. It was based at Gloucester so as to use the wireless telegraphy (W/T) radio station at Birdlip.

November 1940 A civilian reception party was formed by Scottish Aviation Limited (SAL) to accept the aircraft being delivered from North America, and to welcome, feed and accommodate both aircrew and passengers.

17 March 1941 Flying Officer Sarll was posted in to command the RAF Delivery Flight Reception Party at Prestwick.

May 1941 ATFERO came under the control of the Ministry of Aircraft Production (MAP).

15 July 1941 ATFERO became Royal Air Force Ferry Command. Air Chief Marshal Sir Frederick Bowhill became C-in-C at Montreal.

15 July 1941 RAF Transatlantic Reception Party (TRP) formed.

20 July 1941 RAF Ferry Command in control.

15 August 1941 No.44 Group formed within RAF Ferry Command and absorbed OAMCU. Responsible for the Master Control of all non-operational flights outside the United Kingdom. The Transatlantic Air Safety Services Organisation (TASSO) which included Ireland, United Kingdom, Newfoundland and Canada, controlled the flying boat operations between Foynes and Botwood.

15 August 1941 Transatlantic Air Control (TAC) formed at Prestwick and assumed the control of the local area. It was located in the Air Defence HQ at Powbank Mill.

15 August 1941 to 21 October No.44 Group continued the Master Control of North Atlantic and Iceland flights.

15 September 1941 RAF Prestwick transferred from No.27 Group Technical Training Command (TTC) to No.44 Group becoming responsible for Transatlantic Air Control, Transatlantic Reception Party, No.27 Beam Approach Training (BAT) Flight and No.3 Radio School.

21 October 1941 At 1315 hrs, Transatlantic Air Control (TAC) was moved to Redbrae House.

6 November 1941 At 0700 hrs, the Regional Control Centre (RCC) was opened at Redbrae.

6 November 1941 At 1500 hrs, Transatlantic Air Control (TAC) assumed Master Control of the North Atlantic, Bermuda, Iceland and all Russian flights north of 5230N. Overseas Air Control (OAC) at No.44 Group retained control of aircraft south of 5230N United Kingdom – Gibraltar–Malta and Middle East.

January 1942 Control of all flying boats on UK–Gibraltar route handed over to No.19 Group Coastal Command.

25 March 1943 RAF Transport Command formed, RAF Ferry Command renamed No.45 (Air Transport) Group with HQ retained at Montreal, Canada.

1 April 1943 No.45 (Air Transport) Group, renamed No.45 Group.

15 February 1946 No.45 Group reduced to Wing status.

1 May 1946 RAF handed over Transatlantic Air Control (TAC), Approach and Control Tower control to Civilian Ministry of Transport & Civil Aviation (MTCA). The introduction of standard operating procedures (SOP) was delayed until 1 November 1946.

Note: Representatives from Canada, Ireland, Great Britain and the United States had met in Dublin during March 1938 to agree the Transatlantic Air Service Safety Organisation (TASSO). Control, Meteorological, Wireless Telegraphy (W/T) communication, MF Direction Finding (D/F) navigation and alerting services were to be provided for commercial flying boat services and these were located at Botwood in Newfoundland and Foynes in the Republic of Eire. They were to continue in operation throughout World War Two, until replaced by the International Civil Aviation Organisation (ICAO) North Atlantic Regional Manual in 1946.

Bibliography

Andrade, John M., *US Military Designations & Serials Since 1909* (Midland Counties, 1979).

Blue, Allan G., *The B-24 Liberator* (Ian Allan, 1979).

Bowers, Peter M., *Boeing Aircraft Since 1916* (Putnam, 1989).

Bowers, Peter M., *Curtiss Aircraft 1907-1947* (Putnam, 1979).

Bowers, Peter M., *The DC-3 – 50 Years of Legendary Flight* (Tab Books, 1986).

Berry, Peter, *Beechcraft Staggerwing* (Tab Books, 1990).

Francillon, Rene J., *Grumman Aircraft Since 1929* (Putnam, 1989).

Francillon, Rene J., *Lockheed Aircraft Since 1913* (Putnam, 1987).

Francillon, Rene J., *McDonnell Douglas Aircraft Since 1920* Vol. 1 (Putnam, 1988).

Gradidge, J. M. G., *The Douglas DC-3 and its predecessors* (Air Britain, 1984).

Green & Fricker, *The Air Forces of the World* (McDonald & Co., 1958).

Griffin, J. A., *Canadian Military Aircraft 1920–1968* (Canadian War Museum, 1969).

Halley, J. J., *Aeromilitaria* (Air Britain Historians).

McVicar, Don M., *Ferry Command* (Airlife, 1981).

McVicar, Don M., *Ferry Command Pilot* (Ad Astra Books, 1993).

Meadows, Jack, *Aviation News Vol. 22 No. 20* (Hall Park Publishing Ltd, 1994).

Pearcy, Arthur, *The Dakota* (Ian Allan, 1972).

Pearcy, Arthur, *Dakota I to IV RAF* Profile No. 220 (Profile Publications, 1973).

Pearcy, Arthur, *DC-3* (Ballantine, 1975).

Powell, Taffy, *Ferryman* (Airlife, 1982).

Robertson, Bruce, *British Military Aircraft Serials 1878–1987* (Midland Counties, 1987).

Slader, John, *The Fourth Service* (Robert Hale, 1994).

Smith, David J., *Aviation News Vol.22 No.20* (Hall Park Publishing Ltd, 1994).

Smith, Peter C., *Vengeance* (Airlife, 1986).

Stettinius, Edward R. Jr, *Lend-Lease – Weapon for Victory* (Penguin Books, 1944).

Swanborough & Bowers, *United States Military Aircraft Since 1909* (Putnam, 1989).

Swanborough & Bowers, *United States Navy Aircraft Since 1911* (Putnam, 1990).

Thetford, Owen G., *Aircraft of the Royal Air Force Since 1918* (Putnam, 1968).

Thetford, Owen G., *British Naval Aircraft Since 1912* (Putnam, 1991).

Thetford, Owen G., *Camouflage 1939–42 Aircraft* (Harborough, 1946).

Index